Critical Questions in
Persuasion Research

Critical Questions in Persuasion Research

Franklin J. Boster | Christopher J. Carpenter

Michigan State University | Western Illinois University

SAN DIEGO

Bassim Hamadeh, CEO and Publisher
Todd R. Armstrong, Publisher
Michelle Piehl, Senior Project Editor
Abbey Hastings, Production Editor
Abbie Goveia, Graphic Design Assistant
Trey Soto, Licensing Specialist
Natalie Piccotti, Director of Marketing
Kassie Graves, Vice President of Editorial
Jamie Giganti, Director of Academic Publishing

Cover image: Copyright © 2019 iStockphoto LP/MicroStockHub.

Printed in the United States of America.

cognella® | ACADEMIC PUBLISHING
3970 Sorrento Valley Blvd., Ste. 500, San Diego, CA 92121

Brief Contents

Detailed Contents

Preface

What is there, then, to rule out the idea that Helen, too, came under the influence of the spoken word just as unwillingly as if she had been abducted by the violence of visitors? For thought is banished by persuasion. Indeed, persuasion may not have the appearance of compulsion, but it has the same power.

—Gorgias of Leontini, Encomium of Helen

COMMUNICATION FACILITATES TWO PRIMARY FUNCTIONS for humans. On one hand, it allows us to coordinate our actions, promoting our ability to meet our goals; on the other, it aids us in influencing our fellow humans so as to obtain better outcomes for ourselves and perhaps select others. This volume reviews the knowledge generated by social and behavioral scientists pertaining to one form of social influence: persuasion.

In this textbook, we provide an alternative to the usual persuasion textbook structure. Most books look at each type of persuasion research and review them one at a time. We look at eight key controversies in the study of persuasion and cover research and theory that relate to each topic. So rather than have a chapter on a theory, such as functional attitude theory, we discuss that theory as one of several potential ways to resolve a controversy (e.g., how best to tailor or target persuasive messages to a particular audience or how to persuade particularly difficult-to-persuade people).

This organization schema will benefit students by focusing on the more easily remembered pivotal controversies and by showing them how various types of research and theory deal with the important questions in the persuasion process. They will see how various perspectives deal with the big questions in persuasion rather than seeing them as isolated theories. Students will see how research and theory contribute to answering theoretically and practically important general questions. Our approach of focusing on the big questions and how various strands of research and theory help answer these questions will help students integrate mentally what they might otherwise view as disparate areas of persuasion research.

We phrase each of the controversial issues as a question. Sandwiched between an introductory chapter and a concluding chapter, we pose the following eight questions.

- What constitutes a strong persuasive message, and does it matter?
- How do we adapt persuasive messages to diverse audiences?
- Do persuasive messages have side effects?
- How can we manage the buzz?
- How can we maintain attitude change?
- Can a persuasive message be counterproductive?
- How can we encourage resistance to persuasion?
- To what extent does action follow from attitudes?

Focusing on persuasion research as a series of controversies rather than as a list of important variables, contexts, or settled empirical generalizations will also improve students' scientific literacy. They will enter into the controversies and choose for themselves which answers to these key questions have more merit. Current textbooks present a series of findings and theories that often give students the sense of the field of persuasion as a dead and finished area with a series of answers. By framing persuasion as a series of controversies, students will learn the dynamic and exciting way that social science helps them understand human behavior—to which they might someday contribute.

Focusing on controversies also creates a context that draws in research from all the social and behavioral sciences instead of focusing on just one discipline's ideas. In this text, we draw on our home discipline of communication, but we also integrate perspectives from advertising, argumentation, business, cognitive science, marketing, neuroscience, philosophy, political science, psychology, public health, and sociology. No field has a monopoly on understanding how people persuade each other, and we sought to show our readers how research and theory from all of these disciplines inform how we think about the controversies in this book.

Each chapter shares a common structure designed to pull students into each controversy before diving into the various answers generated by theory and research. Initially, we will explain the controversy with multiple examples that students will understand and find relevant to their lives—examples that will both explain the controversy and indicate the importance of them understanding it. Then we will explain the significance of the issue in detail before going into what scholars believe currently and why they believe it. Each chapter will include a few graphs and tables displaying data from original research in the area so that students can visualize the strength of the evidence for the scholarly claims. Most books merely assert that a particular variable has a persuasive effect, but the use of tables and figures will empower students to decide for themselves. These graphic presentations will also help them understand how to conduct persuasion research. The final part of each chapter will explain what we still need to know to understand the issue, uncommon in persuasion textbooks that present the field as though the answers remain settled. By closing with necessary information, we hope it motivates students to conduct their own research.

Several scholars generously reviewed early drafts of some of these chapters and offered us suggestions for improving this textbook. We would like to thank Ryan Goei (University of Minnesota, Duluth), Michael R. Kotowski (University of Tennessee, Knoxville), and Steve Rains (University of Arizona) for their valuable recommendations. We also extend our thanks to the members of Chris's spring 2020 undergraduate Introduction to Persuasion class who also provided helpful and enthusiastic feedback. Finally, Frank acknowledges the mentorship of Thom Solon, Bob Engbretson, Betty Crowther, Gerald Miller, and Jack Hunter; they made this project possible. Chris would like to thank his wife Neala and his parents Mark and Suzan for their unwavering support.

What Is Persuasion?

W HY DID THE ABILITY TO communicate among members of the genus homo and the species sapiens evolve in such a sophisticated manner? One reason involves the importance of making ourselves understood sufficiently well so that we can coordinate our actions (see Misyak et al., 2016 for an example of communication evolving to serve this purpose). For example, once, communication promoted our ancient ancestors' success in planning hunting expeditions. Today, communication facilitates the planning and work of construction crews as they build houses.

A second, and no less important, reason involves influencing other Homo sapiens (Mercier & Sperber, 2011). Sloman and Fernbach (2017) assure us of the very real limits of our individual knowledge and its inadequacy for accomplishing many, perhaps most, of the tasks that we face daily. We become acutely aware of this fact when our plumbing malfunctions, our car fails to start, or our dog becomes ill. Sloman and Fernbach remind us that parts of our bodies, other than our brains, various technologies, and especially *other people,* increase our ability to complete many tasks that otherwise we could not.

To put the matter another way, interdependence characterizes the human condition. In the *Politics* (Barker, 1995), Aristotle described humans as social animals. Baumeister (2005, p., 389-ff) extended this point, describing us as cultural animals. To provide some examples, Baumeister pointed out that social animals, like birds, gain from flying together as a way of presenting a more formidable target to predators, but humans can employ divisions of labor to enhance productivity by orders of magnitude. Social animals solve problems and imitate one another's successes, but humans store and transmit those solutions so that they can pass them on to succeeding generations. Social animals fight off predators and so help and cooperate with close relatives—action that enhances survival and reproduction. On the other hand, cultural animals create institutions, such as police forces, that do for others the same that they do for relatives. Social animals limit violence through the emergence of domestic hierarchies, but cultural animals have more sophisticated systems of dispute resolution involving laws, attorneys, courts, and even moral emotions, such as sympathy and guilt, that constrain aggression.

In sum, other people prove pivotal to our ability to survive and thrive, and more often than we might like to think, we need or want them to conform to our requests or our way of thinking. We may want them to purchase a product, support a cause, vote for a political candidate, help us complete a tax form, help us with a homework assignment, or, if a medical professional, follow a particular diet and exercise regimen, among countless other possibilities. Consequently, the cultural animal Homo sapiens developed varied and extremely sophisticated means of achieving this goal. The subsequent section discusses some of this variance and sophistication by describing various forms that social influence takes, including means control, legitimate power, identification, compliance gaining, and persuasion.

THE UNIVERSE OF SOCIAL INFLUENCE

When one (or more) human affects the thoughts, actions, or both of one or more humans, social influence has occurred. The focus of this book, persuasive communication, forms but one of the variety of ways that humans influence each other. We describe some of the others before focusing on persuasive communication.

Means Control: The Power of Reward and Punishment

Imagine that you volunteer to participate in an experiment. Entering the laboratory, you find eight other people who you come to believe have volunteered for the same experiment. An older adult, clearly the person conducting the experiment, enters the room and asks each of you to take a seat. There are two rows of chairs, five in the front row and four in the back. With the other seats taken, you sit in one of the back seats, which the experimenter subsequently calls seat eight. He then explains that the experiment involves a study of spatial ability and tells you that you will make a number of line-length judgments. He shows you two cardboard sheets. On one, three lines of varying lengths labeled A, B, and C exist. On the other, you see a single unlabeled line (see Figure 1.1). Then he asks the person sitting in the first seat which of the three lines on the first sheet most closely resembles the length of the line on the second sheet. Person 1 answers B, and those

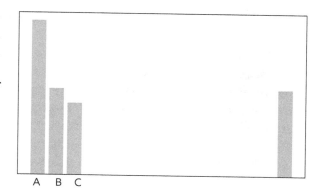

FIGURE 1.1   Asch's line-length judgment task.

sitting in seats two through seven echo his answer. Now you must answer, and you report the plain evidence of your senses: B. The person in the last seat also says B, and you settle back, resigned to having volunteered for a very boring experiment.

The second line length judgment, or trial, presents similar stimuli, with a correct answer of "A" this time. All of you once again report A as the correct answer. On the third trial, you examine the two sheets and decide that C corresponds to the correct answer—and clearly so. Yet Person 1 reports A as the correct answer. Furthermore, those in seats two through seven agree with her! Now the experimenter asks you for the correct answer. What do you do? Do you report the obvious results of your senses, line C, or do you give the same answer as the others, line A?

Even though those participating in this experiment did not, you may have suspected something amiss here. Unlike you, the other eight people in the room did not volunteer for this experiment. Rather, they serve as confederates of the experimenter, trained to provide predetermined answers. The experiment might go on for 20 judgments, with perhaps 12 of them critical trials, on which the other eight people answer incorrectly.

Solomon Asch (1956) conducted this experiment and a number of others like it. He wanted to know the extent to which people would forgo reporting the obvious results of their own senses and conform to the judgment of others. In his experiments, he found that they did so approximately one-third of the time. On average, people gave the same wrong answer as the eight others on one of every three critical trials. Perhaps even more amazing, a careful reading of his paper shows that 75%, three of every four, participants answered incorrectly at least once in an experiment of 12 critical trials. The magnitude of this outcome demands an explanation. Why would so many people make incorrect judgments with the correct answer readily apparent?

As with many features of human behavior, several factors may have driven these responses. Two important and related motives likely contribute the most. First, people conform to obtain **rewards**; second, they conform to escape **punishment**. When others have the ability to reward us for conforming, punishing us for failing to conform, or both, they have **means control** over us; they can help or hinder (the means) our ability to reach our goals.

Reflecting on the rewards that people seek or the punishments that they seek to escape in Asch's experiment eliminates many things that we think of as rewards and punishments. No one holds a gun to the participant's head threatening to pull the trigger if they fail to produce the incorrect answer. No one offers them substantial amounts of money to provide the incorrect answer. Think of how much conformity would occur under such conditions. Alternatively, consider how much conformity would result if the naïve subject in this experiment had friends among the other eight people in the room, or if they did not know the correct answer. The Asch experiment demonstrates the power of means control even with the application of minimal pressure.

An answer emerges when we consider the importance of other people to a cultural animal. Because of the importance of others to us, their **approval** and **disapproval** matter to us, and they matter a lot, even when they are strangers, and even when Asch's subjects knew the correct answer. People find social approval rewarding; they find social disapproval punishing. The desire for the former and the desire to avoid the latter produce powerful forces of social influence.

A classical experiment conducted by Stanley Schachter (1951) and replicated recently by Wesselmann and others (2014) demonstrates the fact that conformity tends to result in the approval of others and that nonconformity tends to result in the disapproval of others. Schachter assembled groups of nine people supposedly to participate as members of discussion groups. Each group included six naïve participants and three confederates, those working for, and under the orders of, the experimenter. The three confederates played different roles in the experiment. One confederate played the "modal" role, taking the same position as most of the members of the group. The "slider" initially took a position deviant from the group, and in the course of the discussion, the person pretended to change to the same position taken by the majority of people in the group. The "deviant" also took a position at odds with other group members, but he stuck to that position throughout the experiment.

Group members read a case about a troubled young man, Johnny Rocco, and then Schachter asked each group member to announce aloud their opinion as to how to treat Johnny in the future, choices ranging from treating him with extreme love and kindness to punishing him harshly for his mistakes. Most of the members favored treating him with more love and kindness than punishment. Thus the slider and the deviant initially took a more pro-punishment stance, whereas the modal confederate aligned himself with the more love and kindness majority. After providing ample time for discussion, Schachter again entered the room and asked the participants to announce aloud once more their opinion of how to treat Johnny in the future. Again, the modal person took the same position as most of the others; the slider now announced that he agreed with the majority as well, but the deviant stuck to his pro-punishment position.

At this point, Schachter announced that he now realized that nine people made it impossible for the group to discuss such issues thoroughly. He said that he did not want to make the choice of who to exclude, so he asked each group member to rate via paper ballot how much they wanted each other group member to continue in the group. Clear results emerged. The modal person and the slider received ratings near the scale midpoint, but the deviant received extremely negative ratings—the most negative of any group member. Some group members added comments to their ratings, with one being "anybody but Bibb" (the deviant's name).

The numbers do not tell the whole story though. Observing the group discussions revealed that naïve participants first tried to convince the slider and the deviant. The deviant (Bibb Latane, later to become a distinguished scholar in his own right) had received extensive training, though, and could and did defend his position skillfully. When they could not convince him, group members verbally abused him and later just ignored him. At no time did the deviant reciprocate the verbal abuse. He just continued to make arguments supporting his position and to offer counterarguments to those with whom he disagreed. Altogether, the deviant received unpleasant treatment from the naïve participants—treatment that the modal person and the slider did not receive. Hence, in this experiment, group members rewarded conformity by providing social approval and punished a lack of conformity by meting out social disapproval. Most of us have had direct experience or have witnessed similar events. Consequently, we can expect people to develop a sensitivity to the relatively pleasant consequences of conformity and the unpleasant consequences of deviance.

As a result of such experiments, we can expect that social approval shapes human behavior in general, and human communication behavior specifically, and, indeed, experiments have produced such results. For instance, in 1955, William Verplanck performed a very simple experiment demonstrating this principle. He had confederates engage people in conversation, instructing his confederates to reinforce positively their conversational partner each time the partner uttered an opinion (i.e., any statement starting with "I think," "I feel," or some similar construction). The reinforcement could consist of a smile, a nod of the head, or a brief "I agree." Verplanck (1955) found that when reinforced positively, conversational partners expressed considerably more opinions than they did in a controlled, nonreinforced interval.

We can expect social disapproval to have a similar impact, and indeed this outcome emerged in an experiment by Crowne and Strickland (1961). In this experiment, the investigators focused on reinforcing plural nouns rather than opinion statements. Replicating Verplanck's experiment by showing that positive reinforcement increased the expression of plural nouns, they also found that when they punished expressions of plural nouns by responding with frowns, horizontal head shakes, and other forms of disapproval, subjects expressed fewer of them.

The power of social disapproval to influence us involves even more subtlety than experiments like Crowne and Strickland's. Janes and Olson (2000) showed that one manifestation of social disapproval, ridicule, or what they termed "jeer power," has just such an effect. When experimental participants viewed a video of another person receiving ridicule, their judgments on a subsequent task conformed more to the judgments of those (fictitious) others than did a control group.

Yet the effect of social disapproval on us reaches its zenith when expressed as ostracism, as toward the end of Schachter's experimental sessions. Williams's (2001) program of ostracism research showed that when others ignore, exclude, or reject us, we suffer decreases in our sense of belonging, our sense of our ability to control our lives, our self-esteem, and our feeling that our *existence has meaning*. In some of Williams's studies, he and his colleagues induced a sense of ostracism in his subjects and observed the accompanying effects. In his experiment, he merely had two other players in an online virtual ball tossing game stop throwing the virtual ball to the naïve subject. The other two players did not actually exist, but the subjects believed that they did and that they had stopped passing the ball to the subject. Some of these effects, belonging, lack of control, self-esteem, and meaningful existence, continued to emerge in a follow-up study in which the experimenter informed the participants that a computer, rather than humans, actually controlled the other players' actions—altogether rough and unpleasant treatment, indeed, and sufficiently powerful to make us susceptible to those who have and use means control pressures to influence us.

Obedience to Authority/Legitimate Power

A holocaust refers to a wide-spread destruction or slaughter. History books report all too many examples of holocausts. Millions of Native Americans died at the hand of Europeans following their landing in North America. Between 1975 and 1979, scholars estimate that Pol Pot and the Khmer Rouge held responsibility for the deaths of approximately two million of their fellow Cambodians. From 1992 to 1995, historians tell us that Bosnian Serbs killed more than 100,000 Bosnian Muslims. Those in power in Nazi-dominated Germany during the years preceding and including World War II (approximately 1933–1945) executed approximately six million Jews. Referring to the last of these horrors, Stanley Milgram wrote, "These inhumane policies may have originated in the mind of a single person, but they could only have been carried out on a massive scale if a very large number of people obeyed orders" (1974, p. 1).

One can better understand Milgram's point when looking at this holocaust from the point of view of the Nazi bureaucracy. For them, killing massive numbers of people presented not a moral problem but rather an engineering problem. How do you go about killing that many people? First, you have to identify those in the targeted group. They do not want to die, so you will have to round them up and then guard them to prevent their escape. You must construct death camps and arrange transportation to them. You must maintain the railroads, the transportation mode of choice, and someone must drive the trains. Someone must manufacture the materials (e.g., gases) to kill them.

Ordinary citizens, not soldiers, would have to perform many of these tasks. For instance, ordinary citizens provided the names of their Jewish neighbors and acquaintances to officials tasked with identifying Jews. Ordinary citizens drove trains to the death camps. Ordinary citizens maintained the railroad tracks. Ordinary citizens with construction skills, such as masons, plumbers, carpenters, and members of other skilled trades, participated in building and maintaining the death camps. Chemists developed the poisonous gases used in the death chambers. Without these acts, fewer would have died. Why did these ordinary citizens perform these tasks? Milgram's answered that in large part they did it, not exclusively but in large part, because authority figures ordered them to do so, and they obeyed these commands. They perceived these authority figures as people who, by virtue of their positions (e.g., military rank or members of the SS or policemen), had a legitimate right to tell them what to do. Being influenced because one believes influencing agents have a legitimate right to tell you what to do and that you have a duty to obey them defines a type of social influence termed obedience to authority or legitimate power.

In retrospect, this explanation seems absurd to many of us. Many prefer attributing this holocaust to Hitler and members of his regime, viewing them as cruel, sadistic, or perhaps psychotic. Some might invoke fear of punishment for failing to conform to explain the conformity of ordinary citizens. No doubt this holocaust included some of these factors. Nevertheless, the case remains strong for obedience as one of the most important factors. Considering the messages that shaped childhood socialization in the Nazi-dominated Germany of the 1930s and 1940s provides an explanation of the crucial role of obedience as a source of social influence.

In this time period, the overwhelming majority of Germans identified as Christians. The Bible provided the dominant, authoritative text for Christians then as now. Biblical passages, particularly stories, transmitted across generations contributed in important ways to the socialization of the populace. And the writers of Biblical texts frequently extolled obedience. Consider an example.

The 22nd chapter of the book of Genesis focuses on the story of Abraham and his son Isaac. Abraham and his wife, Sarah, had long wanted a child but had not produced one. At a very old age, however, Sarah bore a child whom she named Isaac. The Biblical account describes him as very much a beloved son. Nevertheless, in the 22nd chapter of Genesis, God orders Abraham to sacrifice Isaac. Without question, Abraham makes preparations to do so, to the extent of putting wood on an altar, binding Isaac, and placing him on that altar. At this point, God halts the proceedings, orders Abraham to stop, provides an alternate sacrifice in the form of a ram, and praises Abraham for his obedience. Subsequently, Abraham receives rewards for his obedience, but notably, his obedience to authority preceded the rewards or any hint of them. Theologians, and the priests and pastors they influenced, drew the conclusion that obedience to authority, God in this case, represented a moral imperative. Untold numbers of parishioners, and through them numerous generations, religious or not, would receive exposure to this message, with the religious context either included or excluded, and would receive it frequently. Subsequent Christian writers, such as Paul in the 13th chapter of Letter to the Romans, would extend the conclusion to authorities in addition to God. The principle of obedience as a social good would emerge as a central part of children's socialization.

Greek classics provided another important socializing influence on members of the German populace in this era. The virtues of obedience arise in such Greek classics as Sophocles's play, *Antigone*. In this drama, Antigone attempts to secure a proper burial for her brother in defiance of an order from her uncle, King Creon of Thebes. For her defiance, she receives harsh punishment—entombed alive. Although Creon has a change of heart and orders her release, he finds that she has committed suicide. Stories such as this one explore the opposite side of the coin that constitutes the obedience principle: negative outcomes await those who disobey. Once again, stories such as this one, but including many others, formed an important part of childhood socialization.

Socialization experiences such as these provide a context in which we can expect citizens to react obediently to orders from those perceived as authorities. When those authorities have malevolent intent, holocausts can emerge. Nazi Germany has no monopoly on them; they can occur anywhere. Some famous experiments demonstrate that certain conditions can induce ordinary U.S. citizens to act in a similar manner.

Most famous, Stanley Milgram (1974) conducted a series of experiments examining the effect of obedience to authority. A relatively representative sample of people from the New Haven, Connecticut, area participated in these experiments. Replications of the experiment include participants from many countries, a recent partial replication by Burger (2009), and numerous variations.

In its most common form, the Milgram experiment involved persons playing three roles: an experimenter, a learner, and a teacher. He assigned the naïve subject the role of teacher, and confederates filled the roles of experimenter and learner. Upon entering Milgram's lab, subjects heard a cover story explaining (falsely) that the experiment addressed the issue of the effect of punishment on learning. To study this issue, Milgram used a paired-associate learning task. A teacher read a long series of word pairs (e.g., "nice-bottle," "ant-eraser") to the learner. Subsequently, the teacher would read the first word of the pair, and the learner would have to supply the paired word. For example, the teacher might say "nice," and the learner would respond with "bottle." If the learner provided the correct response, Milgram instructed the teacher to go on to the next pair. But if the learner responded incorrectly, or failed to respond, he instructed the teacher to shock the learner before going on to the next pair. Furthermore, with each error, he instructed the teacher to increase the shock by one level (the learner never actually received these shocks)!

Milgram designed the experimental procedure very realistically so that it provided high drama and substantial stress for many of the participants. A large, foreboding gray shock generator loomed in the foreground of the lab. On it, 30 switches appeared, starting with 15 volts and increasing in increments of 15 volts to reach the highest level of 450 volts (remember that 110 volts come through your electrical sockets!). Verbal labels on the shock generator reinforced the strength of the shock that the learner's errors would produce. They began with "slight shock," "moderate shock," and continued in escalating severity until the last two switches read "XXX."

After a rigged drawing, the confederate drew the role of "learner" and the naïve subject drew the role of "teacher" (both slips of paper in the drawing had the label "teacher," and the confederate reported falsely that his said "learner"). The learner mentioned that he had a heart condition and asked if the shocks would endanger him. The experimenter assured him that the shocks would hurt but that they would cause no damage to his health. The teacher received a sample shock of 45 volts to emphasize the pain imposed by the shocks. The experimenter strapped the learner into an apparatus resembling an electric chair, attached electrodes to his wrists, and applied a paste so that the shocks would do no "permanent tissue damage." The experiment then began with the teacher reading the word pairs.

Very quickly, the learner started making errors in a predetermined manner. As the shock level increased, many of the teachers expressed concern about the learner's welfare. Milgram heightened these concerns in some variations of the experiment by having the learner pound on a wall or cry out in pain. In some variations, the learner stopped answering at some point, and teachers received the instruction to interpret no answer as a wrong answer and to shock him. When teachers expressed reluctance to continue the shocks, Milgram inserted an escalating series of verbal prods, phrases such as the following: "Please continue." "The experiment requires that you continue." "It is absolutely essential that you continue." And, "You have no other choice; you must go on." The experimental session terminated in one of two ways: (1) the teacher exhibited complete obedience, shocking the learner at each of the 30 levels and then twice more at 450 volts, or (2) the teacher refused to continue even after the experimenter went through all of the four prods.

The subjects (teachers) in these experiments exhibited a substantial amount of obedience. For instance, in a particularly important experiment in this research program, Milgram demonstrated the powerful effect of physical proximity on obedience. Teachers in the *remote* condition performed their tasks with the learner in another room, and they could neither see nor hear him. Those in the *voice proximity* condition could not see the learner but could hear him voicing his complaints about the painfulness of the shocks. Those in the *proximity* condition could both hear and see the learner through a glass petition. Finally, those in the *touch-proximity* condition sat next to the learner who had to place his hand on a metal plate to receive the shock following an incorrect answer. After the shocks reached a certain level, he refused to continue doing so, and so the experimenter ordered the teacher to place the learner's hand on the plate before administering the shock.

TABLE 1.1   The Relationship Between Proximity and Obedience

	Touch-Proximity	Proximity	Voice Proximity	Remote
Percentage Totally Obedient	30.0	40.0	62.5	65.0
Average Shock Administered	268.1	312.0	367.9	405.0

A summary of the results of this experiment appears in Table 1.1. The pattern of the numbers clearly illustrates the principle that obedience expanded with increased distance from the suffering. They suggest that authorities could expect more people to turn in neighbors or repair railroad tracks than to force people into a gas chamber. Moreover, the sheer magnitude of the numbers proves informative as well. In the remote condition, almost two-thirds of the teachers display complete obedience. Even in the touch-proximity condition, slightly less than 1 in 3 responds with complete obedience. The lowest average shock, found in the touch-proximity condition, exceeds the voltage entering the home through a wall socket by a factor of more than two. We must remember that, far from being Nazis, the subjects in this experiment resembled typical U.S. citizens.

These results testify to the extent to which the socialization process influences us to obey authorities. Notably, the authority in this experiment, the experimenter, held no public office. Should the teacher disobey, he had no ability to punish him by incarceration or physical harm. He merely wore a symbol of authority, a white lab coat that marked him as one whose position allowed him to give orders and that he expected others to obey him in the context of a laboratory. With a sample of relatively typical U.S. citizens and only these minimal credentials, he could still command a massive amount of obedience.

Milgram conducted a number of variations on the voice proximity experiment, the findings of which add nuance to our understanding of the power of a legitimate authority to obtain our obedience. One of these experiments examined sex difference and found none. No evidence emerged that males or females responded to an authority differently. Although socialization experiences continue to differ between the sexes, apparently they remain similar with respect to obedience to authorities.

Milgram also probed conditions that might increase or decrease the amount of obedience found in the voice proximity experiment. In one variation, the naïve subject did not have to shock the learner but rather had only to perform the subsidiary act of reading the word pairs. Under these conditions, 92.5% of subjects exhibited complete obedience. Milgram (1974) commented,

> Any competent manager of a destructive bureaucratic system can arrange his
> personnel so that only the most callous and obtuse are directly involved in vio-
> lence. The greater part of the personnel can consist of men and women who, by
> virtue of their distance from the actual acts of brutality, will feel little strain in

their performance of supportive functions. They will feel doubly absolved from responsibility. First, legitimate authority has given full warrant for their actions. Second, they have not themselves committed brutal physical acts. (p. 122)

In contrast, very little obedience (20% completely obedient) occurred when a peer, rather than the experimenter, gave the order to shock the learner, when two authorities gave contradictory orders (0% completely obedient) or when a peer(s) rebelled (10% complete obedience). The first result indicates that for the subject to conform in this situation, the order must come from an authority. The second and third findings have important implications for authorities who would seek to get others to perform malevolent acts to advance their agenda. They must give consistent orders, and they must suppress any evidence of rebellion, no matter how minor. Hence, King Creon's harsh punishment of the heroine in *Antigone* shows Sophocles's exceptional insight into human behavior.

Although the percentages of completely obedient subjects in these experiments provide important insight into the nature of obedience to authority, they fail to provide a complete story. Some of Milgram's observations about how his subjects acted during the experiment add important nuance. Milgram noted that many of his subjects experienced severe stress, at times manifested verbally, at other times manifested by fitful laughter. The stress of the experiment may have led them to adopt what Milgram characterized as an administrative outlook on the experiment, in contrast to a moral outlook. So, for example, many paid close attention to the details of the experiment (e.g., reading the word pairs with exaggerated care), perhaps as a means of avoiding thinking about the consequences of their actions. They also tended to make a clear distinction between duty to the authority (experimenter) and personal feeling, with duty considered the more important of the two. They might justify this choice in terms of a higher purpose, in this case for the advancement of scientific knowledge about learning, much as Nazis might have justified their actions by appealing to the importance of racial purity. Finally, they tended to derogate the victim (learner), at times blaming him for failing to get the correct answer and so "forcing" them to shock him. Victim derogation occurs commonly when we find ourselves wanting to justify hurting others. It justifies harming others by casting them as less than human. Thus during times of war, we might refer to our enemies using racial epithets, with the same outcome emerging when exhibiting racial discrimination against minority groups. Similarly, those opposing governmental assistant programs might justify their position by characterizing enrollees in the Supplemental Nutrition Assistant Program as stupid, lazy, or both.

The reason that people conformed in the Milgram experiments differs from the reason that people conformed in the Asch experiments. Because many miss the distinction, consider some of the differences. First, Asch's confederates applied implicit influence; they never demanded or even asked the naïve subject to conform. In contrast, Milgram's experimenter applied explicit influence, demanding obedience to his orders. Second,

Asch's subjects failed to understand the extent to which they conformed, some even failing to understand that they did conform at all. In contrast, Milgram's subjects had keen awareness of the fact that they conformed to the experimenter's orders. In fact, their verbal reports at the termination of the experiment often used the fact that the experimenter ordered them to shock the learner to justify their action. Interestingly, this response also characterized a substantial portion of the defense of some Nazis on trial for war crimes after World War II. Finally, the goal of the two experiments differed in a subtle way. In the Asch experiments, Asch strove to produce behavioral homogenization, with everyone giving the same answer, everyone behaving in the same way. In contrast, Milgram's experiments encourage behavioral differentiation. Not everyone did the same thing. Some gave orders, others took orders. Some meted out painful shocks, others received them. Providing food for thought, Milgram suggested that behavioral homogenization characterizes democracies or republican forms of government, whereas obedience emerges as a dominant form of social influence in authoritarian or fascist regimes.

Milgram may overstate this last distinction. Humanist philosophers, such as Henry David Thoreau in *On Civil Disobedience*, assert and argue for the greater importance of individual conscience compared with conformity generally, and with obedience specifically. Alternatively, conservative philosophers, such as Thomas Hobbes in *The Leviathan*, would more likely endorse conformity as more important. Nevertheless, rarely, if ever, would one find an advocate of the view that one should avoid obedience at all costs or that one should embrace obedience to the extent that one obeys orders from a malevolent authority to perform evil acts in the interests of social harmony.

Instead, those examining the issue carefully understand the importance of leadership, know that leaders must issue orders in certain circumstances, and know that followers must obey orders to advance the interests of legitimate and benevolent businesses, governments, and other institutions. Nevertheless, they also realize that therein lies the seed of a potential holocaust. The same obedience to the orders of a highly competent and benevolent authority may transfer to obedience to an incompetent and malevolent authority. People require strong moral compasses to distinguish the two.

Identification

Imagine that you take your child to a psychology lab at prestigious Stanford University. The researchers separate you from your child to show her a short film. You pass a room full of toys and enter into an adjacent observation room where you will watch her play with the toys after the film.

She then enters the room and focuses on an inflatable clown toy, a Bobo Doll. She rushes toward it, and you expect that perhaps she will befriend the toy clown. To your surprise, the inflatable clown receives a vicious assault from her in the form of kicks to the doll, beating the doll with a hammer, and firing a toy gun at the doll. You protest while the researchers busily take notes. "My little darling never plays like this at home and never gets in trouble for fighting the other children at school!" You start to wonder, wait a moment, what did they show her on that film?

Although Bandura et al. (1963) do not report whether the parents watched the children at play in their study, the description of the child assaulting an inflatable doll reflects the results they obtained from showing small children a film of an adult beating up a similar doll. The attacks on the doll by the children occurred substantially less often when the children did not view the filmstrip. In addition, previous ratings of the children's usual level of aggressiveness by their teachers had no relationship with the children's likelihood of engaging in aggressive play. This study shows an early research example of social influence through identification.

Social influence through **identification** occurs when people attempt to model their behavior on an individual or group with whom the person identifies. People act in this manner because they want to resemble the other person or persons as much as possible. This form of influence differs from the kind of means control shown by Asch in that the source manipulates no rewards or punishments. The famous professional basketball player Michael Jordan sold a lot of Gatorade under the slogan "Be Like Mike." Yet Jordan offered no rewards to those who complied and threatened no punishments to those who failed to drink Gatorade. This form of influence differs from obedience because with obedience, the authority directly commands behavior to particular people, whereas when identification occurs, the source may not even know who adopted the modeled behavior. The source may not even know that influence occurred.

When identification occurs, the source does not command behavior, the source displays behavior. Those who identify with the source then try to imitate that behavior to feel more similar to the source. Identification also differs from means control in that someone who adopts a behavior because of identification likely comes to believe in the merits of acting that way, whereas with means control, the target does not usually continue the behavior when the source withdraws rewards and punishments. Similarly, the obedient target performs the behavior because the authority ordered the target to do so, not because the target came to believe in the merits of the action.

Researchers have discovered ways in which identification and modeling behavior can influence people. Altheide and Johnson (1977) offered an ethnographic account of the Billy Graham Crusade in which Graham spoke at large events, drawing thousands of Christians. During these events, Graham would invite to the pulpit those who wanted to "come forward to Christ." It would appear that many people spontaneously walked forward, although about one-half of them came forward because the organization arranged for them to do so in advance. These confederates created a model for the uninitiated to follow and emulate. According to the investigators,

> These strategies promote the respectability of making a public commitment and represent methods calculated to manipulate the consent of the passive, the uncertain, the wary, and the indecisive.

The confederates modeled the desired (by Graham) behavior and many followed their example.

Following Bandura's successful use of filmstrips to influence children to engage in violent play, mass media scholars have long sought to understand processes by which people may imitate the behavior of a character in a narrative mass media presentation. Cohen (2001) explained that some scholars argue that such a character influences behavior because the viewer sees things from the character's point of view; others argue that the viewer sees the character as a friend; and still, others argue for an identification process in which people wish to emulate the character's behavior. Some refer to this latter aspect as "wishful identification."

One study of wishful identification focused on the popular, unscripted television show, *Jersey Shore*. The show presented the adventures of a group of young people who spent most of their time seeking and finding casual sex. The study authors, Bond and Drogos (2014), first conducted a careful content analysis and estimated that the *Jersey Shore* characters engaged in sexual behavior or discussed sex approximately once per minute in an average episode. Following others, they referred to television as the "sexual superpeer," a reference to the likelihood that young viewers would look to television characters as peer models to emulate. Based on a survey of young people who watched the show, they found that responses to a set of questions measuring wishful identification with the *Jersey Shore* characters related positively to the extent to which the survey subjects reported permissive sexual attitudes, which in turn related positively to sexual behavior. Also consistent with the premise that *Jersey Shore* characters provide models to emulate, the authors noted the popularity of Halloween costumes based on *Jersey Shore* characters during the heyday of the show.

Compliance Gaining

We next distinguish persuasive communication from a closely related phenomenon, cases in which a requester approaches a target and asks a favor using scripted techniques. When the requester uses the right combination of phrasing, the likelihood that the target says "yes" increases, even though the target may not have actually developed a positive attitude toward performing the request. For example, consider a case in which someone wearing a badge indicating that she represents the American Cancer Society approaches you. The representative asks you to donate some money. Aside from whether you have money on you or not, your attitude likely shapes your response to the solicitor. In contrast, what if at the end of the request the representative of the charity also said, "Even a penny will help." Now you base your decision on more than just your attitude toward the charity and giving. Now you consider the extent to which your refusal would make you look like a miserly Scrooge who refuses to donate even a measly penny to a worthy cause. The addition of these five words did nothing to convince you of the worthiness of the charity or the value of donating. Yet the pressure to agree with the request increased.

Compliance gaining differs from persuasive communication in several ways. Someone producing persuasive communication tries to change the attitudes of the target so that the target will behave in ways consistent with that attitude, even in the persuasive agent's absence and in all contexts. Compliance gaining focuses on behavior only and usually in a single instance. In addition, persuasive communication deliberately presses for attitude change, often by presenting detailed and compelling arguments. Compliance gaining includes no overt pressure. The scripted parts of the compliance-gaining technique rarely include anything resembling an argument in favor of compliance.

Although you may think that adding a phrase like "even a penny will help" would surely affect very few people's decisions, summaries of the relevant studies indicate that the likelihood of people saying "yes" increases by a factor of 2.41 when a requester adds the phrase "even a penny will help" to their verbal pitch (Andrews et al., 2008). Similarly, you may express skepticism that the phrase "of course, you are free to refuse" would not affect anyone's likelihood of saying "yes." Why would telling people they can say "no" to a request from a stranger increase the likelihood of that person saying "yes?" No one would believe otherwise in the first place, so why would pointing it out matter? Researchers have presented different explanations for why it works, but quantitative research summaries, or meta-analyses, suggest that when a requester adds that phrase or something similar, the target will comply 2.2 times more often than when the request lacks that key phrase (Carpenter, 2013). One study even showed that adding the phrase might have increased compliance when making the request for a person to hold a transparent box that contained an enormous spider (Guéguen et al., 2015).

Other compliance-gaining techniques attempt to manipulate the interaction in more nuanced ways. The foot-in-the-door technique involves two different requests. The first request consists of a very small favor that nearly everyone agrees to perform. Then a second larger request follows. Although most compliance-gaining studies use requests for donations of time or money to charities, one study used the foot-in-the-door to get a date. Young women walking alone in a city on the west coast of France served as the targets. The male requester in the control condition approached each woman and stated, "Hello, I'm sorry to bother you but I was wondering if you were busy now. If not, we could have a drink together if you have some time" (Gueguen et al., 2008, p. 531). With this request, 3.3% of the women agreed. In contrast, when the requester first asked the women if they could give him a light for his cigarette, 15% agreed to his subsequent request to have a drink together. Some of the women may have found the requester more attractive because he smoked. Yet the researchers found a similar rate of compliance (15.8%) when the initial request involved asking for directions to a local landmark. Neither of these requests persuaded the target that the requester would provide more desirable company for a drink, yet the behavior changed for more of the targets.

Another complex technique uses the opposite strategy. For example, imagine a young man who wants his father to give him $10 to see a movie. He first asks his father for $2,000 to buy a used car. The father immediately refuses. The son immediately follows up by asking for a mere $10 instead and gets his money. The researchers who first empirically demonstrated this technique referred to it as the door-in-the-face technique.

The door-in-the-face may also prove useful in situations other than asking for small favors. Gold and Raven (1992) analyzed communication before World War II between the United Kingdom's prime minister Winston Churchill and the American president Franklin Roosevelt. They argued that Churchill used a door-in-the-face strategy to get military aid from Roosevelt. Roosevelt's reluctance to sell arms to the United Kingdom resulted from a fear of upsetting anti-war constituencies in the United States. Then in mid-1940, Churchill sent a telegram to Roosevelt in which he

> asked not only for the old destroyers, but also aircraft, anti-aircraft equipment, steel, raw materials, a promise to continue the supply when British cash was exhausted, and a visit to Ireland and Singapore by a United States naval squadron. (p. 255)

Although Churchill did not receive the contents of his wish list, Roosevelt did supply some "aircraft, anti-aircraft equipment, and steel" (p. 256). Gold and Raven argued that with this message, Churchill had successfully used the door-in-the-face technique. Although one usually does not receive anti-aircraft guns, meta-analyses suggest that requesters using the door-in-the-face increase success by a factor of 1.59 (O'Keefe & Hale, 2001). People who use the door-in-the-face strategy do not persuade the target to adopt a positive attitude toward the requested behavior. Yet the targeted behavior does occur more often when requesters use this technique or any of these compliance-gaining techniques relative to a simple request.

Persuasion

In 1873, Susan B. Anthony gave a brief but compelling address advocating that women receive the right to vote. In 1924, Clarence Darrow presented an impassioned plea in the service of his clients Richard Loeb and Nathan Leopold, who had admitted killing a 14-year-old boy. Darrow sought to obtain a verdict of life in prison, thus preventing them from receiving the death penalty. In 1963, Dr. Martin Luther King Jr. composed *Letter from Birmingham Jail*, in which he defended the principle of nonviolent resistance to combat racism. Seemingly, these authors/speakers designed these texts to address a specific issue: Anthony in regard to her arrest for casting an "illegal" vote, Darrow to obtain a particular verdict, and King to convince local clergy. In fact, the goals appeared broader: Anthony advocating that women receive the right to vote, Darrow eliminating the death penalty, and King appealing to the larger U.S. Christian community. Despite the differences in the authors, the nature of the language employed, the channel employed to transmit the message, and the target audience, these examples share the commonality that they convinced people. They persuaded.

As used in this book, the term **persuasive communication** refers to cases in which a source transmits a message to an audience through some channel with the purpose of changing an attitude. This definition lists six components of this definition: change, attitude, source, message, channel, and audience. To understand this definition requires examining each component.

Changing an attitude refers to modifying, reinforcing, or shaping one. To **modify** an attitude requires making it different from a previous attitude. The Apostle Paul's conversion to Christianity on the road to Damascus described in the *New Testament* (ninth chapter of Acts) exemplifies this type of change. Less dramatically, convincing an opponent of the death penalty to vote for its reinstatement in Michigan provides another example of modification. To **reinforce** an attitude involves making an existing attitude stronger (e.g., by making people more confident or certain in their judgment, more knowledgeable concerning their judgment, or more committed to their judgment). For example, parents of a teenager might continue to point out the advantages of abstaining from premarital intercourse, despite the fact that the teen holds a pro-abstinence attitude, in the hope that the attitude will strengthen and that the probability of continued abstinence will increase. The Republican Party designs messages to reinforce the attitudes of persons who already identify with the Republican Party in the hope that this portion of the electorate will vote, give money to the party, and, generally, promote the party's various agenda. To **shape** an attitude refers to creating one. Likely few of us have formed attitudes about hydroponically grown vegetables or butterfat standards required of dairy herds. Nonetheless, someone interested in promoting the sale of hydroponically grown vegetables, or in decreasing the butterfat content required of dairy herds, might construct messages designed to shape them in a direction favorable to their interests. Furthermore, although some argue that at least some attitudes have a genetic component (Olson et al., 2001), at some point in our lives, most, if not all, of the attitudes we hold presently remain unshaped. Leaders of social movements, well aware of this fact, may seek to foster racial consciousness or environmental awareness, both examples of attitude shaping.

An **attitude** refers to a basic evaluative orientation toward an object. For instance, someone may oppose offshore oil drilling, in which case the person has a negative attitude toward that topic. Alternatively, some may favor a capital gains tax, with such people having a positive attitude toward that tax. For other issues, concepts, and persons one may have no attitude. Moreover, most believe that attitudes emerge from experience shaped, reinforced, and modified by exposure to different persuasive messages; that they endure as opposed to rapidly changing affective states, such as moods; and that they predict action.

Several concepts related to attitude emerge frequently when studying persuasion. Particularly, the concepts: values, ideologies, beliefs, opinions, and behaviors arise often and thus merit definition. Attitudes differ in their generality or abstractness. For example, one's attitude toward war in general lies toward the more abstract end of a continuum ranging from extremely concrete attitudes to extremely abstract ones. In contrast, one's attitude toward war in Syria lies closer to the extremely concrete end of that continuum. The term **value** refers to an exceptionally general or abstract attitude. For example, one could think of attitudes toward security or achievement as values.

An **ideology** refers to having a consistent set of views on a constellation of related attitudes. Hence when one speaks of someone embracing a progressive ideology, one may think of someone who favors making a university education tuition-free, increasing the minimum wage, and increasing taxes on the wealthy, as well as opposing a flat tax, completely market-based solutions to health care, and increases in military spending.

Attitudes differ from **beliefs** in that beliefs involve judgments of the correctness of a proposition rather than an evaluation of it. The term **opinion** refers to the verbal expression of a belief. You can think of beliefs as claims of fact. For example, I may believe that offshore oil drilling in Alaska will result in a decrease in the size of the whale population. I might then express that opinion in a face-to-face conversation with a friend, or I might post it on my blog. Nevertheless, that belief remains independent of your evaluation of it. Some might evaluate a decrease in the size of the whale population negatively and others positively. To provide a different example, I might believe that an increase in the capital gains tax will decrease investment. Those who share my belief might evaluate decreased investment negatively and others positively. At times, persuasion efforts focus on changing beliefs as a means of indirectly influencing attitudes.

Behavior refers to overt action. We shall see later that attitudes affect behavior. Thus by changing people's attitudes, or persuading them, changes in action likely result. Several dimensions of behavior interest those of us who study persuasion. At times, scholars focus on the **frequency** of action (e.g., how often someone attends class). In other cases, the **intensity** of action emerges as the dimension of interest. For example, giving money or working for a political candidate by going door-to-door handing out campaign literature involves relatively intense political activism. In contrast, signing a petition or expressing support for a cause on a social media platform demonstrates less intensity. Behavioral **latency** refers to the speed of action, such as how quickly one moves to purchase a newly marketed electronic device. Finally, **duration** refers to how long action persists (e.g., how long one continues following a New Year's resolution to exercise regularly).

The **source** of a persuasive communication refers to any person, or group of persons, who transmits that persuasive message. Sources differ in numerous ways, with their credibility as one of the most important factors. Most generally, the **message** consists of a set of symbolic stimuli designed with the purpose of changing attitudes. Sources have numerous message design options available when constructing persuasive messages. Many of these options vary in their persuasive effectiveness. The **channel** refs to the medium through which the source transmits the message. Again, sources have options. They can transmit their messages in face-to-face form, written form, in audio, on video, and even in other ways. The **audience** encompasses that set of people targeted by the persuasive message. These audience members may vary considerably on important demographic characteristics, such as age or income. They may differ on psychological characteristics, such as self-esteem or the need for cognition, as well. Subsequent chapters emphasize the importance of these components.

Compared with other forms of social influence (reviewed in Table 1.2), persuasion offers important advantages for the influencing agent because influenced targets have internalized attitudes likely to result in the desired action. Thus, successful persuasion requires less need to monitor the target's subsequent action. For instance, supervisors have less need to surveil a worker who has a strong work ethic, or parents have less need to check up on children who have strong attitudes opposing antisocial activities. Second, influencing agents can expect that those who have internalized certain attitudes will exhibit substantial resistance to counter persuasion. Hence, should coworkers attempt to convince a hardworking employee to slack off on the job, or should your children's friends attempt to convince them to engage in underage drinking, one can expect them to resist. Third, those who have internalized such attitudes may assist in convincing others. Hardworking employees might spread their ideology and create a more productive work environment, or your children may influence their peers to act in a more prosocial manner.

On the other hand, in the short run, influencing agents may find persuasion less effective or efficient than other forms of social influence. For example, parents may find it more efficient or less taxing to threaten their children as a means of gaining their conformity. Alternatively, in response to the practically infinite number of "why" questions that children can generate in response to a parental order, the parent may invoke the obedience principle by exclaiming, "Because I am your parent, and I told you to!" Of course, such influence strategies fail to yield the benefits listed in the preceding paragraph.

TABLE 1.2   Types of Social Influence

Means Control	People conform to someone's commands because that person can manipulate the rewards and punishments they experience
Legitimate Power	People obey someone's commands because they feel that they have a duty to comply with that person's requests
Identification	People model their behavior on an individual or group with whom they identify
Compliance Gaining	Requesters use a scripted technique to change the behavior of a targeted person
Persuasion	A source transmits a message to an audience through some channel with the purpose of changing an attitude

A NOTE ON THE HISTORY OF PERSUASION AS A DOMINANT SOURCE OF SOCIAL INFLUENCE

McGuire (1985) argued that in the course of human history persuasion has rarely emerged as the dominant means of social influence (p. 234). He characterized four eras and geographic locations as times and places when persuasion played the central role in settling economic, political, and social disputes. In these eras, elites found persuasion so sufficiently important that they trained their children in its art and later its science.

Athens in the 4th and 5th centuries BCE demarcates the first era of persuasion's dominance. McGuire dates it from Gorgias's introducing the work of the sophists to Athenians in 427 BCE until 338 BCE when Phillip II of Macedon established a new order in Athens. The Roman Republic in the 1st and 2nd centuries BCE forms the second era of persuasive dominance, the Italian Renaissance the third, and the 20th and 21st centuries CE the fourth. Certainly, one could find examples of other forms of social influence in these times and places as well. The number of wars fought during these periods attests to that fact. One could also find examples of persuasive influence at times other than these four eras. Nonetheless, we should not lose McGuire's primary point. Persuasion has rarely dominated the manner in which we influence one another. Furthermore, no trend has emerged; eras dominated by other types of influence have both preceded and followed eras dominated by persuasive influence. Presently, we see numerous examples of persuasion at work. History reminds us that that state of affairs could change.

THE ETHICS OF PERSUASION

Not infrequently, humans experience conflict. Two or more people might want the same thing, but only one can have it, such as when two coworkers want a promotion to the same position. Two or more people might want different things, but they can only have one thing, such as when a woman wants two children and her husband wants one. On some occasions, but not all, people find it necessary or preferable to manage, if not resolve, conflicts such as these.

When people find it necessary or preferable to manage or resolve conflict, they try to influence others. As discussed previously, social influence techniques vary widely. Historically, physical aggression, such as war, provided a common social influence mechanism. Throughout the recorded history of humankind, the prevalence of wars stands out (cf., Hoffer, 1967). Comparing persuasion and aggression as a means of resolving conflict, McGuire (1985) wrote,

> The tragic vanity of thinking that the word is mightier than the sword is exhibited by the fates of the rhetorical masters of each of the previous centuries of persuasion: Demosthenes, done in by poison under the Macedonians his Philippics

had failed to halt; Cicero, by the knives of the Triumvirs at whom his latter-day Philippics were aimed; and Ramus, in the St. Bartholomew's Day massacre—each dispatched by his inarticulate targets whose brutally effective responses proved that the rhetoricians had spoken against them wisely but not too well. (p. 235)

Certainly, persuasion can evolve into an unsavory event at times. Political posts on social media may spread false beliefs to support the source's position. Advertisers might make exaggerated claims of the wonders of their products. Spouses might say hurtful things to each other as a means of winning an argument. Because of such events, some might deem persuasion morally objectionable. In contrast, however, the skillful, persuasive presentation of an innocent defendant's case at trial or the well-crafted presentation that convinces executives in a business meeting to fund an innovative product also involves persuasion. Such instances fulfill the Quintilian ideal written at the beginning of the 12th book of *Institutio Oratoria* of a good man speaking well. Let us give McGuire (1985) the last word on the subject,

At those more normal times, a few aberrant young who see visions and old who dream dreams may discern that persuasion is the worst possible mode of social mobilization and conflict resolution—except for all the others. (p. 235)

THE STRUCTURE OF THIS BOOK

The next eight chapters address eight issues fundamental to understanding the persuasion process. Chapter 2 examines a central premise long embraced by persuasion scholars; namely, the notion that stronger arguments persuade people more effectively than weaker arguments. Models developed by psychologists challenge that view, arguing that sometimes argument strength does not matter. Chapter 2 examines what constitutes a strong argument from several points of view. The chapter concludes by addressing the nuanced question of the role of argument strength in persuading others. Because message characteristics contribute so substantially to effective persuasion, and because argument strength stands above other message characteristics as the most fundamental, this chapter provides a foundation necessary to gain the benefit of all subsequent chapters.

Humans differ in an abundance of ways, one of which involves the ease with which they change when exposed to persuasive messages, or what persuasion scholars term persuasibility. Even those not very susceptible change their attitudes on certain topics and when exposed to certain kinds of messages. In addition, even the very susceptible resist on some issues and when exposed to some well-crafted persuasive messages. Chapter 3 explores important demographic and psychological characteristics that have an effect on persuasibility.

Medications may target the condition for which physicians prescribed them, but they may also have unintended effects. Sometimes those unintended effects promote one's health; in other cases, they have effects detrimental to one's health. Similarly, even when effective in convincing others, persuasive messages may have unintended consequences or side effects. Chapter 4 explores some of these consequences, such as generalizability and displacement effects, credibility, and message comprehension. Following a persuasive attempt, the influencing agent would like to have changed the audiences' attitude and perhaps related attitudes but also would like to have the audience understand the content of the message, seek out more information congruent with the argument recommendations, and have enhanced respect for the influencing agent. These outcomes may or may not occur, and this chapter explores the conditions under which favorable and detrimental side effects emerge.

Chapter 5 addresses a side effect so important that it deserves special treatment. It examines the frequency with which, with whom, and how people talk about persuasive messages that they have heard. In scholarship, as well as common parlance, people refer to this phenomenon as buzz.

Persuasive messages could have a temporary effect on audience attitudes, perhaps lasting no longer than the targets' completion of the experiment's attitude measures. Alternatively, they could have a long-lasting impact, driving targets' attitudes and action for decades. Chapter 6 explores message and source properties that contribute to the duration, or lack thereof, of persuasive message effects.

A potential outcome of a persuasion attempt involves the audience shifting their attitudes away from, rather than toward, the position advocated in the message. Persuasion scholars refer to this outcome as a "boomerang effect" or a "backfire effect." We shall, however, employ the more cumbersome but (we think) more accurate phrase "counterproductive message effect" (CME). Notably, a CME differs from resistance, which occurs when the audience members do not shift their attitudes in response to an attempt to persuade them. Chapter 7 examines the frequency of such effects, their consistency, the conditions under which they might occur, and their explanation.

Chapter 8 focuses on the opposite of most persuasive attempts. Rather than trying to modify peoples' existing attitudes, it reflects on trying to prevent attitude modification. Put differently, it examines methods of reinforcing existing attitudes, rendering them resistant to subsequent persuasive attempts to modify them. It reviews indicators of attitude resistance. A discussion of the methods of inducing resistance temporarily and permanently ensues. A review of the relative importance of cognitive and motivational elements then follows. The chapter attends closely to the growing body of research addressing the use of inoculation to induce resistance.

Persuasion research generally targets audience attitudes, but one of the enduring controversies in persuasion examines the extent to which attitudes, especially self-reports, predict behavior. Initially, Chapter 9 describes some of the classic research challenging the strength of the attitude-behavior association. Then it addresses recent meta-analytic evidence. A description and evaluation of some of the more thoroughly studied models that address the issue conclude the chapter.

Although each chapter concludes with a summary of the chapter's focal topic, the concluding chapter, Chapter 10, provides a broader summary. It reviews what we think that we know about persuasion and identifies those important pieces of knowledge for which we have equal confidence in our ignorance. It concludes by presenting an agendum for advancing the study of persuasion. With this brief summary, we now turn to grapple with the question of "what constitutes a strong persuasive argument?"

2

What Constitutes a Strong Persuasive Message, and Does It Matter?

Skepticism is the chastity of the intellect.

> —George Santayana, *Skepticism and Animal Faith*

He who will not reason is a bigot, he who cannot reason is a fool, and he who dares not is a slave.

> —Sir William Drummond, *Academical Questions*

M OST WHO HAVE STUDIED PERSUASION have held the belief that the stronger the persuasive message, the more persuasive the message. This chapter attends to Santayana's assertion from *Skepticism and Animal Faith* that begins this chapter by examining this assertion carefully. First, we shall consider what constitutes a strong persuasive message, and we shall do so by looking at the matter from several varying lenses. Metaphorically, we shall circle the phenomenon by asking how logicians, argumentation scholars, social scientists, and communication scientists view the idea. Next, we shall turn to the question of the effect of the strength of the message on the ability to change audience attitudes. This question requires inspecting, and trying to make sense of, the results of a vast number of experiments conducted with the purpose of studying this issue. The fact that different investigators think about message strength differently makes this exercise challenging.

Our everyday language assumes that a stronger argument persuades more than a weak argument. We encourage people to write strong arguments, blame failed persuasion on weak arguments, and explain our own attitude changes with reference to the strong arguments we encountered. Yet if someone asked you right now to describe the features of a "strong" argument, do you think you could do it? You might find yourself merely offering synonyms, such as "compelling" or "persuasive," rather than listing any features. You might have thought "logical," but most of us have not received the kind of training in formal logic required to identify a logical argument from an illogical one. Former Supreme Court Justice Potter Stewart admitted that he could not define pornography but added, "I know it when I see it." Similarly, we may not have the ability to define what constitutes a logical argument but believe that we have the ability to recognize one when we see it. The contents of this chapter will help you identify strong arguments from weak ones and consider the circumstances under which the distinction matters.

In Chapter 1, we defined a persuasive message as a set of symbolic stimuli designed to change attitudes. Although one may have to probe them carefully to see it, these persuasive messages have a structure, a structure referred to as an argument. So, one can reframe the question of what constitutes a persuasive message to the question of what constitutes a persuasive argument. In ordinary discourse, the term "argument" frequently receives poor treatment. Often, people associate argument with irrational anger, the verbal escalation of conflict perhaps involving yelling and screaming, hurt feelings, and, perhaps eventually, violence. Others may associate the term with competition, with someone trying to exert dominance over another (as in "he just wanted to win the argument" or "she just wanted to get her way") and with rude interruptions of other speakers. In scholarly discourse, the term gets used much differently, with much less negative connotations. Nevertheless, all scholars do not use the term uniformly. Nuanced differences in views of what constitutes argument emerge in different sectors of the academia. We shall begin in the philosophy department.

PERSPECTIVES ON ARGUMENT

A Logician's View

The study of both formal and informal logic occupies important places in the curriculum of philosophy departments and has for a very long time. From a logician's point of view, arguments have two distinguishable components: conclusions and premises.

A **conclusion** refers to a statement articulating the point one endorses, or put another way, the position for which one argues. Words such as "therefore," "hence," "thus," "ergo," and "consequently" prepare the listener for the conclusion about to come, and speakers often use them to signal to their audience the coming conclusion. **Premises** refer to statements that provide reasons for the audience to embrace the conclusion.

Logicians distinguish between deductive and inductive arguments. **Deduction** refers to arguments in which conclusions follow necessarily from premises. For instance, someone might argue the following:

A tax decrease will result in a budget deficit within the next year. (Premise 1)

Taxes have decreased. (Premise 2)

Therefore, a budget deficit will occur within the next year. (Conclusion)

Given the definitions of the term "and" (conjunction) and the phrase "if-then," if one accepts the truth of these premises, then one must embrace the conclusion. This form of argument arises so commonly that logicians have given it a name: **modus ponens** (Latin for "mode that affirms"). The following is a symbolic representation:

1. $X \rightarrow Y$ (If X happens, then Y will happen)
2. X (X happened) $\therefore Y$ (Therefore, Y will happen)

Logicians judge deductive arguments by two criteria: (1) validity and (2) soundness. The conclusion of a **valid** deductive argument follows by rules of logic from the premises. If a valid deductive argument also has true premises, then logicians refer to it as *sound*. Of course, not all arguments have these properties. For example, consider the following argument:

If Tom Brady was a movie star, then he would be famous.

Tom Brady is famous.

Thus, Tom Brady is a movie star.

Indeed, Tom Brady has achieved considerable fame—at least among those who follow professional football. And if he engages in an acting career, he may well achieve fame for it. His present fame results from him playing football well, however, not from acting. We symbolize this argument as follows:

1. $X \rightarrow Y$
2. $Y \therefore X$

Logicians know this invalid argument form, or fallacy, so well that it too has a name (although not a prestigious Latin one), "affirming the consequent." They have proven it false, which means that its structure can yield false conclusions even when preceded by true premises.

Now, consider the following argument.

Those who like bacon are intelligent.

Walter likes bacon.

Hence, Walter is intelligent

Once again, we have a modus ponens argument. The structure of the argument assures us of its validity. On the other hand, as much as one of this book's authors (Chris) might like to believe the first premise, we know not to believe it. The argument may meet the validity criterion, but it fails the soundness criterion.

For a logician to judge a deductive argument as strong, it would have to exhibit both validity and soundness. Thus the arguments of those who construct persuasive messages deductively would have to meet these two criteria for a logician to judge their messages as strong.

In contrast with a deductive argument, the conclusions of **inductive** arguments follow from the premises with more or less certainty or higher or lower probability. Inductive arguments comprise the vast majority of interesting arguments. We cannot judge the premises of most arguments as true or false with certainty; instead, we believe them more or less likely.

Consider the first premise of the tax argument presented previously. A tax decrease will result in a budget deficit within the next year. Rewriting it without changing its meaning yields "if a tax decrease occurs now, then a budget deficit will result within the next year." Economists might argue about the accuracy of that statement. Indeed, tax decreases might increase the deficit, but they might also spur economic growth to such an extent that tax receipts increase. If so, the deficit might not change, or it might even decrease. Now reword the second premise slightly to read, "Taxes will decrease next year." Stating it in the future tense requires estimating the likelihood of this event occurring within the next year. One political scientist studying what various lawmakers have said about the likelihood of an impending tax decrease might estimate the likelihood of a tax decrease and the likelihood of no tax decrease as equal. Another might judge the likelihood as very high, yet another might deem the likelihood low. Suppose we expose some people to this argument and then ask them to quantify their belief in each of the premises. Those who rate both premises as highly probable, say 0.9 (probability estimates range from 0.0 to 1.0), likely also rate the conclusion of the argument (a budget deficit will occur within the next year) as more probable than someone who rates both premises as having a low probability, say 0.2. Others who rate one of the premises as a high probability and the other as a low probability would judge the conclusion as intermediate (i.e., between these two extremes). A logician would characterize an inductive persuasive argument as weaker or stronger depending on the probability with which the audience embraced the conclusion; conclusions embraced with high probability constitute strong arguments; conclusions embraced with low probability constitute weak arguments. Notably, logicians, communication scholars, and other social scientists all expect the probability of the premises to determine the probability of the conclusion and thus the strength of the argument (Hample, 1977, 1978, 1979, 1981, 1982; McGuire, 1960; Wyer & Goldberg, 1970).

To this point, the examples have focused on an argument with a pair of premises and a single conclusion. Speakers may extend arguments, however, and they can do so in several ways. For instance, some arguments contain more than two premises. Consider a valid but not sound meteorological argument with five premises.

If it is cloudy today, then there will be precipitation.

Precipitation may take the form of rain or snow.

If the temperature equals or exceeds 32° Fahrenheit, then precipitation takes the form of rain.

If the temperature is less than 32° Fahrenheit, then precipitation takes the form of snow.

It is cloudy today, and the temperature exceeds 32° Fahrenheit.

Therefore, rain is on the way.

Alternatively, argument extension may involve stacking (i.e., using the conclusion of one argument as a premise of another argument). Let us return to the cheery topic of budget deficits for a valid, but not sound, extended argument.

A tax decrease will result in a budget deficit within the next year.

Taxes have been decreased.

Therefore a budget deficit will occur within the next year.

If the budget runs a deficit next year, then the Federal Reserve will raise interest rates.

Thus the Federal Reserve will raise interest rates next year.

If the Federal Reserve raises interest rates next year, then I will not be able to afford a loan to expand my small business.

Hence I will not be able to expand next year.

From the three signpost terms, "therefore," "thus," and "hence," you can see that three conclusions have now emerged.

A third way in which speakers extend arguments involves developing multiple arguments, some of which may entail the same conclusions, others of which may entail different conclusions. For instance, let us reflect on an argument that someone might make to promote the World Health Organization's (WHO) handwashing guidelines.

If you wash your hands effectively, then you will eliminate most germs.

The more germs you can eliminate, the healthier you will be.

To wash your hands effectively requires putting on ample soap, scrubbing the palms, back of the hands, interlacing the fingertips (front and back), scrubbing the fingertips, and rubbing the knuckles. It should take the amount of time necessary to sing "Happy Birthday" twice. While doing these tasks, place the hands under hot water. Then you should dry them with a clean towel (the WHO guidelines).

Therefore, the more you follow the WHO guidelines, the healthier you will be.

An opponent of this procedure might reply with another argument, such as the following:

To follow the WHO guidelines requires that you use an excessive amount of water.

Using an excessive amount of water is wasteful and harms the environment.

Any action harmful to the environment should be avoided.

Therefore, you should ignore the WHO guidelines.

Alternatively, or additionally, one could substitute (or add) "expensive" for "wasteful and harming the environment" and reach the same conclusion.

The structure of arguments suggests a means of evaluating them. Initially, one might evaluate the syntax of the argument by examining if the conclusion follows from the premises by accepted rules of logic. Although cognitively challenging (see Kuhn, 1991; but also Mercier & Sperber, 2011), uncovering a logical fallacy, such as the previously mentioned affirming the consequent error, provides a strong reason to reject the conclusion of the argument.

One of the additional difficulties performing syntactic evaluation arises from the fact that in ordinary discourse, people do not speak in easily recognized and interpreted premises and conclusions. For example, suppose someone generates the following argument against the effectiveness of the United Nations.

If an assembly of people has diverse interests, then they cannot reach firm conclusions.

The United Nations is an assembly of people with diverse interests.

Therefore, the United Nations cannot reach firm conclusions.

This argument has a valid modus ponens structure, albeit of dubious soundness. In ordinary discourse, however, the same point may appear in a less clearly presented manner, such as the following:

The United Nations is an assembly of people with diverse interests, so it has no chance of reaching firm conclusions.

This restatement of the same idea omits the first premise of the argument. Indeed, the speaker may lack awareness of its omission, assuming that everyone would agree with it, despite the fact that it remains quite controversial. Most arguments appearing in ordinary discourse have such missing premises, termed **enthymemes**. The listener bears the burden of making sense of the argument by supplying the missing premise(s), and listeners may do so in ways that favor or do not favor the speaker's conclusion.

A second means of evaluation, **semantic** evaluation, involves examining the truth of the premises. For example, you might evaluate an argument negatively if you deem a premise(s) false or improbable. Alternatively, you may evaluate an argument positively because you deem the premises true or highly probable.

Adding high-quality evidence to the premise of an argument tends to enhance the listeners' endorsement of that premise. Famously, McCroskey (1969; see also Reinard, 1988) defined **evidence** as consisting of a "factual statement originating from a source other than the speaker, objects not created by the speaker, and opinions of persons other than the speaker that are offered in support of the speaker's claims."

So, considering the proposition, "If you wash your hands effectively, you will eliminate most germs," a listener might demand some evidence of the accuracy of the statement prior to believing it. A clinical trial, the results of which appeared in a report in the *New England Journal of Medicine*, showed that over a 1-month period, washing hands by the WHO guidelines eliminated 98.7% of hand germs, but for those who washed in their usual manner, this only eliminated 61.2% of hand germs, provides evidence in the form of a factual statement originating from a source other than the speaker.

Or suppose that in a trial a witness claimed to have carried $10,000 in his wallet. The opposing attorney then asked him for the denominations of the bills, and the witness replied, "Twenties and fifties." The attorney then asked for a recess, went to a nearby bank, and returned with 200, $50 bills. Asking for the witness's wallet, the attorney then demonstrated that the objects would not fit into the witness's wallet. The $50 bills, objects not created by the speaker, would provide strong evidence challenging the witness's original claim.

Or suppose we consider the proposition that rapid climate change has occurred and will continue to do so. Citing the opinions of 100 experts in the area of climate change, all of whom endorse the accuracy of the statement, provides evidence for the claim—this time in the form of opinions offered in support of the speaker's claim.

Notice the high quality of the evidence in each case. The *New England Journal of Medicine* has the reputation of publishing excellent biomedical research. The attorney tried to fit $50 bills into the wallet, not $20s, thus providing a more stringent test of the witness's claim. The expert opinion cited the opinions of experts in the area of climate change, not the opinions of experts in 18th-century French literature. Evidence of low quality adds little to the believability of one's premises. In addition to providing a definition of evidence, McCroskey conducted a number of studies on the effects of including evidence in persuasive messages. In a 1969 article, he found that in most studies, the inclusion of evidence in an argument produced more attitude change both immediately and after several weeks had passed.

In addition to the presence/absence of evidence and the quality of evidence produced by the speaker, one profits from examining premises for examples of **informal fallacies** (Weston, 2000). In contrast with formal fallacies, such as affirming the consequent, which stem from the structure of the argument, informal fallacies often occur in premises. Thus, an awareness of them aids in semantic evaluation. Although informal fallacies abound, three brief examples will suffice to expand the idea of semantic criticism to the realm of informal fallacies.

The **ad hominem** ("to the person" in Latin) attack emerges frequently in common discourse. It involves attacking a person rather than the argument that person advocates:

> It is no surprise that Carl Sagan claims that life is possible on other planets—after all, he is a well-known atheist. So, I don't believe him.

But neither reputation nor motive provide reasons to believe a premise to an argument. Those of questionable repute and motive may advance strong arguments; those with the opposite characteristics may advance weak ones. Hence ad hominem arguments deceive, and logicians properly categorize arguments that attack a person as fallacies ("fallacy" from the Latin "fallax" meaning "deceptive").

The **argument from ignorance** provides another example of an informal fallacy. For example, "There is no evidence to prove that he was not a Communist, so he probably was," typifies this kind of argument. In this example, the person advancing the premise takes unfair advantage of the fact that one cannot prove that someone did not perform some act (unless specifying time and place carefully).

Begging the question, or **circular reasoning**, provides a third example of a common informal fallacy. It involves assuming the truth of the conclusion or using the conclusions as a premise. For example, consider the argument, "God exists because it says so in the Bible, and I know that the Bible is true because God wrote it." The author wants to develop an argument with the conclusion God exists but assumes that God exists when claiming that God wrote the Bible.

To restate a previous and important point, informal fallacies abound in common discourse and sometimes in formal discourse as well. We enhance our critical ability by learning to recognize informal fallacies. Giving us a reason for optimism, a program of empirical research by the Dutch argumentation scholar Frans H. van Eemeren and his colleagues found that, for most of these fallacies, people judge arguments containing them as less reasonable than messages without such fallacies (van Eemeren et al., 2009).

The third type of evaluation, **pragmatic** evaluation, requires examining other lines of argument that entail the same, or different, conclusions. For example, consider the following argument favoring the abolition of the Electoral College.

If we are to have a democracy, then the person elected president should be the candidate chosen by the majority of the people.

We want to live in a democracy.

Therefore, the president should be the candidate selected by the majority of the people.

If an electoral system is such that a candidate can be elected without receiving the vote of a majority of the people, then that system should be eliminated.

As both the 2000 and 2016 presidential elections show, the Electoral College system allows a presidential candidate to be selected without being chosen by a majority of the people.

Ergo, the Electoral College system should be eliminated.

Another line of argument supporting the final conclusion ("ergo") might invoke the principle of protecting those living in non-swing states and that without the Electoral College, politicians would ignore them during the campaign and their interests after the election.

Alternatively, other lines of argument support the Electoral College system. For instance, one might argue,

> If we are to have a government responsive to all the people, then the electoral system must ensure that people from all regions (north, south, east, and west) and interests (from Michigan auto workers to farm hands in Nebraska) have a chance to influence the outcome of the presidential election.
>
> We want a government responsive to all the people.
>
> Hence the electoral system must ensure that people from all regions and interests have a chance to influence the outcome of the presidential election.
>
> Without the Electoral College, these people's interests will not be able to influence the outcome of the presidential election.
>
> Thus the Electoral College must be retained.

Another line of argument supporting the retention of the Electoral College might invoke the principle of opposing the domination of extremely populous states.

We could subject either or both of these arguments to syntactic or semantic evaluation. Notably, these evaluation criteria apply not only to reactions to others' arguments but also serve as guides in constructing one's own arguments.

An Argumentation Scholar's View

Some scholars focus their intellectual efforts on the study of argumentation. One might find these argumentation scholars in departments of communication or philosophy or scattered in various other sectors of the academy. In 1958, one of the most famous of them, the English philosopher Stephen Toulmin, introduced one of the most popular methods of examining arguments. Rather than analyzing arguments as syllogisms, he advocated a new system that argumentation scholars now call the Toulmin's model (Toulmin, 1958). Toulmin believed that the three-part syllogism advanced by logicians since the time of Aristotle failed to explain fully all the potential parts of an argument. Figure 2.1 shows Toulmin's full model.

Data, warrant, and claim represent the key three parts that resemble the two premises and the conclusion the logicians examine in syllogisms. Consider the following syllogism again:

> Those who like bacon are intelligent.
>
> Walter likes bacon.
>
> Hence, Walter is intelligent

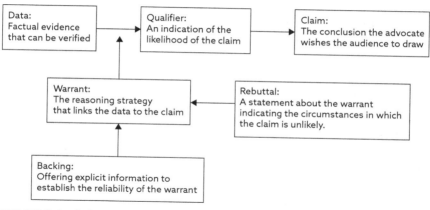

FIGURE 2.1   A depiction of the Toulmin model.

In Toulmin's model, "Hence, Walter is intelligent" represents the **claim**, the new belief the speaker would like the audience to accept. The author of this syllogism wants the audience to believe that Walter has high intelligence. The model would identify "Walter likes bacon" as the data. The **data** (sometimes called grounds) represents the information that the speaker assumes the audience will likely believe and which the speaker wants to use to argue in favor of the claim. After advancing the claim, Toulmin noted that the data responds to the question, "What have you got to go on?" The speaker, trying to convince the audience of Walter's intelligence, offers Walter's bacon consumption as data that will move the audience's beliefs about Walter. The premise we previously identified as unsound, "Those who like bacon are intelligent" represents the **warrant**, the general rule that connects the data to the claim. Toulmin suggested that the warrant answers the question someone might produce concerning the connection between the data and the claim, "How do you get there?"

So far, Toulmin's model does not seem to offer much over the logicians' perspective. But Figure 2.1 shows a number of other pieces not included in the logicians' view of the argument. To illustrate these pieces, we offer the argument: *This bird is a type of penguin, all penguins live south of the equator, and therefore this bird is from south of the equator.* The first statement, identifying the bird as a penguin, represents the data. The assertion that all penguins live south of the equator represents the warrant. The final conclusion denotes the claim.

But in ordinary situations, the audience might not simply accept the truth of the warrant. "How do you know that all penguins live south of the equator?" the audience might ask. Here the originator of the claim about the source of the bird will say, "No penguins in nature have ever been found north of the equator. The zoological record is pretty clear on the point." Such support for the warrant signifies the **backing** in Toulmin's model. The warrant represents the general hypothetical rule meant to connect the data to the claim, but the backing generates factual information that supports the soundness of the warrant. Including such information may greatly contribute to the strength of the argument when doubt about the soundness of the warrant exists. Toulmin noted that on many occasions, the speaker need not state the backing unless someone challenges the warrant.

Toulmin believed that explicitly developing the concept of the backing as separate from the warrant gave his model a clarity that has eluded the logicians who focus on the syllogism. He noted that when the logicians conflate warrants and backing, "they have done so only at the expense of impoverishing our language and disregarding a large number of clues to the proper solutions of their conundrums." The focus on the backing also enables speakers to build stronger arguments by including explicit backing for their warrants. Toulmin claims that the concept of backing also removes the art of constructing a strong argument from formal logical analysis and onto a more realistic footing based on the way people construct arguments in everyday life.

The next part of Toulmin's model, the **qualifier**, indicates "the degree of force which our data confer on our claim in virtue of our warrant." When the warrant indicates that the rule applies universally, one can use phrases such as "definitely," "necessarily," or "must." Yet many warrants do not provide such certainty. Some of our readers who have visited zoos in places north of the equator may have observed penguins living in them. Thus we must temper the conclusion with a sentence like, "Therefore this bird is *almost definitely* from south of the equator." Similarly, we would write the warrant as, "nearly all penguins live south of the equator."

When one wishes to specify the particular cases or situations in which the warrant does not bridge the gap between the data and the claim, Toulmin's model also identifies the **rebuttal**, which indicates exceptions to the warrant. Here our speaker, trying to make claims about the source of a flightless waterfowl, can add, "Unless this bird has escaped from a zoo, it comes from south of the equator."

Both the qualifier and the rebuttal introduce concepts that enable speakers to artic-ulate more clearly the likelihood of their claims. The backing for the warrant adds yet more strength to the argument. One study by communication professor John Reinard (1984) investigated the matter empirically and found backing and rebuttals increased the persuasiveness of an argument. Yet the extent to which qualifiers increased persua-siveness depended on whether the audience judged the issue sufficiently important to them. Specifically, qualifiers only increased persuasiveness when the audience perceived the issue as important. Several studies by advertising researchers have also found that adding backing and warrants generally increases the persuasiveness of advertisements (Kim & Benbasat, 2006; Munch et al., 1993).

A Consequentialist's View

In the study of ethics, consequentialists judge the morality of an action, even an otherwise questionable one, by its consequences. Stealing food from a very rich person for the purpose of feeding a poor, hungry person provides an example of an act that a consequentialist would endorse. Consequentialists view Robin Hood as a very ethical guy.

Some apply this form of reasoning to the question of what constitutes a strong persuasive argument. A summary of their position might read as follows: "Persuasive argument X is strong because the audience thinks it is strong, but persuasive argument Y is weak because the audience thinks it is weak." When hearing this definition, one might respond, "Why does the audience judge X as strong and Y as weak?" Too often consequentialists reply, "Because X is a strong argument and Y is a weak one." Notice the circularity of the position. In fact, it furnishes a perfect example of the "begging the question" fallacy.

Despite the fallacy, this type of thinking creeps into the study of persuasion. For example, psychologists Richard Petty, John Cacioppo, and David Schumann appear to classify arguments for disposable razors as strong or weak on the basis of a preliminary study of undergraduate students (Petty et al., 1981; Petty et al., 1983).

We profit by sensitizing ourselves so that we recognize this fallacy whenever it occurs because it emerges in other ways, particularly in studies of persuasive message effects. For example, you might read a study in which the investigator created two messages and asked a sample of undergraduate students which of the two scared them more. Subsequently, the investigator might give in to the temptation to label the one that most people selected as the "high-fear message" and the other one as the "low-fear message," regardless of the quantity of fear-arousing content in the messages.

A Communication Scholar's View

Communication scholars who study persuasion address two issues when approaching the question, "What constitutes a strong persuasive argument?" On the one hand, we must attend to the logician's and the argumentation scholar's concerns about the structure of argument. On the other hand, we also must examine the relationship between the strength of the argument and the persuasiveness of the argument.

The first concern requires that the conclusion follows from a set of premises and the logical rules that connect them or, in Toulmin's terms, that the claim, as narrowed by the qualifier, follows from the data and the warrant, as narrowed by the rebuttal. Furthermore, the argument requires backing for the warrant. Providing backing entails inserting compelling evidence that makes the warrant more believable or plausible.

The second concern involves investigating the relationship between the strength of the argument and its persuasiveness (i.e., the effectiveness of strong versus weak arguments in changing attitudes). You might think that the assertion "the stronger the argument, the more persuasive the argument" would go unchallenged. Nevertheless, the assertion makes an empirical claim—one about a feature of nature, and nature sometimes surprises us.

Could circumstances require us to reject this empirical claim? Actually, several circumstances might do so. For instance, people might view an argument with informal or formal fallacies or both as equally compelling or perhaps more compelling than an argument without them. Alternatively, people might judge a logically sound argument without evidence, or with low-quality evidence, as equally or more compelling than a sound argument with high-quality evidence. Or our audience might deem a persuasive message with few sound arguments more compelling than a persuasive message with many sound arguments. The question then arises as to how we investigate this matter.

One possibility requires an investigator to construct two persuasive messages on the same topic, say advocating that we all apply sunscreen of at least 45 SPF to all exposed areas of our body 20 minutes before going into the sun. The strong version could consist of several sound arguments with ample amounts of high-quality evidence supporting each premise. The weak version could consist of a single argument containing several formal and informal fallacies and lacking any evidence to buttress the premises of the argument.

The investigator might then assemble a sample of people who agree to participate in a research project and ask them a number of questions, some of which provide an indication of their attitude toward using sunscreen. Perhaps 10 days or so later, the investigator could assign one-half of these participants to read (or listen to or view) the strong version of the persuasive message while assigning the other one-half to read the weak version of the persuasive message. The investigator might then ask the attitude toward sunscreen items again and gauge the extent to which attitudes changed. If those reading the strong version of the message change their attitudes toward sunscreen more in the direction of conforming to the message recommendations (using sunscreen every time you go out in the sun, using at least 45 SPF, and applying 20 minutes before sun exposure) than do those exposed to the weak version of the message, then the investigator has amassed some evidence that strong messages result in more persuasion than weak messages. If the opposite result occurs, or if the investigator finds no differences in attitude change between those exposed to the two different versions of the message, then the outcome questions the idea that strong arguments persuade people more than do weak arguments.

Numerous experiments have, in one form or another, addressed this very question. In the next section, we review some of them.

DO STRONG ARGUMENTS CONVINCE PEOPLE? DO WEAK ARGUMENTS FAIL TO PERSUADE?

The Classical View

As defined in Chapter 1, the term "attitude" refers to the way we evaluate objects. Those formed evaluations depend on us believing certain things as factual, as well as on what we value. Consider an example.

Our imaginary friend, Varda Goslin, believes that those from other countries want to move to the United States because of their membership (by virtue of birth) in persecuted ethnic groups. They might face death if they remain in the countries of their birth, or employers might deny them jobs if they remain in their countries of birth. Or if they have espoused views unpopular to authoritarian governments that rule the countries in which they live, they may face unemployment or death. Varda values freedom from bigotry, such as that based on race or ethnicity or both. Moreover, she values the freedom to spout contrarian views without having to fear for one's safety. So she tends to favor a relatively open immigration policy. She wants to keep out criminals and terrorists, but, otherwise, she evaluates immigration and immigrants favorably.

But Varda sees a post on a social media site and follows a link that exposes her to an argument challenging her views. The source of that argument claims that one of those immigrants might take her job. He adds that immigrants from certain countries come from cultures with rampant crime, that they will bring that culture with them, and that an increase in crime will result. Varda sees no obvious flaws in his reasoning. Although she did not fact-check them, he cites employment and crime statistics supporting his argument. He developed not one but two arguments favoring his anti-immigration stance. Varda values her safety and keeping her job. She had not linked them with the issue of immigration before exposure to this message. Does her previously pro-immigration attitude change? If so, in what way? How much?

The psychologist John French (1956) provided the classical answer to these questions. According to French, Varda would compare and integrate the information contained in this new argument with the information she had that led her to favor a relatively open immigration policy. This integration process results in some of her values favoring an open integration policy, such as opposing bigotry based on race and ethnicity, and others (such as safety) opposing the policy. It also results in some of her beliefs favoring an open immigration policy, such as people immigrate to flee oppression, and others favoring a less open policy, such as immigrants have a high crime rate. French would say that Varda's new attitude (i.e., after exposure to the new message) would favor immigration less than did Varda's old attitude (i.e., the one prior to exposure to the new message), yet Varda would not oppose immigration as much as the person whose message she heard on social media.

Figure 2.2 depicts a continuum of attitudes that provides a way to think about the result of this integration process. You can think of Varda's attitude as potentially ranging from extremely anti-immigration on the far left of the continuum to extremely pro-immigration on the far right of the continuum. The 0 point in the middle of the

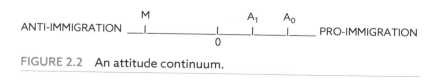

FIGURE 2.2   An attitude continuum.

continuum represents a neutral attitude toward immigration, neither favoring it nor opposing it. M denotes the position on the attitude continuum advocated by the message writer/speaker. A_0 denotes the place on the continuum representing Varda's attitude *prior* to receiving the anti-immigration message, and A_1 represents her attitude *after* exposure to the anti-immigration message. A_0 indicates a very pro-immigration attitude, very far to the right of neutrality. A_1 indicates that she still favors immigration but not as strongly as she did prior to exposure to the anti-immigration message. The distance between A_0 and A_1 marks the direction and extent to which she changed and serves to quantify the strength of the effect of this message on Varda's attitude toward immigration. Notice that had the message produced no effect on Varda's attitude toward immigration, A_0 and A_1 would lie at the same point on the continuum. Notice also that had the message had an even greater effect on Varda's attitude, A_1 would lie closer to the position advocated in the message (i.e., the anti-immigration side of the continuum). In the case of an extremely powerful message, Varda's new attitude might even lie to the left of the neutral point. Central to French's idea, the attitude after exposure to the message always lies as close or closer to the position advocated in the message than does the attitude held prior to exposure to the message.

Communication scholars would expect that strong messages would yield a substantial amount of attitude change in the direction of the position advocated in the message or, put differently, more persuasive impact. Weak messages, on the other hand, would yield little or no change because people like Varda would notice things, such as logical errors, lack of compelling evidence accompanying them, or both.

Data from numerous experiments have produced results consistent with French's thinking (e.g., Anderson, 1971; Boster et al., 1980; Boster et al., 1982; Danes et al., 1978). Others have claimed, however, to have found evidence inconsistent with it. Those others suggest the need for the modification of French's thinking in important ways to account for their findings. The next section explains two suggested modifications of French's position.

Dual-Process Models

In the late 1970s, several social psychologists started to wonder if people always made attitude judgments by carefully integrating new message information into their existing knowledge to produce attitude change, as French and others predicted. One of them, Shelly Chaiken, with her colleague Alison Ledgerwood, explained in a 2012 review that these psychologists wanted to know, "Was careful argument scrutiny the only kind of process by which attitude change could occur? Or might we sometimes change our minds in more efficient, but less effortful, ways?" Dual-process theories of persuasion represent one pattern of answers to these questions, "no" and "yes," respectively.

In 1980, Chaiken first presented the model later known as the heuristic-systematic model (HSM) and elaborated on it with some colleagues in 1989 (Chaiken et al.,

1989). Richard Petty and John Cacioppo first presented their dual-process model, the elaboration likelihood model (ELM), in 1981, and elaborated on it in 1986. The two dual-process models make a variety of predictions, some differing in minor ways from the other. The prediction that concerns us in this chapter deals with circumstances in which the strength or quality of an argument affects the attitudes of the audience.

Petty and Cacioppo's ELM describes what they term the elaboration continuum. This continuum ranges from carefully considering the merits of all of the message arguments (central processing) to ignoring the message claims in favor of simple peripheral cues in the message environment that suggest accepting or rejecting a message position. These cues might include the source's credibility or the sheer number of arguments the speaker presented (peripheral processing). The HSM refers to these two types of cognitive message processing as systematic and heuristic, respectively. Both the HSM and ELM generally predict that the more carefully the audience processes the message, the stronger the effect of message strength and the weaker the effect of peripheral cues. Conversely, they generally predict that the less carefully the audience processes the message, the weaker the effect of message strength and the stronger the effect of peripheral cues. Thus dual-process theories potentially contribute to our understanding of argument strength effects by limiting the effect of argument strength to situations in which the audience carefully considers the message.

The dual-process approach predicts that people will process a message centrally when willing and able to do so. A speaker can induce the members of the audience to process the message centrally by explaining to them that the topic of the argument may greatly affect their own lives. Such an explanation increases what scholars refer to as the listener's **outcome involvement**. And speakers can increase the audience's ability to process centrally by reducing distractions, using simpler language, and discussing issues about which the audience knows a lot. These theories predict that if the audience lacks the willingness, ability, or both to process a message centrally, the strength of the speaker's arguments will not substantially affect the audience members' attitudes. We summarize these theories in Table 2.1.

TABLE 2.1   Summary of Elaboration Likelihood Model Predictions

Peripheral Processing	Central Processing
Causes	Causes
Low outcome-relevant involvement	High outcome-relevant involvement
Low topic knowledge	High topic knowledge
High distraction	Low distraction
Effects	Effects
Persuaded by simple peripheral cues	Persuaded by strong arguments but not weak
Short-term persuasion	Long-lasting persuasion

The HSM describes these processes in more detail and offers a variety of motives for cognitive processing. Chaiken and her colleagues first described the full version of the HSM in 1989. Their theory included the sufficiency principle, which indicates that for any given topic, people have a degree of confidence they require for their judgment. They will then examine the information in the message, putting in enough thought to reach their required level of confidence. Humans generally do not put more effort into a task than required, so once someone has examined a persuasive message to the degree needed to reach the desired amount of judgment confidence, they stop thinking about it. In this way, they strike a balance between confidence in their attitudes and the need to economize in how much cognitive effort they exert. Someone who considers the topic to have little importance will think about the topic very little, instead relying on quick judgment rules or "heuristics" to make the judgment. Principles like "experts are usually right" or "an argument with many pieces of supporting evidence is probably correct," provide examples of the thinking of those engaged in heuristic processing. On the other hand, for extremely important issues, the audience likely will not blindly trust the experts, instead they will carefully consider the arguments. Or put another way, in such circumstances, they engage in systematic processing.

The HSM also differs from the ELM in that it offers alternatives for the role of peripheral cues in addition to the simple trade-off that the ELM presents. The ELM trade-off hypothesis asserts that peripheral cue information, such as a source's credibility, exerts less impact on attitudes as the audience engages in greater depth of processing (i.e., processes more centrally). In contrast, the HSM suggests three possibilities. The first, the attenuation hypothesis, suggests that peripheral cue information may support the message arguments, but if it indicates weakness when paired with strong arguments or strength when paired with weak arguments, then the audience relies on their assessment of the arguments rather than the peripheral cue information. For example, a systematically (centrally) processing audience would rely on the quality of the arguments rather than the sheer number of them. But the HSM also offers the bias hypothesis, which posits that peripheral cue information can influence how people evaluate arguments. For example, an expert source can lead people to judge an argument as stronger than if an inexpert source advanced the exact same argument. Finally, the HSM proposed the additivity hypothesis, which claims that both heuristic and systematic processes can co-occur and jointly influence attitudes. Unfortunately, the HSM does not provide substantial guidance in predicting which of these three options dominate with a given audience and topic.

When dual-process theories of persuasion appeared, many thought them a godsend to persuasion scholars and practitioners. Persuasion researchers had produced many studies on the effects of different aspects of persuasive messages, such as argument strength and source credibility, but across experiments, they found apparently inconsistent effects of those message features on persuasiveness. Initially, dual-process models appeared to offer a clear and consistent explanation of those paradoxical results. Some message aspects affected persuasion when people processed centrally, and others affected persuasion when people processed peripherally. Aspects of argument strength, like the presence of evidence and the use of sound reasoning, would only affect people who processed centrally, whereas other aspects, such as the attractiveness of the speaker or the expertise of the speaker, would only affect those who processed messages peripherally. Initial tests of these theories produced many experiments with results consistent with those predictions.

Criticisms of Dual-Process Theories

Consequently, these theories have enjoyed a great deal of popularity among persuasion researchers, and you will find favorable treatments of them in nearly all persuasion textbooks. Yet their simplicity masks flaws. Initially, although the dual-process theorists talk about two different processes for persuasion, they do not offer much detail on those processes or indicate how to tell which process an audience used when assessing a particular message. This omission makes it difficult for those who want to apply dual-process insights for the purpose of designing messages in practical persuasion situations, such as convincing people to get necessary medical tests, to vote, or to invest their money wisely.

If you want to study something, you need a reliable method of determining when it occurs and when it does not. With so many studies of dual-process models, you might expect that researchers have a good measure for identifying when someone processed the message centrally and when they processed peripherally. Yet despite the dual-process researchers and their students conducting many studies, they have offered no such measure. When communication researchers Paul Mongeau and James Stiff (1993) challenged the theory on that point, the ELM theorist Richard Petty and some of his colleagues (Petty et al., 1993) responded to that critique and pointed to a study that measured processing type by asking the study subjects to report all the thoughts they had when they heard the message. More topic-relevant thoughts meant more cognitive elaboration (central processing). But even then, Petty and his colleagues retreated from that position immediately in a footnote and stated that they did not think counting thoughts produced a good measure of peripheral versus central processing. Although the idea of peripheral and central processing seems very intuitive, we do not know what we need to observe in an audience to determine which type of processing the audience members used when they heard a particular message.

Another critique of dual-process theories questions their ability to predict the effect that a given persuasive message will have on a given audience. These theories and early tests of them appeared to offer clear predictions about what constituted a peripheral cue and what constituted a message argument. Naturally, one expects a theory of persuasion to specify what kind of persuasive messages audiences will find compelling under varying conditions, as well as what kind of persuasive messages audiences likely reject under varying conditions. Yet when pressed on this point, the authors of the ELM exhibit reluctance to provide clear and unambiguous predictions.

In 1986, James Stiff analyzed many of the studies examining what scholars generally think of as a peripheral cue, source credibility, and found that in many experiments, sources high in credibility persuaded people, and sources low in credibility did not, under conditions in which dual-process theories would predict that the audience would process the message centrally. ELM advocates responded by clarifying that any piece of information can serve as a peripheral cue or as a cue to process the message argument centrally. They concluded that source credibility information will sometimes persuade people engaged in peripheral processing and sometimes will persuade people engaged in central processing. They argued that the theory can predict which will happen by the relevancy of the source information to the central merits of the topic (Petty, Kasmer, et al., 1987). James Stiff and Frank Boster (1987) replied by noting the vagueness of such a standard for predicting the pattern of observed source credibility effects from previous experiments, let alone future situations (see also, Petty, Cacioppo, et al., 1987).

For example, Petty and Cacioppo (1980) suggested that in a shampoo advertisement, the attractiveness of the model might serve as an argument because it spoke to the quality of the shampoo. If so, someone strongly interested in the issue of which shampoo to purchase would show a more favorable attitude toward the shampoo advertised with a more attractive model than one picturing a less attractive model. Two marketing researchers, Mary Bitner and Carl Obermiller (1985), responded to that claim by arguing that one could not possibly predict which members of the audience would see the model's hair as a peripheral cue and which would see it as a part of the advertisement's argument. Consider the following example for a moment. When you see an advertisement for shampoo, do you think carefully about it and conclude that the beauty of the model's hair resulted from the shampoo? Or do you attribute the beauty of the model's hair to the skill of professional stylists who made the model's hair look so good for the advertisement? Believing that one's hair will look just as good as the model's because of the shampoo appears an unlikely conclusion to draw by those who engage in careful message scrutiny.

Yet other studies that Petty and Cacioppo reviewed purported to show that the expertise of the message source had little effect when the audience had high outcome involvement and thus processed the message centrally. Consider another example. Why would a centrally processing audience ignore the fact that the author of the message advocating a proposed education policy wrote the message for a high school class assignment as opposed to an essay written by the Carnegie Commission on Education? That piece of information seems important to making an attitude judgment. Stiff and Boster argued that this kind of ambiguity meant that the theory could not predict persuasive outcomes. Petty and colleagues insisted that Stiff and Boster failed to understand the theory. Nonetheless, if we know that the issue matters to the audience, so that audience members will process centrally, we still do not know what kind of information the theory thinks that audience will take into consideration. And if we do not know what kind of information the audience will take into consideration, we do not know how to design persuasive messages to persuade them.

Communication scholar Torsten Reimer and his colleagues (Reimer et al., 2004) claimed that people cannot separate information about the source of a message from the strength of that source's argument. They argued that according to both simple logic and several experiments, argument strength affects the audience's perceptions of the source's expertise. Naturally, if you hear someone making poor arguments with weak evidence, you will tend to infer that the speaker lacks expertise on the topic. Conversely, someone making a well-reasoned case with strong supporting evidence will impress you as highly knowledgeable. Reimer and colleagues argued that this position derives from an Aristotelian argument that speakers establish their credibility by how they deliver their speeches. Their research results show that, indeed, we cannot separate a source's credibility from the strength of that source's arguments (see also Reimer et al., 2005).

Although Reimer and colleagues challenged the extent to which the quality of an argument depends upon the source, earlier work by the social psychologist Solomon Asch argued that the very meaning of the persuasive message depended on the source. Asch argued that researchers need to attend more carefully to the effects of context in interpreting messages. Other researchers suggested that people blindly change their opinion in response to a message if they learn that they approve or disapprove of the source. Asch reanalyzed the data and found that for highly ambiguous statements, meaning could be interpreted in a variety of ways. For example, consider one of the statements from the study, "Those who hold and those who are without property have ever formed two distinct classes." You probably interpret that statement very differently if you think Karl Marx wrote it than if you knew that John Adams, the second president of the United States, said it. Asch's research challenges the clean division of source credibility and arguments in an even more fundamental way than Reimer and colleagues in that Asch demonstrated that sometimes the very *meaning* of the same persuasive message differs if uttered by different sources.

Another area in which dual-process theories struggle concerns the nature of a strong argument. ELM researchers have generally expressed a casual attitude toward the issue. They consider argument quality a methodological challenge, a means to an end of assessing the extent to which an audience has engaged in central or peripheral processing. Rather than trying to explain the nature of a strong versus a weak argument, ELM researchers traditionally combine a variety of features, including stronger evidence, better logic, and more desirable outcomes in the strong message and combine weaker evidence, poor logic, and less desirable outcomes in the weak message. To assess argument strength in their research, they ask an audience to attend to the message carefully and write down the thoughts they had while reading or hearing it. If positive thoughts account for 65% or more of the audience's thoughts about the message, they label it "strong." If positive thoughts account for less than 35% of the audience's thoughts about the message, they label it "weak." Yet they never explore precisely what that thought-listing technique actually measures. As it turns out, it may not indicate anything about argument strength.

In 1989, two marketing researchers, Charles Areni and Richard Lutz, examined some of the kinds of message topics that ELM researchers used to study the effects of strong and weak arguments. One set of arguments came from consumer studies and dealt with a shaving razor advertisement. Another set came from studies with undergraduates that dealt with requiring undergraduate students to pass a comprehensive exam to graduate. As expected, the strong arguments contained better reasoning and stronger evidence than the weak arguments. Yet they noticed that the strong arguments also promised more desirable outcomes than the weak arguments. For example, the strong argument for the shaving razor included the claim that it had "unsurpassed sharpness," whereas the weak argument informed the audience that the razor "floats in water." They wondered, when an audience processes centrally, do they even notice the better reasoning in the strong arguments, or do they just notice the more desirable features?

Subsequently, Areni and Lutz (1988) conducted a study in which they induced the subjects to process centrally. They read a message either from the previous razor advertisement study or from the comprehensive exam study, and they read either the strong or the weak version of the argument. The subjects rated each of the claims in the message that they read on a response scale ranging from "unlikely" to "likely" to indicate their perception of the truth of the claim, as well as a scale ranging from "bad" to "good" to indicate the extent to which they liked that claim's outcomes. Areni and Lutz found that for both topics, the subjects rated the strong arguments as making claims for better outcomes (on the "good" side of the response scale) than the weak arguments. But they did not see the strong arguments as any more likely true than the weak ones.

As discussed previously, we expect to find stronger arguments more believable than weaker arguments. Yet the subjects in Areni and Lutz's study did not rate the claims presented in the strong arguments as substantially more likely than those made by the weak arguments. Several follow-up studies by other researchers have found that when they induced the audience to process centrally, arguments that promised more desirable outcomes proved more persuasive than arguments that promised less desirable outcomes (Hustinx et al., 2007). In contrast, motivating the audience to use central processing did not influence the likelihood that messages that included logical, well-supported claims would result in more persuasion than poorly argued claims. This pattern of results may explain why, when Chris examined many of the studies on central versus peripheral processing and strong versus weak arguments, the ELM predictions did not usually work when communication researchers conducted the study (Carpenter, 2015). Perhaps communication researchers focused on what argumentation scholars and logicians would call strong and weak arguments rather than simply promising more or less desirable outcomes as some of the psychologists had done.

This issue of more or less desirable arguments also illustrates another problem with the way dual-process researchers study argument strength. When communication researchers such as McCroskey studied the presence or absence of evidence, they would write a message that made a number of claims to support a particular advocacy. For one-half of the audience, the message would include evidence, and for the other one-half, it would not. But the claims remained the same in both messages. On the other hand, many ELM studies used the strong and weak comprehensive exam arguments used by Petty and Cacioppo. The strong arguments suggest that if the university required a comprehensive exam as a graduation requirement, then the likelihood of students getting high-paying jobs increased, professors would improve their teaching, and all seniors would not have to take other final exams in their courses. The weak arguments promised that the testing companies would make more money, university enrollment would increase, and that the students would experience more anxiety. The strong arguments make very different claims than the weak ones so that scholars cannot separate whatever argument strength effects might exist from the effect of the completely different claims made in the message. Had Petty and Cacioppo simply varied the support for the positive outcomes described in the strong arguments, then they would have induced strong versus weak arguments. Instead, they induced a mixture of issues so that many of the ELM studies cannot help us determine if argument strength effects only occur for the centrally processing audience.

So dual-process theories of persuasion initially showed much promise in integrating the research examining the effects of various message features, such as source credibility and argument strength. But after researchers began testing some of these predictions and trying to clarify the theories, problems emerged that cast doubt on their utility. The key concept, message elaboration or depth of cognitive processing, remains so unclear that no one has managed to find an adequate method of measuring it. The role of source information remains muddied, remaining inextricably bound with argument strength. The nature of argument strength, as consequentialists conceive it, another pivotal concept in dual-process models, also remains unclear, if not inadequate, after decades of research. And some research suggests that dual-process models do not so much predict when the strength of the argument will affect persuasion, as they tell us when the audience will notice that the message promises better outcomes for them. Next, we examine how an alternative idea addressing the effect of argument strength, the unimodel, not only critiques the dual-process approach but also offers an interesting alternative to it.

The Unimodel

The unimodel seeks to address some of the shortcomings of dual-process ideas by collapsing the distinction between peripheral cues and arguments into a single category labeled "evidence" and collapsing the two processes into a single process termed "reasoning from evidence." Social psychologists Arie Kruglanski and Erik Thompson presented the idea initially in 1999. The unimodel asserts that rather than trying to place information into different categories, such as peripheral cues and arguments, we can think of any piece of information (evidence) in a persuasive message as arrayed on several important dimensions. The extent to which a piece of evidence proves more or less relevant to the conclusion the speaker advocates forms one particularly important dimension. They explained,

> Relevance, in turn, implies a prior linkage between general categories such that affirmation of one in a specific case (observation of the evidence) affects one's belief in the other (e.g., warrants the conclusion). (p. 89)

Although Kruglanski and Thompson did not mention Toulmin, one may think of their concept of relevance as similar to the strength of the warrant in Toulmin's model. On the other hand, they did link their concepts to the logician's concept of argument, such that evidence forms one of an argument's premises and the extent to which the evidence proves relevant to the conclusion forms another premise. The conclusion following from these premises addresses what the speaker wishes the audience to believe.

According to the unimodel, a source's credibility can prove more or less relevant to a conclusion, just like any other piece of evidence. For example, mentioning that the speaker earned a Ph.D. in climatology provides strong evidence for the truth of the speaker's claims about climate change. In contrast, that same speaker's Ph.D. in climatology has no relevance when she makes claims about how many hours of sleep college students need. Similarly, if speakers advance the premise that the results of research studies using large samples provide a better indication of the accuracy of the results than research studies employing small samples, then these speakers have provided strong evidence for their conclusion. The speaker's credentials and the relationship between sample size and the accuracy of results both provide evidence in the unimodel's conceptualization of the persuasion process, albeit evidence of a slightly different nature.

The unimodel also offers the advantage of producing clear predictions concerning when a piece of information will persuade the audience. Kruglanski and Thompson (1999) wrote,

> If the information is lengthy, complex, or unclear, the distillation of intelligible evidence may require a considerable amount of processing motivation and capacity. Similarly, if processing motivation and capacity are relatively low, only relatively simple and straightforward evidence will register, and thus exert a significant persuasive impact. (p. 90)

These criteria reduce to an estimate of the difficulty created for a particular person in comprehending the information and understanding that information's relevance to the conclusion. Information difficult to process will only affect audience members' attitudes if they devote enough cognitive effort to comprehend it and apply it to their attitudes. If audience members fail to devote the required effort, or if they cannot do so, then the information will not affect the audience members' attitude.

Given these postulates, the unimodel makes predictions about when the speaker's credibility will affect the audience members' attitudes. Kruglanski and Thompson presented a series of experiments investigating this point. In these studies, they consistently found that the length and complexity of the information determined whether that information changed the persuasiveness of a message for a peripherally or centrally processing audience. In one study, they presented the subjects with long and complex source credibility information. The peripherally processing subjects ignored it, but the highly credible source proved more persuasive than the low credibility source for the centrally processing subjects. Similarly, they conducted a study that included both very simple and short arguments, as well as long and complex arguments. The peripherally processing subjects focused on the simple arguments and accepted the message recommendations when they read strong, but not weak, simple arguments. The centrally processing subjects focused on the complex arguments and again accepted the message recommendations when they read strong, but not weak, complex arguments. These studies demonstrate the unimodel's prediction that information does not vary by type (i.e., peripheral cues or message arguments) but by length and complexity. So the unimodel does predict when source credibility and argument strength will affect the persuasiveness of a message more effectively than dual-process models.

Subsequent unimodel research also demonstrated the importance of the relevance of argument strength. The first set of studies by Kruglanski and Thompson used the same comprehensive exam arguments as previous ELM research. One set of studies by an Italian social psychologist named Antonio Pierro and colleagues (2004) systematically examined the importance of the unimodel's concept of "relevance" to argument strength effects. They conducted a series of experiments on advertisements for consumer goods in which they induced the audience to have low or high involvement (peripheral or central processing in ELM terms). They found that various aspects of argument relevance affected the attitudes of their subjects more when those subjects had high involvement. But it did not matter that subjects received information associated with argument strength (aspects of the products) or information associated with a peripheral cue (proportion of consumers who reported high satisfaction with the product). In both cases making the information more relevant affected the audience's attitudes, especially the high-involvement group. The low-involvement group, on the other hand, generally reported attitudes more consistent with whatever information they encountered first, regardless of that information's relevance. This study suggests that the unimodel's conceptualization of argument relevance may have less susceptibility to the criticisms of the ELM conceptualization of argument strength.

We began this section by inquiring about the extent to which the effects of argument quality depend on other factors. Early persuasion research suggested that argument strength would always persuade audiences as long as the audiences understood the arguments properly. In contrast, dual-process theories claimed that argument strength only persuaded audiences when those audience members felt motivated to produce a correct attitude and when they could devote the necessary amount of cognitive effort to understanding the arguments.

Yet problems emerged with the dual-process perspective. Proponents found it difficult to describe what a pivotal concept, central processing, entailed so no agreed upon measure of it exists, even after decades of research. They failed increasingly to provide clear predictions about the role of important components of the persuasion process, such as source credibility. Compounding these difficulties, other researchers have found it difficult to untangle argument strength effects from source credibility effects. An additional obstacle emerged from the ambiguous definition of argument strength found in dual-process thinking, with a deeper investigation finding that what dual-process experiments termed argument strength often meant little more than promising the audience better outcomes.

The unimodel solves many of these problems. Kruglanski and Thompson claim that any piece of information in an argument will persuade when the audience both can and will devote the necessary cognitive resources to understanding it and its connection to the argument's conclusion. As a qualifying point, they do go on to write that sometimes audiences will ignore simple information in favor of more diagnostic information in the arguments. The unimodel further proposes a definition of argument strength that returns us to the ideas advanced by the logicians and argumentation scholars. Putting the matter in language with which logicians and argumentation scholars find more comfortable, the unimodel specifies that argument quality depends on the extent to which the audience believes the warrant connecting the evidence with the conclusion.

One wonders then how much improvement several decades of persuasion research has added to the simple advice that the audience needs to understand the message and that the message must offer strong evidence that makes a clear connection with the argument claim. For sure, that assertion oversimplifies dual-process research. Persuasion scholars working in the dual process and now the unimodel traditions have identified a number of aspects of the persuasion context that affect the ability and willingness of the audience to devote the necessary cognitive effort to comprehend the message. The HSM's sufficiency principle, for example, offers a powerful method of assessing how much effort the audience will likely exert to understand any given message. The critiques of these positions have also illuminated important points that demand continued research, such as the possibility that the quality of evidence has less importance for persuading the audience than what the speaker promises. Dual-process theories may not have lived up to their early promise, but they have raised a variety of important issues into, and spurred a great deal of research addressing, matters that otherwise would remain neglected.

Conclusion

We opened this chapter with quotations indicating the value of logical reasoning and identifying as fools those who do not use their logical faculties. We reviewed perspectives from logicians, argumentation scholars, social scientists, and communication scientists on how to produce arguments that would impress those who used logical reasoning to the fullest. Yet we also discovered that humans will not use their reason to the fullest every time they encounter a persuasive message. When the topic does not concern us, we may only produce a cursory examination of the simplest aspects of the topic rather than using more complex rules of logic to assess an argument. Perhaps, then, a strong argument not only offers sound logic but also must offer the audience a reason to care.

3

How Do We Adapt Persuasive Messages to Diverse Audiences?

Humanist: But no persuasive message could ever appeal to everyone. Because everyone is unique, you have to create a unique message for every person. That task is impossible. Thus persuasion is impossible. You must admit that everything is unique. Even every coin is unique, if for no other reason than the time of its minting.

Pragmatist: Yes, but for some purposes, like getting gum from a gumball machine, any coin will do. So it is with persuasive messages.

P EOPLE EXHIBIT MARKED DIFFERENCES ACROSS many characteristics. We vary in obvious physical characteristics, such as height, weight, and eye color. We also vary in less obvious physical characteristics, such as blood pressure and heart rate, high-density lipoprotein levels and low-density lipoprotein (LDL) levels, and lung capacity. We differ in the type of culture in which we live. For example, those living in some cultures embrace individualism more than collectivism, and those living in other cultures have the opposite orientation. Some have steep hierarchies, others considerably less so. Anthropologists characterize some cultures as high context, others as low context. Within any culture, people differ demographically. Some define themselves as female, others male, and others have different, sometimes multiple, gender identities. We differ in age, occupation, amount of formal education, racial identification, wealth, and the geographical region in which we live. Even within demographic categories, we differ in social attitudes. Some view themselves as political conservatives, others as liberals, and still others have alternative political affiliations. Some value achievement highly, others less so. Some endorse authoritarian positions, whereas others reject them. We differ in even less obvious and, therefore, less easy to detect ways as well. We might term these characteristics as "psychological." For instance, we judge some as more extroverted than others, some as more conscientious than others, some as more open than others, some as more agreeable than others, and some as more neurotic than others.

This chapter addresses the role of individual differences in response to persuasive messages. First, we examine persuasibility. Introducing this term acknowledges that people have greater or lesser susceptibility to persuasive messages.

Nevertheless, even those with low persuasibility might change their attitudes on certain topics and with certain kinds of messages. Moreover, even those with high persuasibility may resist changing their attitudes on some issues, even when exposed to strong persuasive messages. It remains an article of faith, however, that all of us will change our attitudes when exposed to the right source transmitting the right argument through the right channel. We shall return to that article of faith at the end of this chapter. The second matter to consider in this chapter requires that we examine how to target and then to tailor persuasive messages likely to appeal to specific persons or narrowly defined groups of persons with a set of common characteristics.

PERSUASIBILITY

Persuasibility refers to an individual difference (i.e., a characteristic that distinguishes people). Specifically, it refers to the difference in susceptibility to influence from persuasive messages. At one end of the spectrum, some people frequently change their attitudes in response to persuasive messages. At the other end of the same spectrum, other people strongly resist changing their attitudes when exposed to any persuasive message. Likely, most of us fall between these extremes.

Notably, this dimension of individual differences does not concern itself with the issue involved, the source of the persuasive message, the characteristics of the persuasive message, or the channel through which the source transmits the message. Let us engage in a thought experiment together. Suppose that we expose a large number of people to many different types of persuasive messages on many different issues. Let us also suppose that these messages come from many different sources and that these sources communicate these messages through varying channels, sometimes face-to-face, other times through an audio message, other times via a video message, and yet other times through a written message. Now, suppose that we also have the ability to assess for all people if their attitude changed in response to each message. And if so, by how much? We would then refer to those people who, on average, changed their attitudes most often, and by the greatest amount, as having high persuasibility. In contrast, we would refer to those who, on average, changed their attitudes least often, and by the least amount, as having low persuasibility. For those between the two extremes, phrases such as "moderately persuasible," "moderately highly persuasible," "moderately low in persuasibility," would apply. The limits of our gradations of persuasibility would result only from the limitation of our vocabulary to produce terms to distinguish quantities of persuasibility. Alternatively, we might find a way to quantify the number of times people changed their attitudes, the amount by which they changed, and then integrate these two numbers into a quantitative index describing persuasibility. For instance, perhaps we could develop a measure that ranged from 0 to 100 with the property that the higher the number, the more persuasible the person.

Assuming this task completed, the next task that persuasion scientists would pursue involves asking with what might persuasibility associate. Might height, weight, or eye color correlate with persuasibility? Not likely. For example, we would doubt that we would find those with blue eyes easier to convince than those with brown eyes. Might less obvious physical characteristics matter? Again, not likely. We have no reason to expect to find it easier to persuade those with high LDL than those with low LDL. In contrast, we do have reasons to suspect demographic differences.

Sex/Gender: A Demographic Difference

We shall use the term "sex" to refer to a biological difference, and the term "gender" to refer to socially created differences in the sexual group with which one identifies. Socialization refers to the process of learning how to act (or not act) in ways that gain the approval of others and avoid the disapproval of others. The process of socialization often differs in some important ways for females and males, with stereotypes growing from these differences. Pertinent to sex/gender differences in persuasibility,

Alice Eagly (1978) pointed out that females learn to assume a role of dependence and submissiveness more than do males. Accompanying this process, females come to view themselves stereotypically as more accommodating, more easily influenced, and less analytic than males, and men learn to share these perceptions. In contrast, men come to view themselves as more unwavering, intelligent, and rational than females. Once again, women learn to share these perceptions. Importantly, these tendencies do not apply to everyone or to an equal extent among those to whom they do apply. Instead, they characterize many, but not all, and among those to whom they apply, they apply in lesser measure for some than for others.

Eagly reasoned that, given differential socialization based on sex/gender, one would expect to find a sex difference in persuasibility, with females more persuasible than males. In two major review articles (Eagly, 1978; Eagly & Carli, 1981), she reached three important conclusions. First, she reported evidence of a sex difference, with women more persuasible than men. Second, her findings revealed a small, although not trivial, observed difference. And third, she observed an inconsistency in the effect across experiments. Put differently, some experiments reported a sex difference, whereas others did not. Her findings raise two important questions for us: (1) what determines when a relatively large versus a relatively small sex difference in persuasibility occurs, and (2) when relatively large effects occur, why do they do so?

Interesting answers to these questions emerged in a recent series of experiments by psychologists Eaton et al. (2017). In this program of research, Eaton et al. made use of a technique called "priming." **Priming** refers to creating experiences that increase the likelihood of bringing a particular idea to mind (see Kunda, 1999, pp. 22–23 for an overview). Eaton et al. created sets both of female primes and of male primes by asking their experimental participants to unscramble sentences. For example, they might ask their participants to construct a coherent sentence from the following words, "doll her sister a got birthday on her." The correct unscrambling would produce the sentence, "Her sister got a doll on her birthday." This unscramble problem provides an example of a female prime, only one of several given to the participants. An example of a male prime might require unscrambling "gave boy his football father a the" ("the father gave his boy a football"). They also included control, or neutral, primes, such as, "banana breakfast had pancakes for they" ("they had banana pancakes for breakfast"). As a result of these tasks, we can expect that the thoughts of those exposed to several female primes focus on females and feminine matters to a considerable extent, thus invoking stereotypes associated with that sex/gender, such as accommodating and unanalytical. Moreover, we can expect that the thoughts of those exposed to several male primes focus on males and masculine matters, thus invoking stereotypes associated with that sex/gender, such as unwavering and rational. Furthermore, we can expect that the control primes invoked neither female nor male stereotypes.

Eaton et al. exposed some female participants to female primes, others to male primes, and yet others to control primes. In addition, and very importantly, they exposed some males to female primes, others to male primes, and yet others to control primes. Then they exposed participants to either weak or strong arguments opposing the death penalty—a topic found in a pilot study as neither female oriented nor male oriented.

These experiments produced clear and striking results. When exposed to control primes, strong arguments led to considerable persuasion in the form of agreement with message recommendations, whereas weak arguments led to very little persuasion/agreement with message recommendations. This result characterized both the females and the males who received the control primes. Similarly, those who received the male primes exhibited the same pattern—persuaded by the strong arguments and unconvinced by the weak arguments—and again this outcome occurred both for the females and the males who received the male primes. In stark contrast, however, those receiving the female primes did not distinguish the weak and strong arguments. Instead, they found both equally persuasive. Furthermore, they found the weak argument more persuasive than did those receiving either the control or male primes. Critically, this pattern occurred both for the female respondents and for the male respondents!

Eaton et al. pursued the matter. Female stereotypes, such as more accommodating and less analytical, and their male counterparts, unwavering and analytical, hint at two different reasons for a sex difference in persuasion. On the one hand, female primes might result in a stronger tendency to *yield* to persuasion attempts than male primes (more persuasibility)—the accommodating stereotype. Alternatively, however, female primes might result in people *processing* persuasive messages relatively superficially and uncritically, whereas male primes might result in careful and critical scrutiny of persuasive messages. Conceivably, either or both reasons could contribute to the observed difference.

Eaton et al.'s research indicated that priming female stereotypes results in less careful and critical examination of persuasive messages than priming male stereotypes. Little evidence emerged to suggest that priming female stereotypes led to more overall accommodation than priming male stereotypes.

Therefore, these results challenge the claim that women and men differ inherently in persuasibility. Stating the matter another way, women exhibit no stronger a tendency to yield to persuasive arguments than do men. Instead, men and women alike yield more when exposed to features of the persuasion context that prime sex/gender and bring to mind the associated stereotypes.

How then do we explain Eagly's observed sex difference in persuasion? After all, the experiments that provided the evidence for her review did not involve priming female or male stereotypes. Or might they have? Neither Eagly nor Eaton explain specifically how that might happen but consider one possibility. Perhaps simple features of an experiment provide subtle primes that remind us of our sex/gender. One way in which that reminder might occur involves the common and simple task of experimenters asking their experimental subjects to indicate on a questionnaire if they identify as female or male. If tasks as simple as this one do serve as primes, then consider how many times small, but important, details like this one arise in our everyday interactions and the importance they have for our susceptibility to persuasive messages.

Aging: A Second Important Demographic Difference

Scholars have advanced and tested various ideas about the relationship between age and persuasibility. Existing evidence, although always subject to modification by future research, converges to recommend one of them, the life-stages hypothesis, over the others. Nevertheless, reviewing the discarded hypotheses serves the important function of showing what others have found incorrect.

The life-long openness explanation asserts that no differences in persuasibility emerge over the life course. Put differently, this idea proposes that age has no effect on the ease or difficulty associated with trying to persuade people. Because scholars have found that differences do emerge, however, we must discard this possibility.

The persistence explanation claims that attitudes form during preadult socialization and that they change very little subsequently. Because investigators have found that people remain open to changing their minds even as relatively young adults, this explanation fails. One failure of this explanation results from setting the point at which peoples' attitudes crystallize, or become permanent, too early in the life course.

The increasing persistence explanation conceives of persuasibility as a continuous process that remains uniform across the life course. As we age, we find ourselves, and others find us, as steadily less and less easy to convince. Inconsistent with this idea, scholars report discontinuities or gaps in the life course. Persuading those in certain age ranges proves easier; persuading those in other age ranges proves substantially more challenging.

The impressionable years explanation shares an important similarity with, but differs in one important way from, the persistence explanation. Proponents of this position claimed that attitudes crystallize, but they do so later in the life course than the persistence explanation would have us believe—somewhere in one's 20s, perhaps even into one's early 30s (Krosnick & Alwin, 1989; Newcomb, 1961; Newcomb et al., 1967; Sears, 1986). Until this point, attitudes remain relatively malleable or open to change. After this point, malleability decreases rapidly until attitudes reach a point at which they change little, if at all. As Jon Krosnick and Duane Alwin (1989) explained it, "The historical environment in which a young person becomes an active participant in the adult world shapes the basic values, attitudes, and world views formed during those years. Once the period of early socialization has passed, this hypothesis argues, its residuals are fixed within individuals, and these core orientations are unlikely to change" (p. 416). They go on to qualify this conclusion somewhat, noting that

> "young people may evidence higher levels of attitude change not because of greater susceptibility but rather because of greater exposure to change-inducing

events. Indeed, this is quite plausible: People probably experience more major life shifts between ages 18 and 25 than at any other point in the life cycle. These changes may include graduating from high school, going to college, graduating from college, starting a first job, getting married, becoming a parent, moving from one place of residence to another, and so on" (p. 423).

The impressionable years hypothesis likely has it correct that prior to a certain age, perhaps our late 20s or early 30s, we find ourselves more susceptible to persuasive influences than we do in certain other parts of the life course. But might the same outcome occur for those in their later years as well, perhaps those in their late 60s and older? Applying recent advances in statistical knowledge to this problem, Penny Visser and Jon Krosnick (1998) reported that, indeed, such a pattern emerges. They refer to this pattern and its accompanying explanation as the previously mentioned life-stages explanation.

To summarize the life-stages explanation, it advances the claim that both in early adulthood and in the latter stages of the life cycle, people exhibit more susceptibility to persuasion than they do in the middle years. Moreover, as mentioned, careful analyses of relevant data indicate that this pattern more accurately characterizes persuasibility over the life course. To provide an adequate account of these data, the life-stages explanation must show (1) why young adults remain very susceptible to persuasive appeals, (2) why old adults exhibit the same high susceptibility, and (3) why those in middle age do not.

The explanation of the susceptibility of young adults parallels the impressionable years explanation mentioned previously. During young adulthood, people form attitudes that help them make sense of the environment in which they find themselves. For example, attitudes about the importance of economic security, such as the importance of saving money or the wisdom of investing in the stock market, among those coming into young adulthood during the Greater Depression of the 1930s (and extending into the 1940s) formed in response to an insecure economic present and an uncertain economic future. The formation of these attitudes would have had to take into account these dire conditions. Once formed, changing them would provide a formidable obstacle.

Those advocating the life-stages hypothesis assert that the greater susceptibility of older people to persuasion involves several factors. For example, attitudes toward particular issues can become obsolete with changing times. For example, the attack on the World Trade Center and the Pentagon on September 11, 2001 may have changed many older people's attitudes toward war, as it involved a relatively novel element—namely, an attack on the mainland of the United States, whereas the experience with war for the elderly involved battles fought on foreign soil. Furthermore, as Visser and Krosnick pointed out, the meaning of attitudes may change. Civil rights, once associated with the integration of schools and residences, now may refer to the redistribution of resources to offset past inequalities, and attitudes toward this issue may change as a result. In addition, Ahreem Ahn and Dongwon Min (2018) argued that older adults try to regulate emotion as a way of maintaining a positive affective state more than do younger adults. Generally, those in a positive affect state change their attitudes in response to persuasion messages more so than do those in a neutral or negative affective state, providing yet another reason for increased persuasibility among older adults. Finally, with increasing age comes a well-documented decrease in cognitive ability (Verhaeghen & Salthouse, 1997). Decreasing cognitive ability results in a decrease in one's ability to pick out logical flaws, lack of evidence, and other characteristics of weak arguments, thus making one more susceptible to them.

In contrast, the life-stage hypothesis advocates claim that in middle age, we come to assume roles associated with increasing social power. Eaton et al. (2009) showed that in middle age, people come to assume more occupational power. Increasingly, they make and enforce social norms, assume leadership roles, and make important decisions. And as Eaton et al. go on to show, people entering such positions come to value resoluteness more than flexibility in their attitudes as befits their newly acquired social roles. Consequently, persuading them becomes a more difficult task.

One must take caution not to overstate the magnitude of the effect of aging on persuasion. Like the sex/gender effect, the research reveals a nontrivial, but modest, effect of aging on persuasion. Those in middle age do change their minds; young adults and older people do resist. Nonetheless, the former group changes less than the latter two groups, on average.

In addition, considerable nuance qualifies these findings. For example, as Carolyn Yoon and colleagues (2005) suggested, topic may matter. For instance, convincing older people about health issues may provide more of a challenge than persuading certain other age groups. And although older adults may find themselves more susceptible to the "truth effect" (i.e., more likely to believe repeated information) and change more in response to emotional appeals, nonemotional appeals may not sway them as much as other age groups.

Dogmatism: A Psychological Characteristic

A trait that affects persuasibility emerged from the thinking and research of social psychologist Milton Rokeach (1960). He described a trait called dogmatism, which referred to closed-mindedness. His conceptualization of dogmatism focused on the extent to which people can objectively evaluate messages from others based on the merits of their arguments. One would expect to have difficulty persuading people with high levels of this trait. Yet Rokeach also explained that dogmatic people have difficulty objectively evaluating a message because they have difficulty separating how they feel about the speaker from the quality of what the speaker said. On the one hand, their minds close to new information, but on the other hand, they blindly follow the dictates of sources they respect.

Consistent with highly dogmatic people as resistant to new information, some research emphasizes the difficulty in persuading the highly dogmatic. One study found that they rate articles with which they agree more favorably than articles with which they disagree (Kleck & Wheaton, 1967). Another found that they choose to read articles with which they agree more often than they choose to read articles with which they disagree, a phenomenon referred to as "selective exposure" (Innes, 1978). One pair of researchers tested the "bogus stranger" paradigm with high and low dogmatic people (Palmer & Kalin, 1985). They described an upcoming interaction with a stranger. Then they described that stranger's political beliefs. Generally, people dislike strangers who disagree with them, but they found that especially true of high dogmatics. In addition, a few studies have shown that highly dogmatic persons change their attitudes less in response to persuasive messages (Jones & Dieker, 1968; Miller, 1965).

Yet research evidence also shows that trusted sources can persuade highly dogmatic people and do so easily. One study found more powerful source credibility effects in audiences composed of highly dogmatic participants (Harvey & Hayes, 1972). Furthermore, a few studies report that highly dogmatic people change their attitudes *more* easily (Bostrom, 1964; Cronkhite & Goetz, 1971).

Recent developments that incorporate better ways of measuring dogmatism may prove fruitful in explaining inconsistency in this body of research. In 2006, two communication scholars, Shearman and Levine, developed a new version of the dogmatism scale (see Appendix 3.1 for the Shearman and Levine scale). They noted that the original Rokeach measure tried to cover a variety of different pieces that did not really fit together very well. In particular, they found that the obedience to authority part of the measure did not associate strongly with the closed-mindedness part. They argued that closed-mindedness and obedience to authority, although related, do not measure the same thing as Rokeach had thought. That finding may explain some of the inconsistencies in previous research. Unfortunately, no one has used Shearman and Levine's new measure to assess persuasibility, so we do not yet know if it will produce more consistent results than Rokeach's measure.

A group of social psychologists, Price et al. (2015), recently published a new measure of open-minded cognitive style. Rather than trying to include all the different parts of dogmatism, they argued that specifically conceptualizing people's willingness to consider a variety of perspectives as a personality trait will offer a more fruitful path for future investigations. Unfortunately, like the Shearman and Levine measure, no one has yet published any studies linking their measure of open-mindedness to persuasibility. Nevertheless, these newer measures may help reinvigorate this classic area of persuasion research in years to come.

Need for Cognition: A Psychological Characteristic

Investigators have found that a second important psychological characteristic, the need for cognition (NC), also affects persuasibility. John Cacioppo and his colleagues (1982) defined NC as an intrinsic motive that leads to a tendency to engage in and enjoy effortful cognitive activity (thinking). People range from those having a very low NC (*cognitive misers*) to those having a very high NC (*chronic cognizers*).

Cacioppo and his colleagues (Cacioppo et al., 1984) developed a set of items, the responses to which provide scholars with an indication of where respondents lie on the continuum that ranges from cognitive misers (low NC) to chronic cognizers (high NC) (see Appendix 3.2 for the Cacioppo and Petty scale). A clearer understanding of the idea of NC results from examining the content of some of these items.

For instance, those with a high NC would agree with items such as, "I would prefer complex to simple problems," "I find satisfaction in deliberating hard and for long hours," and "I prefer my life to be filled with puzzles that I must solve." In contrast, those with a low NC would disagree with these statements. Alternatively, those with a low NC would agree with items such as, "I only think as hard as I have to," "Thinking is not my idea of fun," and "Learning new ways to think doesn't excite me very much." In contrast, those with a high NC would disagree with these statements.

Extensive research has uncovered a number of interesting and important characteristics of NC (Cacioppo et al., 1996). For example, people's NC may change over the course of their lives. In addition, no evidence of sex/gender differences has emerged; on average, males and females have comparable NC. Furthermore, to anticipate a thought that may have arisen in your mind, NC differs from the intelligence quotient (IQ). Thus not all exceptionally smart people have high NC, nor do those with lower IQ necessarily lack it. The two ideas correlate positively but only modestly. Moreover, when exposed to a message, those with high NC tend to recall more of the content of the message than do those with low NC. Finally, one might think that those with high NC would exhibit more objectivity when exposed to messages. Nevertheless, research findings have indicated their susceptibility to certain biases, such as mood and priming effects.

Pertinent to the matter of persuasibility, Cacioppo and colleagues report that those with a high NC have stronger attitudes than low NC. Not only do they resist changing their attitudes to a greater extent than do those with a low NC, but also their attitudes both persist over time and predict their actions more accurately than do those with a low NC. Thus, generally, the difficulty in persuading someone increases as NC increases; persuading someone with a high NC provides more of a challenge than persuading someone with a low NC.

But this simple statement of the relationship between NC and persuasibility masks some important nuance. For instance, those with a high NC distinguish sharply between strong and weak arguments, whereas those with a low NC fail to distinguish argument quality as clearly. This difference affects how those varying in NC respond subsequently to persuasive arguments. Although not as susceptible to persuasive appeals, those high in NC change their attitudes to a greater extent in response to strong persuasive messages than to weak ones. In contrast, although more susceptible to persuasive appeals, those low in NC change their attitudes to approximately the same extent in response to strong and weak persuasive appeals. For them, argument quality has little effect on the extent to which they change their minds. Instead, peripheral (heuristic) cues may exert a stronger effect on their attitudinal judgments.

More recent evidence suggests an additional qualification. In a series of experiments, British social psychologist Geoffrey Haddock and his colleagues (2008) showed that cognitively-oriented persuasive messages affect the attitudinal judgments of those with a high NC to a greater extent than do affectively-oriented persuasive messages. And the opposite pattern emerges for those low in NC; namely, affectively-oriented persuasive messages affect their attitudinal judgments more than do cognitively-oriented judgments. Likely, emerging research examining NC will add more details and insight into the relationship between NC and persuasibility.

Self-Esteem: A Psychological Characteristic

A considerable body of research has established a tie between a third psychological attribute, self-esteem, and persuasibility. Sociologist Morris Rosenberg (1965, 1979) provided a useful and straightforward definition of self-esteem, describing it as a persons' negative or positive evaluation or orientation toward themselves. An older label that scholars applied to this idea, ego strength, reflects the same idea. Those with low self-esteem or low ego strength think of themselves more negatively than those with high self-esteem or high ego strength.

So, for example, someone with very high self-esteem would agree strongly with statements such as this one from the Rosenberg Self-Esteem Scale, "On the whole, I am satisfied with myself," and disagree strongly with statements such as, "I wish that I could have more respect for myself." In contrast, those with low self-esteem would likely disagree strongly with the former and agree strongly with the latter. Those less extreme would provide less extreme responses to items such as these two. For example, they might report that they merely agree or disagree or that they neither agree nor disagree (see Appendix 3.3 for the Rosenberg scale).

Scholars tend to think of self-esteem as a trait, referring to it as chronic self-esteem. Nonetheless, we realize that self-esteem might vary somewhat depending on circumstances, referring to such temporary changes as acute self-esteem (also known as state self-esteem). For instance, even those who view themselves positively have bad days. They may fail an exam, get bawled out at work by their supervisors, or let down a loved one. In such cases, their normally high chronic self-esteem would decrease so that they would experience relatively (for them) low acute self-esteem for a brief period. Similar, even those who view themselves negatively have positive experiences that may elevate their self-esteem temporarily. They may get a high score on an exam that they had expected to fail, receive praise from their supervisor in the presence of their coworkers, or receive a coveted award for community service. For some time after such experiences, those with chronically low self-esteem would have relatively (for them) high acute self-esteem.

Notably, a person's self-esteem may not correspond perfectly with others' observations of the person's self-worth. Consider a high school student whom we shall refer as Allison. Those who know Allison might think of her as very accomplished. She received the honor of induction into the National Honor Society, plays as the star striker on the soccer team, and serves as a volunteer at a local assisted living facility. She also has a highly visible supporting role in this year's production of the school's musical. Nevertheless, Allison might have relatively low self-esteem because, in her eyes, she fails to live up to her own (perhaps unrealistic) expectations. In a similar manner, we can think of people who might have relatively high self-esteem despite the fact that others would view them as having accomplished little. Generally, then, if people have a positive ideal view of themselves, then their self-esteem would depend on the difference, or discrepancy, between their ideal view and their actual view of themselves (Higgins, 1987).

At any specific point in time, our self-esteem may result from recent events that affected our self-evaluation, as well as from differences between our ideal and actual selves, such as those in the Allison example from the preceding paragraph. They may also arise from two important sources, which we might term "personal" and "relational" bases of self-esteem (Sanaktekin & Sundar, 2008). The former refers to our sense of self-worth. The latter refers to the success (at least of others' perceptions of that success) of the social groups to which we belong and how that success or lack thereof affects our view of ourselves. We tend to believe that membership in successful groups reflects well upon us and that membership in unsuccessful groups does not (Poole et al., 1998). As an example, psychologist Robert Cialdini and his colleagues (1976) found that students tended to associate themselves with their school's football team in various ways when their team won but distanced themselves when their team lost.

Studies that examine the relationship between self-esteem and persuasibility focus on chronic self-esteem. Psychologist-turned-communication-scholar, Nancy Rhodes, along with her colleague (1992), conducted a thorough and rigorous review of this area of research. Their review indicated that both people with low self-esteem and people with high self-esteem changed their attitudes less in response to persuasive messages than did those with moderate self-esteem. Interestingly, although those low in self-esteem and those high in self-esteem resisted persuasive appeals equally, they appeared to do so for different reasons.

Those with low self-esteem tend not to "receive" the message. Defense mechanisms motivated by psychological self-protection may prevent them from attending carefully to the message, or lead them to fail to comprehend it thoroughly, or both. In contrast, those with high self-esteem resist changing their attitudes because they have a substantial amount of confidence in their attitudinal judgments so that they do not yield easily. Because they exhibit less defensiveness than those with low self-esteem, those with moderate self-esteem attend to and comprehend more of the message than do their low self-esteem counterparts. And because they have less confidence in their opinions, they tend to yield more to persuasive appeals than do their high self-esteem counterparts. Consequently, they have higher persuasibility than those either low or high in self-esteem.

Interestingly, a large amount of heterogeneity (differences across studies) emerged from Rhodes's review. This fact implies that much remains yet undiscovered about the relationship between self-esteem and persuasibility.

Intelligence: A Brief Note on a Psychological Attribute

Intelligence refers to our capacity to learn and to apply that knowledge. Rhodes and her colleagues also reviewed evidence pertaining to intelligence and persuasibility. Although they anticipated that the relationship between intelligence and persuasibility would mirror the same pattern as the relationship between self-esteem and persuasibility, instead they found a simpler relationship. The highly intelligent resisted persuasive appeals more than did those with lower intelligence. Their analyses revealed a modest and heterogeneous effect so, as with self-esteem, much remains undiscovered about the relationship between intelligence and persuasibility. Rhodes attributes this effect to differences in yielding, specifically to the stronger ability to counterargue that characterizes those of higher intelligence. Only the best of arguments can convince them because they tend to know more about the content of any given persuasive message, and they can apply that knowledge to seek out any flaws or omissions in the persuasive message. Those with lower intelligence have less of these abilities and, consequently, yield to persuasive message recommendations to a greater extent.

Nature and Nurture

As mentioned in the first chapter, most think of attitudes forming from our life experiences. So, for instance, Sister Agnes Gonxha Bojaxhiu, more commonly known as Mother Teresa, observed extreme poverty among those on the streets outside the convent in Calcutta where she taught. These experiences shaped her attitudes toward the poor and led her to move from behind the convent walls to the streets as a means of reducing the suffering that she observed. Similarly, most think that experiences lead to attitude reinforcement or attitude change as well. So male delegates' refusal to allow female participation in the World Anti-Slavery Convention may have reinforced Elizabeth Cady Stanton's attitudes toward women's rights, and St. Paul's epiphany on the Damascus Road described in the Acts of the Apostles may have modified his religious attitudes.

Nevertheless, might scholars construct a reasonable case for our genes (nature) affecting the attitudes that we hold? James Olson et al. (2001), among others, think so. To understand their position, we must examine the logic of the twin experiment. A useful place to begin requires making a distinction between monozygotic (MZ), or identical twins, and dizygotic (DZ), or fraternal twins. The former twins share the exact same genetic material; the latter share no more genetic material than what one would expect any two siblings to share. Consequently, if a sample of MZ twins exhibits more similarity on some trait than does a sample of DZ twins, then that fact constitutes evidence that nature has some effect on the development of that trait.

Olson and his colleagues took care to explain what does and does not constitute an effect of nature. They wrote,

> "It is extremely unlikely that there are direct, one-to-one connections between genes and attitudes (e.g., a gene that causes attitudes toward capital punishment) or even many-to-one connections (e.g., a set of genes that, together, determine attitudes toward capital punishment). Rather, genes probably establish general predispositions or natural inclinations, which then shape environmental experiences in ways that increase the likelihood of the individual developing specific traits and attitudes. For example, children who are naturally small for their age might be picked on by other children more than their larger peers. As a result, these children might develop anxieties about social interaction, with consequences for their personality (e.g., introversion) and their attitudes (e.g., dislike for parties)" (p. 846).

They also provide a cautionary note on the limitation of twin studies. So, for example, they point out that among those living in a homogeneous environment (i.e., everyone living under the same conditions), individual differences must result from genetic effects and that, for a homogeneous gene pool, individual differences must result from environmental effects. The latter produces some peculiar results. For example, most people have four limbs, so most individual differences in the number of limbs among people in a given population must result from environmental causes. Yet none among us would question the fact that genetic factors exert a causal effect on the number of limbs that humans have.

Nevertheless, few of us live in a homogeneous environment and few of us live among others in what anyone would describe as a homogeneous gene pool. Instead, the differences among us result from (at the least) our genes, our shared environments, and our unshared environments. And, fortunately, behavioral geneticists have developed techniques for dividing individual differences into these categories.

Olson and his colleagues show that a good number of very different attitudes have a substantial genetic, or heritable, component. Their counterintuitive findings begin to make more sense when they point out that these effects result from a causal sequence in which nature affects many dimensions of our personalities, such as sociability. Subsequently, these personality traits affect our attitudes. For example, those high in sociability likely have a more positive attitude toward taking leadership positions than do those lower in sociability. Thus our genetic inheritance might affect the nature of our personalities, which, in turn, affects our attitudes on certain topics. Hence one can then say that our genetic inheritance affects our attitudes indirectly—as mediated by certain personality traits.

AUDIENCE ADAPTATION

Communicating effectively requires that those transmitting messages that inform others, persuade others, or both must consider carefully those who comprise the audience. So much consensus surrounds this proposition so as to lend it the status of an axiom, and communication scholars refer to this axiom as audience adaptation.

Examining some historical examples of effective communication suggests that the focal communicators understood their audiences well. For example, the first few words of Lincoln's Gettysburg Address, "Four score and seven years ago," evoke the language of the King James Version (KJV) of the Bible, a document with which his audience would have had close familiarity. The KJV commonly employs this linguistic construction, such as in "the days of our years are threescore and ten; and if by reason of strength they be fourscore years" (Psalm 90:10, KJV). Similarly, Biblical references, such as comparing his actions to 8th-century-BCE prophets, as well as to those of the Apostle Paul, which characterize Dr. Martin Luther King Jr's "Letter from a Birmingham Jail," resonated with the Christian and Jewish clergy to whom Dr. King appealed (Wills, 1992).

Less dramatically, and far removed from a religious context, sociologist Joan Emerson (1970) pointed out that gynecologists sensitive to the feelings of those they treated tended to begin their examination employing phrases such as, "let your knees fall apart" rather than phrases their audience might view as vulgar, such as, "spread your legs." And when trying to comfort a patient who has just undergone a radical mastectomy, one would profit from understanding that the patient's primary concern revolves around living rather than physical appearance.

Generic, Targeted, and Tailored Persuasive Messages

Communication scholars Gerald Miller and Mark Steinberg (1975) offered a useful way to think about audience adaptation. They described three levels of knowing a person. Suppose that you meet a stranger walking around on 6th Street in Muscatine, Iowa. You might guess that this person grew up in the United States and has whatever traits you think characterizes people with that background. Based on that cultural-level information, you might predict that the person likes apple pie, knows the words to the national anthem, and easily locates Washington, D.C. on a map. Miller and Steinberg also included a person's apparent ethnicity based on skin color and other physical indicators in their description of the cultural level, so you might infer a little more from observing those attributes. But you might also exhibit surprise if you say "hi" and the person replies, "Guten tag, ich spreche kein Englisch" ("Good day, I do not speak English") in German. Lacking precision, cultural-level information would too often lead you to false conclusions.

Next, Miller and Steinberg (1975) described the sociological level. Here you know at least some of the groups to which people belong. You might see a man at Potter

Park in Lansing, Michigan. Because the man has a baby in his arms, you might label him a "father." He might also wear a T-shirt bearing the message "Cyclist 4ever" from which you would guess that he likes riding a bicycle. You might see indicators of youth and conclude he has not yet reached 30 years of age. Each of these cues provides sociological-level information. This kind of information improves your ability to explain and predict someone's behavior compared with cultural information, but it still lacks quite a bit of precision. The man might look young for his 45 years, the child in his arms his nephew, and the T-shirt purchased from the local Goodwill store where, because he finds himself between jobs, he gets most of his clothing.

Finally, Miller and Steinberg (1975) described the **interpersonal level** where you know information specific to the person in question. You might know that she likes polar bearing, volunteers her time to work at a soup kitchen on her days off work, and that she prefers daffodils to any other type of flower. Miller and Steinberg argued that with interpersonal-level information, you can explain and predict someone's behavior better than with only sociological-level or cultural-level information. At least you know where to find her if you want to ask her out on a date, where to take her on a date, and what kind of flowers to give her.

Now suppose that you want to solicit donations for the Relay for Life, an event that raises money for cancer research. If soliciting from a target person you know well, let us refer to her as Varda, the interpersonal-level information that you have about Varda might enhance your success. For instance, you might frame what you say by coupling the facts that the event supports cancer research, and her sister, Vered, benefited from recent advances in breast cancer research. But what do you say when trying to obtain a donation from a stranger? Let us refer to him as Thomas. Your observations suggest that Thomas has reached middle age. Equipped with only this sociological-level information, you might find a point of emphasis that appeals to middle-aged males, such as "some of the money will go to fund research investigating cures for prostate cancer." Alternatively, you may know nothing about the audience, save cultural information, such as that they live in the United States. In such a case, your persuasive message appears even less personalized. For instance, you might send a direct mail message emphasizing that money solicited for the Relay for Life will go to a good cause.

These examples illustrate that persuasive messages vary in their audience adaptation which, in turn, depends on knowledge of the persuasive target audience. We shall refer to messages predicated on cultural-level information only as **generic**, those based on sociological information as **targeted**, and those stemming from interpersonal information as **tailored**. As Figure 3.1 illustrates, one might profitably think of the degree of persuasive message personalization as arrayed on a continuum ranging from the most generic (least personalized) to the most tailored (most personalized).

Some research findings would lead us to suspect that the more personalized appeal to Varda would result in a higher likelihood of success than the less personalized appeal to Thomas and the appeal to Thomas as more successful than the direct mail message.

GENERIC	TARGETED	TAILORED
(Cultural Level)	(Sociological Level)	(Interpersonal Level)

LEAST PERSONALIZED   MOST PERSONALIZED

FIGURE 3.1   The persuasive message personalization continuum.

The communication researchers Yan Huang and Fuyuan Shen (2016) conducted a thorough review of studies that examined using cultural-level information to persuade people to adopt healthier behaviors as a means of reducing cancer risk. They found that messages that tried to adapt to their audience at the broadest cultural level produced small effects, but that messages adapted more specifically to aspects of someone's culture, such as their values and religious beliefs, had more persuasive success. And communication scholars Jos Hornikx and Daniel O'Keefe (2009), examining cultural-level information as a means of adapting persuasive messages in a variety of contexts, also generally found small effects.

Others have attempted to persuade people by targeting, based on knowing the kinds of groups to which the audience belongs (the sociological level). Advertisers might target older people based on the kinds of products that they believe older people need. If you want to know about those kinds of products, watch some game shows. Advertisers seem to think older people watch such programs, and so they pay to place their advertisements there. During popular sports events, such as American football games, advertisers buy time for commercials for beer based on the belief that people who watch football like to drink beer. But plenty of people who watch football rarely drink beer (Frank), and plenty of beer drinkers do not like football (Chris), so you can see how such adaptation lacks precision. At best, that kind of adaptation slightly increases the chances that interested consumers will buy a particular product.

Frequently, applied communication scientists and public health officials try to persuade people based on sociological information. For example, some public health officials have used focus groups to find out what messages persuade blue-collar workers, Hispanics, or young mothers. Sometimes these efforts produce modest gains in the proportion of people who quit smoking, eat fruits and vegetables, or vaccinate their children. But in other cases, their persuasion attempts fail, yielding no more attitude or behavior change than a generic, nontargeted message.

Tailoring relies on more personalized information to develop persuasive messages. And at this point, a critical question emerges; namely, "On what do we tailor to obtain the maximum persuasive effectiveness?" Put another way, existing theory and data fail to provide a clear guide as to what information to include and to exclude when developing a tailored persuasive message. Interestingly, clinical psychologists face this difficulty when trying to modify their patients' behavior. Treating each patient individually requires that they acquire unique information on that patient and that they then decide what information to include and, by elimination, to exclude in their treatment program (Watzlawick et al., 1974).

Some research given the label "tailoring" has confused targeting and tailoring, suggesting, for example, that messages developed to convince smoking mothers (as opposed to other smokers) to stop smoking constitutes a tailored message. We would apply the term "targeting" to this example, as the set of mothers who smoke forms a demographic category that would mask important individual differences within this sociological group. These individual within-category differences, such as personality differences, might strongly affect the ability to persuade this audience.

Some others have equated greater message specificity with tailoring (Chua et al., 2009). So, for example, a message such as "smokes 30 cigarettes a day" provides more specificity than "smokes a lot of cigarettes." Once again, this message characteristic (specificity) does little to tailor the message to unique, or relatively unique, characteristics of those one wishes to convince.

Approach/Avoidance Motivation

Yet others have tried to tailor by matching persuasive message characteristics with motivational orientations, such as the tendency to approach or avoid (Updegraff et al., 2007). The former refers to those driven primarily to seek positive outcomes; the latter refers to those driven primarily to escape negative outcomes. Thus some have argued that those with an approach orientation find gain-framed messages (those emphasizing the benefits from adopting the persuasive message recommendations) more persuasive, whereas those with an avoidance orientation find loss-framed messages (those emphasizing the costs of failing to adopt the persuasive message recommendations) more persuasive.

Personality

And yet others have employed personality information to tailor persuasive messages. At present, the dominant view of personality focuses on five traits: (1) openness to experience, (2) conscientiousness, (3) extraversion, (4) agreeableness, and (5) neuroticism (OCEAN, see McCrae & Costa, 1987). Inventiveness and curiosity mark those high in openness to experience. Such people would tend to agree with statements such as "I am full of ideas," and "I am quick to understand things." Efficiency and organization characterize those high in conscientiousness. They would tend to endorse statements such as, "I follow a schedule," and "I pay attention to details." Outgoing and energetic people score high in extraversion. They likely agree with statements such as, "I feel comfortable around people," and "I talk to a lot of different people at parties." Especially friendly and cooperative people score high on agreeableness. They endorse statements such as, "I take time out for others," and "I make others feel at ease." Finally, sensitivity and nervousness characterize those high in neuroticism. Highly neurotic people endorse statements such as, "I get irritated easily," and "I have mood swings."

Developing persuasive messages for each of these five personality traits contrasts the personalization of persuasive messages that accompanies targeting and tailoring. Suppose that we target our persuasive messages based on the marital status of the target. We could develop messages to persuade members of the following groups: (1) married, (2) divorced and not remarried/separated/absent spouse, (3) never married, and (4) widowed. In contrast, suppose that we divided each of the OCEAN traits into those low or high on that trait. Then $2^5 = 32$ (two levels of each OCEAN trait taken to the power equaling the number of traits, 5) distinctions. Scholars could develop tailored persuasive messages for people in each of these 32 categories. And if we wanted to divide each of the OCEAN traits into three categories, we could distinguish $3^5 = 243$ types of people. For each of these 243 types, we could create a personalized message.

Hirsh et al. (2012) took a simpler approach by developing five persuasive messages, each designed to persuade people high on one of the five OCEAN traits. They report a modest persuasive advantage for their tailored messages. And in 2015, Turkish information science researchers Alkış and Temizel (2015) found that the six general persuasive strategies identified by social psychologist Robert Cialdini (2008) tended to change attitudes more for certain types of personalities than others. For example, very extroverted people tended to agree more with persuasive messages based on appeals to the scarcity of a product, whereas people very open to new experiences tended to agree less with persuasive strategies rooted in obeying authority.

You may wonder about the practicality of this research. How could you know the personality profile of every potential person you want to persuade? You cannot expect them to complete the OCEAN questionnaire, then wait while you score it and design a persuasive message based on that information, and then try to convince them. An alternative strategy estimates people's personalities based on their social media behavior. Youyou et al. (2015) found they could estimate people's personalities based on what kinds of things they "liked" on Facebook. Based on comparisons to previous research, they claimed that after their subjects had chosen 300 "likes," they could estimate their subjects' personality scores better than peoples' spouses could. For example, they claimed that people who "liked" a particular member of the cast of *Jersey Shore* tended to have high extroversion.

Naturally, some have tested the extent to which these estimates of personality derived from social media help them tailor persuasive messages. Matz et al. (2017), again, used patterns of who or what Facebook users "liked" to estimate personality traits. But they took it a step further, subsequently exposing those with a high level of that trait to a message designed to persuade them (matched) or exposing them to a message designed to persuade those with a low level of that trait (mismatched). For instance, they would identify highly extroverted people and either show them an advertisement on Facebook for beauty products that matched a highly extroverted person or a mismatched message designed to persuade someone low in extroversion. The results indicated a persuasive advantage for matched messages, as they clicked on the matched advertisements more often. Thus Matz and colleagues demonstrated the ability to use previous research on connections between "likes" and personality traits to design more effective persuasive messages. They claimed to increase persuasiveness in some cases based on knowing only a single item their audience had "liked" on Facebook. Other computer science researchers report similar successes estimating personality and matching messages with their targets' Twitter comments.

Yet the big-five personality traits still represent a somewhat broad approach to understanding someone and using that information to choose a tailored persuasive message. As mentioned previously, if we wanted to divide each of the OCEAN traits into three categories, we could distinguish $3^5 = 243$ types of people so that we could conceivably generate 243 persuasive messages to appeal to them. Nevertheless, this approach falls far short of designing a persuasive message tailored uniquely to each and every person. Presently, we estimate that 7.7 billion humans live on Earth. The number 243 falls far short of 7.7 billion.

Attitude Functions

One approach that might get us nearer the 7.7 billion mark requires examining unique features of each and every human, and one way to accomplish that goal involves understanding the function served by and the structure of the target attitude of each person. Let us first consider **attitude functions**.

Functional attitude theory attempts to determine why people have the attitudes they have. A social psychologist named Daniel Katz (1960) argued that even though two people might have the same degree of liking or disliking for an attitude object, their reasons for liking or disliking the object sometimes serve very different functions for each person. Katz observed, "Unless we know the psychological need which is met by the holding of an attitude, we are in a poor position to predict when and how it will change" (p. 170).

Katz distinguished four functions that attitudes serve. The **utilitarian** (or instrumental or adjustive) function refers to attitudes that promote features of the environment that we find rewarding and prevent those features of the environment that we find punitive. For example, for students who accrue a substantial amount of debt in the course of pursuing their education, their attitude toward a slate of political candidates may hinge on whether those candidates support student loan forgiveness. If a candidate does support their view on student loan forgiveness, then students for whom their attitudes serve a utilitarian function develop a more favorable attitude toward the candidate; if the candidate does not, then they develop a less favorable attitude toward the candidate.

The **ego-defensive** function refers to the tendency for people to take measures to preserve their sense of themselves, or their self-concept (or self-identity). At times, people may find it necessary to protect themselves against unacceptable internal impulses. For instance, some might experience deep feelings of inferiority and attempt to defend their sense of themselves as valuable people by masking the inferiority feelings with negative attitudes toward minority groups. They may then assert that, by comparison, their own demographic group exhibits superior valued characteristics, such as intelligence, strength, or morality. By extension, they too come to feel superior or perhaps less inferior.

At other times, protection against outside threats might arise. For some people, perhaps for many or even most of us, our jobs and the skill with which we perform them form a central part of our self-identity. For such people, negative attitudes toward robots might develop, not only because they find robots a threat to their job security (utilitarian function) but also because to lose their jobs would threaten a central part of their self-identity (e.g., "I am a skilled truck driver").

Katz's **value-expressive** function refers to those attitudes that exist to promote self-expression. By expressing them, one can present oneself to others in a particular way that might result in receiving social approval from valued others, gaining entry into valued reference groups, or both. So, for example, valuing independence more than equality might result in pro-business, antigovernmental regulation attitudes, and a career as a business executive. Expressing such attitudes might gain the approval of other like-minded persons and land one a position as chair of the local Chamber of Commerce.

Finally, attitudes that serve to promote Katz's **knowledge** function help us make sense of our experiences. Consequently, they may make our environment more understandable and predictable so that we can deal with it more effectively (e.g., safe, prosperous). For instance, one might embrace negative attitudes toward smoking because we want to live a long life and because we believe that refraining from smoking will promote that goal. On the other hand, stereotypical attitudes may emerge for exactly this reason as well. We might think that they make our environment understandable, and by creating a self-fulfilling prophecy, they might actually do so.

Katz's description and subsequent discussion of these four functions risks providing an overly simple portrait of the functions that attitudes serve. One oversimplification involves the possibility that any given attitude might serve more than one function. If an attitude serves multiple functions, then the question arises as to the extent to which an attitude serves each of the functions (Herek, 1987). Put differently, rather than think of an attitude serving a utilitarian function, or an ego-defense function, or a value-expressive function, or a knowledge function, instead we might think of an attitude serving each of these functions to some extent (including perhaps zero in some cases). So Chris's attitude toward non-fossil-fuel energy sources might serve to a considerable extent the utilitarian function and to a lesser extent the value-expressive and knowledge functions, but it may serve no ego-defensive function. In contrast, his attitude toward intercollegiate debate may very much serve an ego-defense function and value-expressive functions but have little to do with the utilitarian and knowledge functions.

Scholars have challenged Katz's thinking and generated alternative lists of attitude functions (Herek, 1986; Smith et al., 1956). Nevertheless, no consensus has arisen as to a complete set of attitude functions. Disagreements notwithstanding, agreement has emerged as to how to use the knowledge of attitude functions to persuade people. Using either personality characteristics (Snyder & DeBono, 1985) or direct self-report measures to assess the extent to which any given persons' attitude serves a particular attitude function (Clary & Snyder, 1992; both of which provide less than perfect methods of identifying the extent to which an attitude serves a particular function), adapting persuasive messages so that they *match* the function served by the attitude enhances persuasion (Carpenter, 2012).

As an example, suppose that you have the task of marketing a single malt scotch, let us call it Glen Bampot. To someone with an attitude serving a utilitarian function, you might emphasize the benefits of the spirit, perhaps something like, "Looking for great taste at an affordable price? Your drink is Glen Bampot. It stands alone." In contrast, to someone with an attitude serving a value-expressive function, you might emphasize the image of the spirit. The background imagine shows a picture of an exclusive club: dark paneling, bookshelves filled with classic titles, and large overstuffed leather furniture. In the fore-ground, imagine a bottle of the beautiful dark amber, Glen Bampot, sitting on a pedestal, surrounded by elegant crystal glasses with a caption underneath the picture reading, "Those who move among the elite require an elite scotch. That scotch is Glen Bampot."

Attitude Structure

Some who study **attitude structures** think of them as networks (Dalege et al., 2016). Consider how we might construct a network for one person's attitude toward Glen Bampot. This network might include beliefs about Glen Bampot, affect toward Glen Bampot (such as feelings or emotions), and the evaluation of Glen Bampot. Figure 3.2 depicts part of the network that represents some-one's, let us call him Malcolm, attitude toward Glen Bampot.

One cluster of beliefs, depicted in blue, represents a set of three positively related beliefs that Malcolm has about the flavor of this brand of Scotch. He views it as strong (i.e., high alcohol content), and he characterizes the taste as both smoky and having traces of peat. A second cluster of three

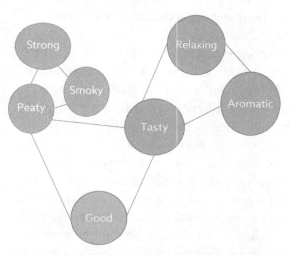

FIGURE 3.2   The structure of Malcolm's attitude toward Glen Bambot.

positively related beliefs, depicted in green, represent a second set of evaluative beliefs that characterize the experience of drinking Glen Bampot. He finds both the smell and the taste appealing and believes that drinking it relaxes him. Finally, a third lone concept, or node, completes the diagram. "Good" represents an overall evaluation of the product and most closely resembles what we have defined as an "attitude."

Notice that the beliefs "peaty" and "tasty" link both with each other, let us say positively, and with the evaluation of the product (good). Suppose that Malcolm finds scotch with traces of peat in it tasty. And suppose further that he evaluates tasty spirits positively. This network of beliefs then provides an account of why/how he reaches this judgment. And it also provides strategies for changing his attitude.

One strategy involves designing messages tailored to change Malcolm's evaluation of one of the nodes in his attitudinal network, say peaty scotch. In this way, we might also change the valence of the relationship between two nodes, say from positive to negative. So, for instance, we might cite botanical evidence that peat frequently has high concentrations of various molds and medical evidence that molds have negative effects on respiratory health. By making the belief that Glen Bampot has peat less appealing, we may make its evaluation less positive (i.e., good).

A second strategy involves adding nodes. For example, we might tailor a message adding the criteria of "price" and "quality" to Malcolm's attitudinal network. Specifically, we might argue that Malcolm could get an equivalent or better product, say Glen Boidheach, for a considerably reduced price. We might amass evidence that the firm that distills Glen Bambot once produced a great scotch but that a recent recession forced it to cut costs and to compromise quality so as to maintain profit margins and to pay exorbitant executive salaries. We could produce testimonials from highly credible sources (those who really know quality scotch) to the effect that they have noticed the decline. We might claim that the Glen Bambot distillery now lives on reputation and no longer on quality.

Notice that we could merge information about attitude functions and attitude structure to tailor even more precisely. For instance, if Malcolm's attitude toward scotch served predominately utilitarian or knowledge functions, then these two message strategies match well.

Neuroscience

Recently, interest in tailoring persuasive messages has expanded to include scholars with interests in cognitive neuroscience. We can expect persuasive messages to have observable effects on brain activity of the sort that one could detect with functional magnetic resonance imaging (fMRI). The fMRI technique relies on the coupling of neural activity and blood flow. Specifically, activity in an area of the brain results in increased blood flow to that area. Conceivably, using this technique, persuasion scholars could test the effect of persuasive messages on the pattern of activity in varying brain regions. Because research has linked certain patterns of neural activity to changing attitudes and behavior, messages that activate these regions emerge as potentially effective persuasive messages. Put differently, persuasive messages induce patterns of neural activity, which may provide a useful, but almost certainly imperfect, indicator of certain cognitive states (e.g., information processing). This brain activity/cognitive state(s), in turn, then mediates the effect of the message on persuasion outcomes, such as attitude change. Notably, however, to pursue this method of tailoring, we would still need to know upon which attributes to tailor the messages that we plan to test.

Recent work by Schmalzle and colleagues (2015), however, suggested a more nuanced conclusion. They reported that strong messages, or powerful speeches as they term them, produce similar neural patterns across persons. These results suggest the possibility that the strong motivational forces unleashed by powerful persuasive messages may prove so powerful that they overwhelm the effect of tailored persuasive messages. Notably, weaker messages produced less similar neural patterns across persons, opening the possibility that tailoring might have a stronger effect on such weak persuasive messages and a weak or no impact on very strong persuasive messages. Experimental outcomes such as these suggest that tailoring might increase persuasion but perhaps not as substantially as many believe.

RETURNING TO THAT MATTER OF FAITH

Previously in this chapter, we wrote of an article of faith—namely, that the right argument from the right source transmitted through the right channel can persuade anyone. What constitutes the message may differ for different people, as might the source and channel. But anyone would change their attitude when exposed to the properly tailored message. We now reexamine that article of faith.

Suppose that scholars or practitioners try to test this article of faith. But despite their best efforts, they tailor their message on an ineffective attribute. For example, they might construct a message designed to persuade Harry to vote for politician Kami based on Harry's big-five personality (OCEAN) profile when in reality, to convince Harry on this matter, a message matching Harry's value-expressive attitude function holds the key to changing his mind. Now what?

Well, first of all, the persuasion attempt fails. Harry does not have a more positive attitude toward Kami after message exposure, and he does not vote for her. Now, what can we conclude about tailoring?

We could attribute the failure to improper tailoring, assuming, of course, that we knew the key attribute on which to tailor. But, of course, we would not know that attribute, or else we would have tailored our message on it in the first place. Alternatively, we could reject our article of faith.

In contrast, suppose that the OCEAN profile provides the uniquely correct way to convince Harry so that he changes his attitude in the direction of greater favorability for Kami, and he votes for her. That result allows us to affirm our article of faith, but it has limitations. We have only persuaded one person on one issue. There remains a finite but very large number of other people and other issues. Will the article of faith still hold for them?

Suppose that reality reveals our article of faith as false. We cannot prove it false because we can always conclude that any failure of tailoring to convince people results from improper tailoring. But suppose reality reveals our article of faith as true. Again, we cannot prove it so because we may (and maybe more frequently than we would like to) tailor only to a limited number of people. Consequently, we cannot really test this idea, and it remains an article of faith.

So, how might we make some progress in determining the truth of this article of faith? One way would involve considering the plausibility of a counterexample. Might some persons never change their minds on some issues? German political scientist Elisabeth Noelle-Neumann (1974) certainly thought so. In her work on the spiral of silence, she pointed to two groups of people who might find no message persuasive on certain topics, labeling them as the hardcore and the avant-garde.

Noelle-Neumann's research focused on how when we perceive that we hold minority opinions we avoid advocating those opinions and, instead, remain silent. The primary reason that she provided for this behavior revolves around the fear of social isolation that might accompany advocating what we perceive as an unpopular position. So, for instance, we might favor political candidate X, but if we judge that most other people prefer candidate Y, we tend not to try to convince others to vote for X or even to defend our own preference. Instead, we remain silent. She identified the hardcore and the avant-garde as relatively immune from such a fear of isolation. The hardcore believe strongly in their positions. They tend toward nonconformity, and they do not fear holding positions that might alienate them from others. The avant-garde also believe strongly in their positions, and they see their views as ahead of the times. Both the hardcore and the avant-garde speak out because the majority view does not compel them to change their minds. Consequently, we can expect to have difficulty convincing them.

The existence of these two kinds of people cast doubt on our article of faith in the right message, source, and channel persuading everyone. On the other hand, Noelle-Neumann identified them as relatively rare. So our article of faith might hold for the vast majority of humankind. Nonetheless, we must keep in mind exceptions, such as the hardcore and the avant-garde.

Conclusion

To conclude this chapter, let us consider where on the message personalization continuum (Figure 3.1) we might prefer our persuasive message to lie so that we might maximize the number of people we persuade. As we move from generic messages

TABLE 3.1 The Number of People Reached (N), Resulting From Different Ranges and Different Probabilities of Effectiveness

Range	P	N
10,000	0.01	100
1,000	0.20	200
100	0.50	50
10	0.80	8
1	1.00	1

to tailored messages, we can expect to have a higher probability of persuading any given target. On the other hand, we could reach massive numbers of people with generic messages, whereas by definition, each specifically tailored message would appeal effectively to a very few people, perhaps only one person. Holding resources, such as time and money, constant, one could find a point on this continuum that maximizes the number of people persuaded by a single message. Table 3.1 provides an example.

In Table 3.1 *range* denotes the number of people exposed to our message. We allow that value to vary from 10,000 people to one person in this example. The letter "*p*" denotes the probability of persuading the target. For the sake of illustrating the principle, we shall assume either that the message persuades the target or that it does not. Finally, "*N*" represents the number of people persuaded. Given fixed resources, one would likely use generic messages to attempt to convince 10,000, whereas one could tailor very precisely when only attempting to persuade one person. Generally, the higher the range, the more generic the message. Consequently, the probability of persuading the target person(s) increases as the range decreases, reflecting the fact that decreased range corresponds to more precise tailoring. With ranges of 10, 100, and 1,000, we could target/tailor, in more or less detail, the message for the audience.

As Table 3.1 illustrates, in this case, a relatively crudely targeted persuasive message that convinces 20% of 1,000 people proves most successful. It convinces 200 people, and neither the generic message sent to 10,000 people or the more precisely targeted/tailored messages sent to smaller audiences convinces nearly as many. So the message maximizing the number of people persuaded lies toward the generic side of the personalization continuum, albeit not at the most extreme end of that continuum. Results of specific persuasion efforts, such as campaigns, will not always replicate this outcome. Rather, the point of the example lies in the way in which it focuses our persuasive efforts. When our persuasive goal involves convincing as many people as possible, say with a health communication campaign addressing the importance of eating a sufficient amount of fruits and vegetables, both the effectiveness of the message (p) and the number of people we can reach determine the extent to which we meet our goal.

Appendix 3.1

The Shearman and Levine (2006) Dogmatism Scale

Items

1. There is a clear line between what is right and what is wrong.
2. People who disagree with me are usually wrong.
3. Having multiple perspectives on an issue is usually desirable. [R]
4. I'm the type of person who questions authority. [R]
5. When I disagree with someone else, I think it is perfectly acceptable to agree to disagree. [R]
6. I am confident in the correctness of my beliefs.
7. There is a single correct way to do most things.
8. People should respect authority.
9. I am a person who is strongly committed to my beliefs.
10. Diversity of opinion and background is valuable in any group or organization. [R]
11. It is important to be open to different points of view. [R]
12. I am a "my way or the highway" type of person.
13. I will not compromise on the things that are really important to me.
14. There are often many different acceptable ways to solve a problem. [R]
15. I consider myself to be very open-minded. [R]
16. Few things in life are truly black and white; instead, I see gray areas on most topics. [R]
17. Different points of views should be encouraged. [R]
18. People who are in a position of authority have the right to tell others what to do.
19. People who are very different from us can be dangerous.

20. I am "set in my ways."

21. When I make a decision, I stick with it.

22. It is usually wise to seek out expert opinions before making decisions.

23. I like having a set routine.

Response Scale:

   5 = Agree Strongly

   4 = Agree

   3 = Neither Agree nor Disagree

   2 = Disagree

   1 = Disagree Strongly

Note: Items marked with an "[R]" are to be reflected, or reverse coded, i.e., "Disagree Strongly" = 1, "Disagree" = 2. "Neither Agree nor Disagree" = 3, "Agree" = 2, "Agree Strongly" = 1.

Appendix 3.2

The Cacioppo and Petty (1982) Need for Cognition Scale

Items

1. I would prefer complex to simple problems.
2. I like to have the responsibility of handling a situation that requires a lot of thinking.
3. Thinking is not my idea of fun.*
4. I would rather do something that requires little thought than something that is sure to challenge my thinking abilities.*
5. I try to anticipate and avoid situations where there is likely a chance I will have to think in depth about something.*
6. I find satisfaction in deliberating hard and for long hours.
7. I only think as hard as I have to.*
8. I prefer to think about small, daily projects to long-term ones.*
9. I like tasks that require little thought once I've learned them.*
10. The idea of relying on thought to make my way to the top appeals to me.
11. I really enjoy a task that involves coming up with new solutions to problems.
12. Learning new ways to think doesn't excite me very much.*
13. I prefer my life to be filled with puzzles that I must solve.
14. The notion of thinking abstractly is appealing to me.
15. I would prefer a task that is intellectual, difficult, and important to one that is somewhat important but does not require much thought.
16. I feel relief rather than satisfaction after completing a task that required a lot of mental effort.*
17. It's enough for me that something gets the job done; I don't care how or why it works.*
18. I usually end up deliberating about issues even when they do not affect me personally.

John T. Cacioppo, Richard E. Petty, and Chuan Feng Kao, from "The Efficient Assessment of Need for Cognition," *Journal of Personality Assessment*, vol. 48, no. 3, p. 307. Copyright © 1984 by Taylor & Francis Group.

Response Scale:

    +4 = Very Strong Agreement

    +3 = Strong Agreement

    +2 = Moderate Agreement

    +1 = Slight Agreement

     0 = Neither Agreement Nor Disagreement

    −1 = Slight Disagreement

    −2 = Moderate Disagreement

    −3 = Strong Disagreement

    −4 = Very Strong Disagreement

Note: Items with a * are to be reflected.

Appendix 3.3

The Rosenberg (1965) Self-Esteem Scale

Items

1. On the whole, I am satisfied with myself.
2. At times I think I am no good at all. *
3. I feel that I have a number of good qualities.
4. I am able to do things as well as most other people.
5. I feel I do not have much to be proud of. *
6. I certainly feel useless at times. *
7. I feel that I'm a person of worth, at least on an equal plane with others.
8. I wish I could have more respect for myself. *
9. All in all, I am inclined to feel that I am a failure. *
10. I take a positive attitude toward myself.

Response Scale:

4 = Strongly Agree

3 = Agree

2 = Disagree

1 = Strongly Disagree

Note: Items with a * are to be reflected.

4

Do Persuasive Messages Have Side Effects?

Dissent is taken as an insult because it condemns another's judgment.

—Baltasar Gracián

FACEBOOK OFFERS MANY OPPORTUNITIES TO deepen and maintain social connections, but sometimes finding out the political beliefs of your acquaintances results in disappointment. You open the Facebook app and start scrolling through and see that a friendly person you know from your workplace posted an argument about politics that you find personally repellant. That coworker may have known that his message would fail to persuade everyone, but he probably did not expect it to cause people to dislike him. Some people may or may not have even read the message or understood it. Some may have read it and spent a few moments thinking about why they think the author's message fails. In this chapter, we focus on some negative persuasive side effects. But we also examine some positive side effects, such as an anti-tanning advertisement (hereafter, ads) that encourages people to quit self-tanning, as well as to try to learn more about the dangers of skin cancer. We shall look at both types.

In this chapter, we look at a variety of potential side effects of persuasion. Most persuasion research studies the effects of persuasive message variations on a single targeted attitude. Such research can include changing the attitude in the direction desired by the communicator or in a direction opposite to the communicator's wishes. We cover these effects in the other chapters. But a single cause rarely has a single effect. Some of these side effects involve processes that may result in attitude change (e.g., message learning). Some affect the persuasion process minimally in the short term (relationship with the source). We start by examining the learning of message content and the initial thoughts about the message. Then we look at related attitudes that our persuasive messages might also change by examining generalization and displacement effects. Then we examine how persuasive messages might affect how we perceive the source of the message's credibility and possibly our relationship with the source. Naturally, affecting our relationships with people also affects our ability to persuade them in the future. Finally, we close by examining situations in which a persuasive message motivates people to try to learn more about a particular topic in some cases and less about a topic in others.

MESSAGE COMPREHENSION

Before someone can change your attitude and behavior, you first must reach some degree of comprehension of what that source wants you to believe and why they think you should believe it. You may not comprehend some messages at all, like the many ads you see online that you completely ignore. Or you may comprehend a message completely and understand all its parts, such as when you carefully read an argument on Facebook about the consistency of Earth's shape with a flat disk or with a sphere. In most cases, comprehension falls between those extremes.

The social psychologist William McGuire (1968) argued that to persuade someone, that person must first comprehend your message. That may seem like an obvious point, but not everyone agreed with him then and not everyone does now. For example, another social psychologist, Anthony Greenwald (1968), argued that message comprehension does not affect the persuasiveness of a message. His cognitive response model claims that the extent to which the audience thinks more positive thoughts than negative thoughts during and after exposure to a persuasive message predicts persuasion directly, regardless of whether the audience fully understands the message. His cognitive response model formed the basis of the still very popular dual-process theories of persuasion. So, we shall first look at a few studies that demonstrated that comprehension matters, at least some of the time, and then we shall discuss a model that tries to explain when comprehension has greater or weaker effects on message acceptance. That way we can get a sense of whether comprehension of the message helps explain the likelihood of message acceptance by the audience.

To demonstrate the importance of the comprehension of the message, we have to figure out how to measure comprehension. Most researchers investigating message comprehension expose their subjects to a persuasive message and then give them a pop quiz on the contents of that message afterward. If a given subject truly understands the message, then they likely retain the message content and recall it successfully on the pop quiz. Then the researcher also measures the attitudes of their subjects and checks to see how strongly the subjects' recall of the message predicts their attitudes toward the message topic. The stronger the recall-attitude correlation, the stronger the effect of comprehension of the message on the message's persuasiveness in that case.

One particularly clever study by social psychologists Kurt Frey and Alice Eagly (1993) demonstrated that message comprehension may affect persuasion more than previous persuasion researchers had thought. They argued that people participating in a persuasion study know the researcher expects them to listen carefully to the message. But they wondered what would happen in a persuasion study in which the subjects did not even know the study had started. For one-half of their subjects, when they arrived at the lab, the experimenter told them to wait so that the experimenter could fetch some forms. While they waited, a research assistant sat in the same room, ostensibly making notes on some tape recordings. The tape recording the assistant listened to played at a sufficient volume for the subject to hear and it "happened" to contain the target persuasive message. So, the subjects in that condition could listen carefully or not. The researcher told the other one-half of the subjects to listen to the taped message without the subterfuge involving the research assistant. All subjects responded to a message recall measure and an attitude toward the topic measure. The researchers found a substantially stronger correlation between recall and attitudes when the subjects "happened" to hear the message and could choose to listen or not versus when the experimenter instructed them to listen to the message. That study found evidence consistent with the claim that, at least some of the time, message comprehension substantially affects message persuasiveness (see also Eagly, 1974; Regan & Cheng, 1973).

Online Versus Memory-Based Processing

Yet not all studies have found a substantial relationship between recall and attitudes. The social psychologists Reid Hastie and Bernadette Park (1986) provided one interesting explanation for these disparate findings. They argued that sometimes people form an attitude while they listen to or read the message. They called that **online processing**. Under those circumstances, people decide how they feel about the topic of the message during message exposure. Imagine that you see an advertisement for a new restaurant opening in your town, and you decide right away whether you like it. It seems that the menu contains a number of excellent-looking bacon dishes, and you love anything with bacon in it. Later, if someone asks you how you feel about that restaurant, you can answer right away because you made up your mind and can easily recall your attitude.

But you probably do not make a decision about every product for which you see an ad. For example, you might see one for a restaurant that does not have any locations within 200 miles of where you live. Because of the distance, you have no reason to form an attitude about it, so you do not. Hastie and Park (1986) argued that many of the persuasive messages we encounter do not interest us enough to motivate us to form an attitude. Yet we sometimes retain some of that information we learned. Suppose someone tells you that a distant restaurant plans to open a location near your house in a few weeks. That friend then asks if you want to go when it opens. Suddenly, you do need an attitude because you need to decide if you like that restaurant enough to pay to eat there. So you search through your memory and, based on what you can recall, you form an attitude about that restaurant. When you have to construct a new attitude based on what you can recall, Hastie and Park refer to the process as **memory-based processing**.

In memory-based processing, message comprehension does predict the extent to which people adopt attitudes consistent with the message. What you can recall from persuasive messages about a topic strongly influences your attitude. So, with memory-based processing, a strong recall-attitude correlation will likely result. But if you have already made up your mind about an attitude object using online processing in response to one or more persuasive messages, then it does not matter what information about the attitude object you recall. You simply recall the attitude, regardless of what else you might remember about the attitude object.

Hastie and Park actually developed the memory-based versus online distinction to help explain how people develop impressions of someone from a description of that person. They explained that many studies in the impression-formation research literature would show study subjects a list of positive and negative traits about a particular target person. Then they would take away the list and ask the subjects to recall as many of those traits as they could. Next, the researchers would ask the subjects how much they liked the target person. They wanted to know if the extent to which subjects remembered mostly positive traits relative to negative traits would correlate positively with the extent to which they reported a favorable impression of the target person. The favorability of your impression of someone and your attitude toward that person generally refer to the same concept. Consistent with the distinction between memory-based and online processing, the strength of that correlation depends on what instructions the subjects received from the experimenters. When the investigator instructed the subjects to memorize the list, a stronger recall-attitude correlation emerged than when the investigator instructed them to use the list to form an impression.

A similar situation might arise in your life. Suppose you have a classmate named Alex about whom you have never thought much. Then your friend Sam says that she has a romantic interest in Alex and wants to know what you think. You would probably try to remember all the information you could think of about Alex. You might recall mostly positive information about Alex, perhaps that he says funny things and tends to dress well. Or you might recall mostly negative things, perhaps that he complains a lot and leaves trash around his desk. What you can recall about Alex will probably have a big effect on the report about him that you provide to your friend Sam. You might forget important negative information or important positive information, but what you recall will form the basis of your judgment.

On the other hand, imagine that your friend Sam asked you at the beginning of the semester to keep an eye on Alex because she had an interest in him. After a few weeks of surveillance, you would probably have an attitude about Alex to report to Sam. You might not recall everything that helped you decide about Alex, but you could give Sam your summary judgment.

Some persuasion researchers wanted to know if similar processes operate for more traditional persuasive messages about public policy topics. The social psychologists Diane Mackie and Arlene Asuncion (1990) tried similar experiments with topics such as gun regulations, oil drilling, and the use of the SAT. They tried a variety of techniques to encourage memory-based processing, such as asking their subjects to find all the verbs in the message, proofread it for grammar, or memorize it. In the online processing conditions, they asked participants to evaluate the strength of the message. In all cases, subjects received a mixture of pro and con arguments on the topics. To assess recall of the message, they looked at the ratio of pro and con elements of the message that each subject recalled. When the subjects received the memory-based processing instructions, the ratio of pro and con elements they recalled tended to correlate with support for the proposal. Alternatively, those asked to evaluate argument strength showed a substantially weaker relationship between message recall and their attitudes. These studies suggest that the distinction between memory-based and online processing matters for a variety of persuasion contexts.

We do not develop attitudes regarding most of the topics we encounter in our day-to-day lives, so we probably use memory-based processing most of the time. In fact, we probably do not remember any of the content from the persuasion attempts that swirl around us every day. If we processed online every persuasive message we encountered, we would have an attitude toward every online mattress company for which we hear an ad. On the other hand, for topics of particular importance to us, we might show a greater tendency to process online. Think of a situation in which you may have gotten into an argument with someone about politics, sports, movies, etc. Can you recall all of your opponent's arguments? Or can you just recall your dislike of their arguments? If that matches your experience, you likely used online processing. In contrast, if you believe you have a strong argument, you want the audience to remember it and recall it later because message comprehension clearly has a positive effect on persuasion at least some of the time. As McGuire argued, you cannot yield to a message you have not first comprehended. But what makes a message more or less comprehensible?

What Makes a Message More or Less Comprehensible

The complexity of the language in the message can substantially contribute to the extent to which the audience can comprehend the message. Advertising researcher Tina Lowrey (1998) argued that several aspects of grammar contribute to the complexity of the message. Passive voice, in which the object of the sentence comes before the subject of the sentence, increases complexity relative to active voice. For example, the sentence, "The cat knocked over the glass" has the active voice structure, whereas the sentence "The glass was knocked over by the cat" has the passive voice structure. Negations also contribute to complexity, such as "The cat ensured that the glass did not remain on the table" relative to the positively stated "The cat knocked the glass off the table." In addition, left-branching sentences increase complexity relative to right-branching sentences. The sentence, "Because the cat wanted to see the glass fall, he knocked the glass onto the floor" shows left-branching, whereas the sentence, "The cat knocked the glass on the floor because he wanted to see it fall" shows right-branching. Lowrey found that advertising messages containing such complex constructions like these made it harder for subjects in her studies to comprehend the messages.

Distractions can also reduce your audience's comprehension of a message. Researchers have distracted their subjects in a variety of ways. In one early study, the social psychologists Leon Festinger and Nathan Maccoby (1965) showed their subjects a filmstrip in which a professor argued against colleges having fraternities. One-half of the subjects saw and heard the professor, whereas the others heard the professor's speech while a humorous short silent film played as the visual. In another study by Deidre Haslett (1976), all subjects heard an audio recording of a speech in which the speaker argued for the "compulsory vasectomisation of all males who have produced three or more offspring" (pp. 85–86). To our knowledge, no other persuasion study has used that topic. Haslett had her subjects perform a variety of distracting tasks, such as writing down numbers they saw appearing on a screen or calling the numbers out as they saw them. A meta-analysis by the communication researcher David Buller (1986) found that distracted subjects generally comprehended less of the message, thereby reducing the persuasiveness of the messages relative to undistracted audiences.

You may now think that you always want your audience to comprehend the message very well. But consider this: What if your message contains weak, unsupported arguments? Several studies have shown that the effect of weakening message comprehension may depend on the strength of the arguments in the message. Part of a study Chris and Frank (Carpenter & Boster, 2013a) worked on together presented their subjects with a message containing very easy to comprehend arguments or arguments with very complex structures, based on Lowrey's (1998) sentence structure inductions. The message also contained either arguments that included strong support and credible sources (strong arguments) or arguments with weak support and questionable sources (weak arguments). As expected, for those exposed to the strong arguments, making the arguments harder to understand weakened the persuasiveness of the arguments. But for those exposed to the weak arguments, making them harder to understand enhanced their persuasiveness (see Hafer and colleagues, 1996, for a similar finding). These studies suggest that although comprehension helps those with a strong case for their proposal, it may hurt those with the weaker case.

THINKING ABOUT THE MESSAGE

We mentioned previously that although some persuasion researchers believe persuasion requires comprehension of the message, others believe that the valence of the thoughts (negative and positive) that the audience has predicts persuasive outcomes the best. The memory-based versus online processing distinction suggests that comprehension has the strongest effects on persuasion when the audience uses memory-based processing. But the thoughts people have when exposed to a persuasive message may have a stronger effect when the audience employs online processing.

Negative Thoughts

Many persuasion researchers have focused on trying to understand negative thoughts—thoughts that help the audience resist the message. When some audiences encounter a persuasive message, they might vocally inform the speaker why the speaker's message lacks persuasiveness, perhaps even heckling the speaker. Some of us even resort to pointing out loudly the logical and evidentiary errors of people on television, even with no one else present. But, usually, persuasion researchers examine how the negative thoughts people have about the persuasive message enable them to feel comfortable retaining their original attitude rather than moving their position closer to the speaker's.

Consider a situation in which you see a political advertisement for a candidate you dislike. The candidate promises to fight for ordinary people like you, and you think to yourself, "Yeah, then why did you get caught taking bribes?" Similarly, sometimes your negative thoughts will include considering other information that the speaker did not address. Or sometimes you might simply think, "Ha! Vote for you? Fat chance, jerk!"

We have a variety of ways to resist persuasion. The social psychologists Julia Jacks and Kimberly Cameron (2003) described some of the more often studied routes. They use the term counterarguing to describe the thoughts of an audience member when that person thinks of reasons that disagree with the speaker's claims, or as they put it, "Direct rebuttal of message arguments" (p. 146). You might see an advertisement for a car dealer who claims to offer honest deals and recall how several of your friends felt the car dealer had ripped them off. You might also choose to reject the message by rejecting the speaker using source derogation such that you decide that something about the source indicates that they do not deserve credence. For example, you might see a celebrity selling life insurance and think to yourself, "What does he know about life insurance? He's an actor, not an accountant!"

On the other hand, some people may not engage directly with sources or their arguments. Instead, they might engage in attitude bolstering so that they focus on reasons for the superiority of their original position. You might see an ad for a politician and instead of thinking of reasons why you would not vote for that politician, you consider reasons why you support that politician's opponent. Social validation offers another option in which you think about all of the people who agree with your original position and draw confidence in your attitudes from that thought. People who smoke cigarettes might resist a public service announcement about the dangers of smoking by thinking, "All my friends smoke; it can't be that dangerous." Jacks and Cameron also identify **negative affect** as an additional means of resisting persuasion such that the audience merely feels negative emotions and resists the message that way. This last one seems like it cannot exist on its own without one of the others operating as well. How can a persuasive message anger you if you do not think about it? Perhaps emotional responses merely intensify one of the types of negative thoughts.

A persuasive message may cause the audience to think any of these types of negative thoughts and thereby fail to change their attitudes. Thus the potential side effects of trying to persuade someone include the possibility that people think negative thoughts and resist the persuasive message. As you might imagine, persuasion researchers have attempted to reduce the likelihood that the audience will produce negative thoughts.

Preventing the audience from thinking in general represents one commonly studied method of preventing the audience from thinking negative thoughts. The social psychologists Leon Festinger and Nathan Maccoby (1964) wrote about distraction as a method of creating a "passive listener" (p. 360) who, while distracted, cannot think any of the various types of negative thoughts we just described. But you probably recall that we just told you that distraction can prevent the audience from comprehending the message as well. If the audience cannot understand the message in the first place, the persuader profits little from also preventing the audience from thinking negative thoughts.

One way out of this dilemma focuses on the extent to which the distraction disrupts audience cognition. Communication researchers John Vohs and Roger Garrett (1968) proposed a Goldilocks solution such that there exists a sweet spot of distraction for any given audience and any given message. When you distract the audience a little, you may leave them with just enough cognitive ability to comprehend the message but not enough for them to have the cognitive resources left over to think many negative thoughts about the message. Too much distraction, however, prevents the audience from understanding the message. A meta-analysis by the communication scholar Mark Hamilton and psychologist John Hunter (1998) examined many of the studies on this issue and found evidence consistent with this proposition such that when one mildly distracts the audience during message exposure, counterarguing decreases, whereas when one strongly distracts the audience, comprehension decreases. Only mild distraction helps increase persuasion.

Several objections to using distraction to persuade people may have occurred to you. You might consider persuasion through distraction unethical because the source tries deliberately to prevent the audience from thinking. In addition, researchers have not produced a standard method of scaling the extent of distraction. What counts as mild? As strong? Furthermore, the amount of distraction may likely need to match the complexity of the message. If the message contains extremely difficult to comprehend arguments, even a mild distraction might prevent message comprehension. Other scholars have instead focused their attention on a more enjoyable way to reduce counterarguing: embedding persuasive messages in stories.

Narratives

In 1983, a film aired on American television called *The Day After*, which depicted the effects of a conflict that included nuclear weapons between the United States and the USSR. As you might imagine, life after nuclear devastation appeared grim. The social psychologists Janet Schofield and Mark Pavelchak (1989) measured people's intentions of engaging in antinuclear activism 2 weeks before the movie aired. They then measured the same intentions 1 week afterward. On average, people who had watched the movie showed stronger intentions to engage in activism. The design of their study prevents us from ruling out the possibility that people who planned to change their activism anyway also had a higher likelihood of watching, but many people likely changed their intentions as a result of viewing the film.

Melanie Green and Timothy Brock (2000) argued that when people experience a narrative of some kind, regardless of whether they read it, watch it, or hear it, they might produce fewer negative thoughts about the message, especially counterarguing. They showed that part of the reason for the reduction in negative thoughts occurs because the audience feels **transported** into the story such that people feel lost in it, focusing instead on the story unfolding to the exclusion of other thoughts. If the story contains information or arguments that can influence someone's attitudes, that story can then persuade people in the same way that the anti-nuclear weapons film encouraged people to try to reduce the likelihood of nuclear conflict.

A summary of the research on narratives in persuasion showed that such efforts tend to persuade people, although the effect emerges inconsistently (Braddock & Dillard, 2016). If you have ever tried writing a story, you know that capturing your audience's attention often proves challenging. Boring stories persuade few people. Consequently, researchers in this area face the twin difficulties of writing a good story and finding ways to sneak in persuasive content. But using narratives to persuade has attracted a considerable amount of research interest in recent years, so advances in this area may help identify ways of improving the success rate of this method of reducing the negative thoughts that tend to occur when people resist a persuasive message.

But consider another possibility. What if the people who watched *The Day After* not only changed their minds about nuclear weapons but also changed their minds about nuclear power generation? Or perhaps they held fast to their pro-nuclear weapons attitudes but instead changed their attitudes about chemical weapons?

GENERALIZATION AND DISPLACEMENT

Persuasion scholars have long believed that our attitudes do not exist as closed-off entities, isolated from each other in our minds. Instead, some think that our attitudes connect with each other to a greater or lesser degree (Tannenbaum, 1967). Your attitudes toward space exploration funding connect weakly if at all with your attitude toward green tea. In contrast, perhaps your attitude toward green tea connects strongly with your attitude toward black tea. Hence, if someone convinces you that cool, sophisticated people drink black tea, you may develop a more favorable attitude toward both black tea and green tea. But your improved attitude toward black tea will probably not affect your attitude toward funding for space exploration.

Psychologist Tina Glaser and her colleagues (2015) have pointed out that if attitudes possess linkages with each other, then attitudes in networks of associations associated with attitude structures such as these might produce lateral attitude change effects. Specifically, they may generate either generalization or displacement effects. A generalization effect refers to a situation in which a persuasive message modifies not only the focal attitude but also a related attitude. For example, a persuasive message designed to change an audience member's attitude in the direction of higher favorability toward recycling might do so, and the message might have the added effect of changing that audience member's attitude on the idea of installing solar panels so that they find themselves more favorable toward the idea of installing them.

A displacement effect arises when the persuasive message fails to change the focal attitude but does change related attitudes in the desired direction. Returning to the previous example, the message may not modify the audience member's attitude toward recycling, but it may result in that audience member favoring solar panel installation to a greater extent. Alternatively, consider someone whose friend lectures him on the need to act more responsibly by quitting smoking. The recipient of that lecture may resist the speaker making demands regarding his smoking habits, but the idea of acting more responsibly might sink in and motivate him to curtail his alcohol consumption.

The idea of displacement effects may strike you as peculiar, but consider one possible reason why they might occur. Suppose that you find yourself in a position in which you must make an evaluation of a member of a disliked minority group, say a skinhead. In an attempt to appear objective, you try to suppress, and succeed in suppressing, your dislike of skinheads when making this judgment. Nevertheless, if asked subsequently about what you see as a related attitude object, say an aggressive young man riding a motorcycle, all of the reasons you dislike skinheads that you recently suppressed might come to mind. You might then apply them to this new (and in your mind similar) person, thus leading you to evaluate him more negatively than you otherwise might have. Glaser and colleagues admitted that substantially more research has demonstrated the existence of generalization effects, whereas relatively few studies have reported displacement effects. Yet the relative frequency of either of these effects in persuasion situations remains unknown and in need of additional research.

Psychologist John Hunter and his colleagues (1976) argued that attitudes such as those regarding green and black tea show a connection because people likely possess a superordinate attitude toward tea that includes all types of tea. They proposed a particular type of network of attitudes to explain this process called a hierarchical model (see Figure 4.1). The superordinate attitude toward hot drinks may include tea, coffee, and hot chocolate. They argued that generalization effects occur strongly in a downward direction with the more abstract attitudes higher up and the more specific attitudes further down. Suppose Mark had never liked recycling, but he adopted more pro-environmental attitudes to impress Allison, who often expresses pro-environment attitudes. Hunter's model predicts that such an attitude change would generalize to change Mark's recycling attitude, as well as Mark's attitude toward solar energy. But Hunter's model would not predict that Mark would adopt more progressive political attitudes in general because the model argues that generalization only happens downward in the structure, and progressive political attitudes exist at a higher degree of abstraction than pro-environmental attitudes.

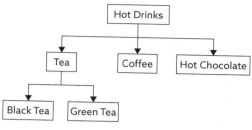

FIGURE 4.1   A hierarchical model of hot drinks attitudes.

Glaser and colleagues (2015) described similar hierarchical models and several models of attitude networks but left the question open regarding which model of attitude organization can best predict which attitudes will generalize to or displace which other attitudes. For example, in Figure 4.2, we see that black tea has connections to many different attitudes. Some of these connections might apply to green tea too, such as "drinks in fancy cups" or "bitter-tasting beverages," but perhaps "British culture" might not connect to green tea. Therefore, if someone positively changed your attitude toward drinks in fancy cups, would that generalize to black tea? What if you had very positive attitudes toward anything associated with British culture, and you decided to start drinking black tea? Would your new affection for black tea transfer to green tea, even though you do not associate green tea with British culture? The best way to construct attitude network models remains unclear. Does each person have a uniquely different attitude network? If so, how can we predict when a persuasive message will generalize to or even displace other attitudes? Alternatively, can we develop messages that will influence people's attitude structures such that the generalizations we want to happen become more likely?

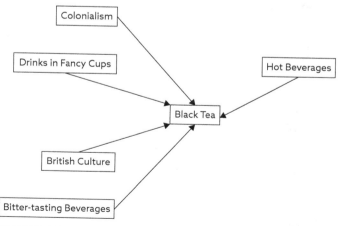

FIGURE 4.2   A network model of black tea attitudes.

Another way to think about attitude networks concerns the consistency among the various parts. Philosophers Paul Thagard and Karsten Verbeurgt (1998) argued for a model focused not only on connections among attitudes (and beliefs, experiences, values, etc.) but also on how attitudes constrain each other. In their model, two attitudes cohere if a positive attitude toward one necessitates a positive attitude toward the other. For example, you could enjoy Disney films in general and feel constrained to enjoy any new film that the company produces. Alternatively, if you like your close friend, you may feel you should agree with your friend's political preferences. Incoherence exists when a positive attitude toward one object constrains you to have a negative attitude toward a related object (and vice versa). For example, if you like your friend, you may feel constrained to dislike someone who abruptly breaks up with your friend to date someone else. Thagard and Verbeurgt argued that you try to keep as many of these constraints as possible in a state of balance. But what do you do if you like Disney movies and your closest friend tells you he hates the new Disney movie? Thagard and Verbeurgt suggested that we weigh these constraints so that they have more or less importance. Consequently, we try to balance as many of the important ones as possible. Some of their models may offer useful guidance for determining when attitude generalization and displacement will have a greater chance of occurring.

Models of attitude networks may offer powerful ways to explain and predict generalization, and researchers continue to work on understanding the connection among attitudes to determine when generalization and displacement might occur. Such modeling has implications for applied research too. For example, Krcmar and Green (2000) found connections among a variety of risky behaviors such as problem drinking, vandalism, and drug use. Their research found that particular types of mass media consumption tend to associate positively or negatively or decrease these behaviors as a group, possibly through generalization processes.

Returning to the situation in which your close friend expresses a contrary opinion about Disney films, how do you resolve your previous positive impression of your friend's taste in films with this new information? If you feel strongly that Disney never makes a bad film, the side effect of your friend's attempt to persuade you otherwise might result in a revision of your estimate of that friend's taste.

PERCEPTIONS OF THE SOURCE

In public speaking classes, we often teach students the three types of artistic proofs from Aristotle: (1) ethos, (2) pathos, and (3) logos. We usually teach ethos to mean **credibility**, and we encourage our students to add a few sentences early on in their speeches that inform the audience of their credentials to "establish ethos." Yet when Aristotle described ethos, he referred to the content of the speech in general as constructed "to make the speaker worthy of credence" (335 BCE/1991 CE, p. 38). Essentially, the way you make your persuasive pitch can change how the audience perceives you, especially your credibility.

One dimension of credibility, **expertise**, refers to the extent to which you possess the relevant knowledge to produce arguments backed by facts for the audience on that topic. The audience might perceive that you have high expertise in rocket science, or they might perceive you have high expertise in plumbing. Most of us will not require the expertise of the rocket scientist, but most of us will require the expertise of a plumber, usually at the worst time possible. You can have expertise because of education or training in an area like rocket science or plumbing. You can also have expertise because of your life experiences, surviving cancer for example.

Prominent communication researcher James McCroskey (1969) published a series of studies demonstrating that speakers who include evidence not only persuade others more effectively but also convince the audience that they have higher expertise in the topic area. So, in addition to persuading people, including evidence tended to have the side effect of making the speaker seem to have greater expertise. McCroskey argued that for speakers who already possessed high expertise, adding evidence does not provide much of a boost in credibility. In contrast, when the audience did not already perceive that the speaker possessed expertise on the topic, the addition of evidence had a stronger positive effect on that speaker's perceived expertise.

A study by communication scholar Torsten Reimer and his colleagues demonstrated a similar effect concerning the quality of arguments (Reimer et al., 2004). When the source of the message used arguments with sound reasoning and strong support, the audience perceived the speaker to have higher source expertise. Conversely, the subjects perceived a speaker with weak reasoning and weak support to possess lower source expertise. These findings raise the possibility that strong arguments add to your persuasiveness both by giving people plausible reasons to adopt your proposal and boosting your perceived expertise.

Similarly, you may have a friend on one of the social media platforms who likes to share links to information. If that friend shares consistently good information from reputable sources, you may increase your estimate of that friend's expertise. On the other hand, many of us have social media friends who never seem to bother checking the legitimacy of their sources before they post. Perhaps they post wild claims about political figures or health information of dubious validity. After a while, you probably just scroll past anything that friend posts or perhaps you use one of the site's or app's blocking features so that you do not see that friend's posts anymore. If you think this frequent poster of nonsense does not know any better, you likely conclude that the person has low expertise. On the other hand, if you think this person knowingly posts inaccurate information, then you might harbor doubts about one of the other two dimensions of credibility.

In addition to expertise, Aristotle also identified two other aspects of speaker credibility: trustworthiness and goodwill. Work by McCroskey and Tevin (1999) demonstrated that Aristotle's three types of credibility do form three separate types. Trustworthiness refers to the extent to which the audience believes the speaker will try to tell them the truth. Goodwill refers to the extent to which the audience believes the speaker has their best interests at heart.

The way the speaker tries to persuade may also have the side effect of changing the audience's perceptions of the speaker's trustworthiness. To increase your audience's perception that they should trust you, you might try to create the expectation that you hold a position opposite to the one you plan on advocating. Priester and Petty (1995) described a speaker as having either worked for pro-environmental groups against business interests or having worked for pro-business groups against environmental groups. The speaker then spoke forcefully for the pro-environmental position in both conditions. The subjects in that study rated the speaker with a pro-business background as more honest than the speaker with the pro-environment background, even though they both gave the same speech. A follow-up study on political campaign ads found that subjects who saw an ad for a politician named David Hunter who praised his opponent rated Hunter more positively than those who saw an ad in which Hunter attacked his opponent (Combs & Keller, 2010).

Although there exists a variety of approaches to increasing expertise and trustworthiness, researchers have paid comparatively little attention to goodwill. During the months preceding the American presidential election, you can find news programs full of interviews with "ordinary people" who insist that one candidate or another has their best interests at heart. How does a political candidate convince people they have goodwill toward them? One might expect that speaking against one's own interest might promote perceptions of goodwill just as it does trustworthiness. Emphasizing similarity between the speaker and the audience generally causes the audience to like the speaker better (Byrne, 1971), perhaps that too might help one's perceived goodwill. We certainly see politicians emphasizing their similarities with their constituents. Chris lives in Iowa, so the political ads he sees often include the candidate wearing jeans and looking thoughtfully at rows of crops while talking to a farmer. Persuasion research would profit by researchers directly addressing this neglected aspect of credibility.

Consider situations in which someone trying to persuade others lacks one or two of these three parts of credibility. Suppose you have taken your car to a mechanic for a small, inexpensive repair. After performing the repair, the mechanic attempts to convince you to replace the timing belt in your car. The mechanic might demonstrate expertise by discussing in detail the importance of the timing belt, the average life span of the part, and how the failure of that part would result in even more expensive repairs. The mechanic might demonstrate trustworthiness by telling you that you probably will not require any other expensive repairs for a few more years. That information would mean not paying the mechanic again for a few more years, so this mechanic must be honest. Nevertheless, you might still hesitate because you keep thinking that this mechanic just wants to make more money. Then the mechanic tells you about how he knows how you feel, that he had a friend who put a lot of money into a car because a mechanic told him to do so, but then the car broke down permanently a few months later. Hence, he understands why you hesitate. To thank you for your patronage, he decides to give you a discount on the labor cost. That last part convinces you that this mechanic really does care and wants you to drive safely.

On the other hand, Chris once had a mechanic who recommended that he get his timing belt replaced (these things happen to Chris a lot). Chris said he would think about it and went home and looked into it. He found out from the car's manufacturer that his model of car did not have a timing belt. Instead, his car had a timing chain designed to last for the life of the car. That mechanic immediately lost all three types of credibility, and now Chris goes to a different mechanic—one that he trusts much more.

Aristotle developed his three types of credibility for use in public speaking situations. Yet persuasion also occurs between two people who have a close relationship. Sometimes your friend or your romantic partner disagrees with you on a point important enough that you try to change their mind. What you say may affect any of these three types of credibility in that situation. In addition, what you say may also affect your relationship with the person.

RELATIONSHIP WITH THE SOURCE

When examining the side effects of trying to persuade someone, we also need to consider that the attempt might alter our relationship with that person, potentially in a negative way. Even if you successfully persuaded your significant other, for example, the attempt may have upset that person. As James Dillard and Mary Fitzpatrick (1985) observed in their study of persuasion in marriages, "In marital as in martial affairs, there are many pyrrhic victories" (p. 420). They studied 51 married couples' interactions and found that when one partner used persuasive strategies that relied on claiming some kind of authority over the other, one or both partners tended to report less marital happiness. Couples reporting higher marital happiness tended to use influence strategies that relied on their shared values instead. They pointed out, however, that they cannot rule out the possibility that strategy use stemmed from the degree of marital happiness rather than causing changes in marital happiness.

Another study conducted by public health researchers Lewis and Rook (1999) examined the amount of pressure people received from a recent interaction in which someone they knew tried to persuade them to adopt healthier behavior. Most of the subjects reported on a situation in which a romantic relationship partner tried to change their behavior. They found a positive relationship between the intensity of pressure and healthy behavior change. Conversely, they also found a positive relationship between pressure and experiencing negative emotions. When your spouse tells you to quit smoking, you might do it, but you might also feel a bit irritable about it.

We may infirm our relationships when we try to persuade our friends, family, and romantic partners because the targets of our attempts might feel insulted. Communication researcher Steve Wilson and his colleagues (1998) adapted an earlier theory about politeness that focuses on positive and negative face. You insult someone's positive face by stating or implying that the person has low social value. You insult their negative face by stating or implying that you have a right to tell that person what to do rather than letting them decide for themselves. Wilson and his colleagues noted these kinds of insults arise in cases of asking people for favors, giving them advice, and demanding someone live up to an obligation.

In a review of this literature, Dillard and Knobloch (2011) noted that any attempt at persuasion can insult both positive and negative face. Suppose you decide to try to convince your friend Kyle that the St. Louis Cardinals professional baseball team plays better than his preferred New York Mets. Simply trying to convince Kyle puts into question Kyle's intelligence because he holds such an obviously incorrect opinion about the merits of the obviously inferior New York Mets. Thus, our message insults his positive face. Furthermore, your message implies that one cannot rely on Kyle to choose baseball teams and that his preferences should give way to yours. Thus you also insult Kyle's negative face by challenging his autonomy in baseball team preferences.

You can start to see why persuasion inherently risks your relationships with people. We wrote this persuasion textbook, so, clearly, we think the benefits sometimes outweigh the risks. As Lewis and Rook reported, people adopted healthier behaviors when pressured by people they knew well. Nevertheless, you may decide in some cases that the potential costs outweigh the potential gains. A few years ago, Chris helped conduct a study with the communication researchers Ioana Cionea and Cameron Piercy (2017). They surveyed a group of undergraduates and asked each to discuss a case in which they engaged in an argument on Facebook. Many of them reported the argument had damaged their relationship with someone else involved. We strongly advocate avoiding the Pyrrhic victories about which Dillard and Fitzpatrick warned us.

WANTING TO LEARN MORE: INFORMATION SEEKING

Our last side effect of a persuasive message concerns what the audience does after message exposure. Usually, someone constructing a persuasive message does so with the goal of changing the audience's attitude and thereby changing the audience's behavior. Suppose Noelle watches a public service announcement concerning the importance of wearing sunscreen to prevent skin cancer. She might decide to start wearing sunscreen because the message offered good reasons for doing so. Then Noelle might find the outcomes associated with skin cancer so disturbing that she decides she wants to learn about other ways to protect herself. She then goes to the American Cancer Society's website and reads about early detection of skin cancer. The additional information may even strengthen her attitude so that she ignores peer pressure to go to a tanning salon. Noelle's decision to learn more represents information seeking—when people attempt to find more information about a topic after exposure to a persuasive message.

As you might imagine, those who seek to use persuasion theory to influence the public to adopt healthier behavior sometimes seek to cause not only a change in the target behavior but also encourage information seeking about the topic. As the communication researchers Monique Turner and colleagues (2006) noted, "Although health-related information seeking can lead to a deeper understanding of disease symptoms, prevention tactics, or effective cures, people are not always motivated to seek such information on their own" (p. 131). They conducted a pair of studies in which subjects answered questions on a computer-based survey. The investigators informed them that the computer program would provide a personalized risk profile for either skin cancer (study 1) or diabetes (study 2). In both studies, the investigators assigned the risk ratings randomly. People who received a high-risk rating reported a stronger intention to seek more information about the topic.

A study by Neuwirth and colleagues (2000) tried to persuade students that the fluorescent lighting in classrooms necessitated wearing sunglasses to avoid harming their test scores. They experimentally varied the extent to which the message included either a high risk of the problem or a low risk. Similar to Turner et al.'s findings, they report that students who thought they had a higher risk of the problem reported a stronger intention of finding out more information. The researchers did, of course, inform their subjects at the end of the study that the researchers had made up the fluorescent lighting problem.

In the political context, Valentino and colleagues (2004) looked at a situation in which a persuasive message may have reduced the likelihood of their subjects seeking information. They exposed them to either a political ad or a control ad about a different topic. Then they allowed them to visit websites with political information about the candidates in that election. For subjects who began the experiment with low political knowledge, the political ad had no effect on how many issues they looked at on the website. In contrast, for those who had high political knowledge, they looked at the website *more* after seeing the control messages than if they had seen the political advertisement. Valentino et al. argued that for the highly politically knowledgeable, the ad filled their need to learn about the candidate. In contrast, when the politically knowledgeable viewers had not just learned from the advertisement, they took the opportunity to seek information.

As a collection, these studies tend to point to the importance of information sufficiency. The communication researchers Griffin and colleagues (1999) explained that in contexts such as health, people have an amount of information they feel they need to deal adequately with a situation or issue. When they perceive that they have an insufficient amount of information, they seek out more. When they perceive that they have enough information, they stop seeking more. Persuasive messages can make people feel like they do not have enough information, perhaps by informing them that some negative outcome threatens their health or safety, as in the case of the health studies we just discussed. Alternatively, the political study we just discussed showed a case in which a persuasive message gave some people the impression that they now had enough information and did not require substantially more.

Griffin and colleagues (1999) predicted that a variety of variables about health information messages might positively predict information seeking. A meta-analysis by Z. Janet Yang and colleagues (2014) tested the extent to which those variables predicted information seeking. They found that, across studies, information sufficiency predicted information seeking very well, such that the more people thought they had sufficient information, the less information they sought. They argued that information sufficiency, along with a sense of social pressure to get more information, offered sufficient predictive power for information seeking without needing other variables. This line of research suggests that, in general, your persuasive message might encourage information seeking if you manage to convince audience members that they do not know enough about a subject to make the decisions they need to make.

On the other hand, claiming that information sufficiency predicts information seeking nears tautology. Generally, you act when motivated. So saying that people seek information when they feel they do not have enough information does not help us predict information seeking very well. If you told anti-tobacco researchers that you discovered that the motivation to quit smoking predicts quitting smoking, they would not find your insight particularly helpful. So ongoing research in this area needs to focus on determining what kinds of messages result in people feeling that they lack sufficient information. But what if you see a persuasive message, and you become fed up with hearing about the issue and decide to avoid the topic altogether?

WANTING TO LEARN LESS: SELECTIVE EXPOSURE

Sometimes people try to avoid persuasive messages about a topic. Some of us get so tired of political ads during election season that we use the mute option to silence the scary voice-overs during television commercials or click the "skip" option on ads presented online. Given the wide variety of information available, your options for responding to a persuasive message you disagree with include actively trying to avoid it and similar messages in the future. If you smoke cigarettes, and you see an anti-smoking billboard that highlights the effect of secondhand smoke, you might feel guilty. At that point, you might try to avoid looking at that billboard and perhaps even persuasive messages about secondhand smoke in general. The phrase selective exposure describes situations in which people attempt to avoid particular kinds of persuasive messages, usually those that oppose their current attitudinal stance on an issue.

One interesting study (Ryan & Brader, 2017) tested for selective exposure effects with political ads on Facebook. The investigators used people's Facebook profile information during the 2012 presidential election to determine if an American user supported Governor Mitt Romney or President Barack Obama. They then bought ads that promised, if clicked on, to take the user to a news report containing new economic information that would harm either the Romney or Obama campaign. First, as you might guess, few people clicked at all, perhaps showing a general selective exposure effect against seeing any political information. For those who did click, the results showed that they clicked more often on ads promising information against the other party's candidate. People showed substantially less interest in information that might harm their preferred candidate's chances of election or reelection.

People engage in selective exposure for a variety of reasons. For instance, they might avoid information that threatens attitudes that they consider particularly important to them (Festinger, 1957). They might also avoid information that shows their behavior increases their risk for unpleasant or life-threatening health outcomes (Witte, 1992). In either case, sometimes people avoid messages that tell them that their actions or thoughts require serious modification. Yet these people may need to change the most. Consequently, they may form the population we most want to reach. Such difficulties provide challenges for those wishing to persuade the public.

Conclusion

Very few causes have only one effect. When you set out to persuade someone, you may want to consider all of the other effects your persuasive attempt could produce. Your audience might understand your position better but then think negative thoughts about it. They might change their mind about something related. Your audience might like or respect you more or less than they did before. They might decide that they want to learn more and go looking for more information. This latter possibility can produce mixed results because people vary in their information literacy and might believe false information that encourages poor behavior. For example, Chris might find a website that claims that the healthiest diet includes several servings of bacon per day, information that he would like to hear but that will not likely improve his health if followed. The persuasion research literature demonstrates empirically that these possibilities exist, but it has not developed sufficiently to make predictions about these issues as accurately as we would like for use in applied settings. To close on a positive note, however, contemporary researchers continue to take these issues up and make progress.

5

How Can We Manage the Buzz?

That ideas should freely spread from one to another over the globe, for the moral and mutual instruction of man, and improvement of his condition, seems to have been peculiarly and benevolently designed by nature, when she made them, like fire, expansible over all space, without lessening their density in any point, and like the air in which we breathe, move, and have our physical being, incapable of confinement or exclusive appropriation.

—Thomas Jefferson

T HE SIDE EFFECTS MENTIONED IN the preceding chapter do not provide an exhaustive list of all possible outcomes that result from trying to persuade someone. This chapter focuses on an additional side effect, one we believe sufficiently important to merit separate examination. We shall refer to it as the "buzz" (Rosen, 2000). It differs from the other side effects discussed in Chapter 4, though, in that it involves changing attitudes, albeit not merely those of a single persuasive target.

The bulk of persuasion research focuses on how members of a captive audience respond to a persuasive message to which the investigator exposes them. The focal response usually involves changes in attitude; perhaps it also includes changes in beliefs, behavioral intentions, and behavior. Then the experiment ends. As Chapter 4 demonstrates, however, additional important effects may follow. So, terminating the experiment does not necessarily signal the end of the effects of the persuasion process.

Another extension of the persuasion process follows from the fact that people tend to talk with one another about the persuasive messages they have heard or read. A persuasive message may have changed their minds about a political candidate, introduced them to a new product or service that they want to try, or reinforced their conviction that the federal government should legalize recreational marijuana. Excited about the matter, they want to share their new point of view with others and so engage them in conversation about it. Or a persuasive message advocating a law prohibiting hate speech may have so angered them that they want to convince everyone with whom they communicate that free speech should remain unfettered. Or they may have heard a speech in which the speaker advocated the abolition of the Electoral College, and they want to see how others react to this position as a way of helping them make up their minds about the issue. All of these examples describe ways in which persuasive messages might create buzz.

By **buzz** we shall mean the extent to which, and the ways in which, people discuss with others the merits of arguments raised in persuasive discourse. Some might experience relatively simple versions of buzz. Members of juries discuss with one another the facts and the merits of the arguments they hear during the course of a trial (see Boster et al., 1991). Or some may spend a considerable amount of time in meetings in which they debate the merits and disadvantages of various policy alternatives upon which they have received briefings (Boster et al., 1982; Boster et al., 1980). But buzz may emerge in more complex ways. For example, it may occur in larger social systems in which the issues that compose the substance of the buzz have widespread ramifications. In addition, the persons who spread the buzz, as well as the targets of buzz, may not know each other.

The concept of buzz raises a host of questions, some of which we can begin addressing and others for which we lack adequate knowledge to begin addressing: Will a persuasive message spark discussion with others? If so, how many? Who will speak the most? To whom will they speak? What will they say? What effect(s), if any, will emerge?

AN EXAMPLE OF BUZZ-SHAPING ATTITUDES

We shall start by raising a basic question about buzz; namely, can buzz *shape* (as opposed to modify or reinforce) attitudes? A clever experiment by communication scholars John Hocking and colleagues (1977) provides an answer to this question. The Hocking et al. experiment examined intra-audience effects or the effect of others in our immediate physical environment on our judgments, affect, and behavior.

In the Hocking et al. experiment, students volunteered to participate in an extra credit assignment, with the investigators suggesting that they would have to write a short paper about their experiences observing people in a bar. So the students went to a bar on one of two nights, supposedly for the purpose of infiltrating and observing communication behavior. Approximately one-half of them went the first night; the other half went the second night. A local band played both nights, and the investigators convinced the band to help with the experiment by playing the same set in the same way both nights. As this band had considerable experience, this task proved easy for them. Moreover, a few observers (confederates of the experimenters) attended both nights and reported that they had indeed played uniformly.

This bar held approximately 200 people, nearly at full capacity both nights. On both nights, the experimenters planted a number of confederates in the audience. These confederates, unknown to the student subjects, wanted to make it appear either that they liked the band or that they did not like the band. On one of the nights, these confederates responded enthusiastically to the band. They applauded loud and long. They danced. They called for encores. On the other night, the confederates ignored the band. They talked among themselves. They did not applaud, dance, or call for an encore.

When the students returned to class approximately a week later, their professor distributed a short questionnaire that asked them about their experiences at the bar. Among other things, the students responded to items asking for their evaluation of the band. Their responses indicated that they thought others had liked the band more on the night when the confederates responded positively to the band and that they also liked the band more on the night when the confederates responded positively. If they saw the band on the night in which the confederates provided the positive feedback, then they also reported staying longer and expressed a stronger desire to see the band again. In sum, Hocking et al. (1977) demonstrated that what we infer from the behavior of others around us can *shape* our attitudes. And *they do not even have to say anything to us* to have that kind of impact!

AN EXAMPLE OF BUZZ-MODIFYING ATTITUDES

But can the buzz also *modify* our existing attitudes? Revisiting a less well-known part of the history of World War II (WWII) proves instructive (see Wansink, 2002, for a detailed account). During WWII, civilians in the United States experienced a meat shortage because much of the best cuts of meat went to the soldiers fighting the war. As a result, some people in the United States suffered from protein deficiency. To address this problem while continuing to ship the best cuts of meat to the troops, the federal government embarked on a program to persuade U.S. citizens to purchase and consume nonstandard cuts of meat (e.g., liver, kidneys, brains, hearts, tongue), items toward which U.S. States citizens had a decidedly negative attitude. Social scientists, led by the eminent anthropologist Margaret Mead and the equally eminent psychologist Kurt Lewin, tackled the problem of convincing citizens to eat these cuts of meat (see Lewin, 1947).

Their program of research produced novel insights and strategies to promote U.S. citizens eating these products. Contrary to the conventional wisdom of the time, their data showed that it made sense to focus on convincing housewives, as housewives purchased, prepared, and served the food in most households.

They also found it important to restructure the norms around family meat consumption. For example, they labeled these cuts of meat "organ meat" or "variety meat" as a means of making them appear more acceptable. They disseminated the phrase "organ meats are foods that patriots eat" so that complaining about eating them would appear unpatriotic. Because people tended to view these meats as things to discard or things eaten by poor people, they sought to change those perceptions by getting adults, particularly the housewives, to eat them, finding that if they did so, the remainder of the family tended to eat them as well.

Mead and Lewin also found it necessary both to find effective incentives to consume these meats, such as their availability and cost, and to discover ways to reduce barriers to eating them. To reduce barriers, they presented the food as SAFE: **s**elected, **a**vailable, **f**amiliar, and **e**xactly as expected. So, for instance, they found that when they prepared organ meats and served them in ways that looked similar to more familiar cuts of meat, people found them more palatable. They also discovered that making them look familiar in cut, shape, and packaging made them more acceptable. The strategy of initially introducing them as side dishes led to greater acceptance as well, as did introducing them gradually and increasing their variety.

One series of experiments in this research program focused on contrasting two methods of convincing housewives to serve these nonstandard cuts of meat (Lewin, 1947; Wansink, 2002). The *lecture method* involved having the housewives listen to an expert's arguments for serving them, how to prepare them, and other related issues. The *discussion method* involved housewives talking about this matter among themselves. Lewin (1947) found the discussion method five times more effective than the lecture method in getting housewives to serve organ meats! A difference of a similar magnitude also emerged with children's willingness to eat them. Furthermore, the effects lasted longer, presumably because these housewives had a greater public commitment to their position. The buzz generated in these discussion groups resulted in a substantial increase in the consumption of organ meats—a change that decreased soon after the end of WWII when the domestic meat shortage ended.

FAILING TO CONTROL THE BUZZ: AN EXAMPLE OF HOW CAMPAIGNS MAY FAIL

Communication campaigns consist of large-scale efforts of finite but relatively long duration that seek to persuade large numbers of people to change their attitudes, beliefs, and behaviors. The phrase "large scale" implies that those who initiate campaigns employ mass media, and often multiple media, and do so extensively. Examples of communication campaigns include a political candidate's attempt to gain votes, efforts on the part of the public health community to reduce smoking, or the environmental community trying to convince us to use less energy (see Rice & Atkin, 2013, for additional and specific examples). But despite the best of intentions, they do not always succeed (Snyder & Hamilton, 2002), although some argue persuasively that failure occurs less often now as a result of advances in our knowledge of how to conduct them (Noar, 2006).

Those designing campaigns may try to flood the message environment with public service announcements (PSAs) advocating their point of view and in this way control the message environment. By **message environment**, we mean the number and mixture of messages on a specific topic to which people receive exposure. So, for example, a communication campaign designed to reduce alcohol-impaired driving will result in the transmission of numerous messages over myriad channels with the intent of exposing as many people as possible to those many messages advocating that they avoid drinking and driving. By so doing, they may also hope to drive out, or create an absence of, any messages to the contrary—namely, those messages encouraging drinking and driving or minimizing the potential danger associated with drinking and driving.

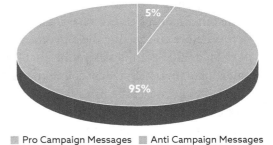

Pro Campaign Messages ▪ Anti Campaign Messages

FIGURE 5.1 Effective control of the message environment.

Figure 5.1 depicts a campaign that effectively controlled a message environment. In this hypothetical case, 95% of the messages to which people receive exposure on this topic support the campaign's point of view. Figure 5.2 depicts less-effective control of the message environment. In this hypothetical case, perhaps one involving a very controversial topic, the campaign controls only 50% of the message environment. The remaining 50% consists of messages that seek to thwart the campaign's persuasive goal. The 50% of the messages opposing the campaign could, as might occur in a

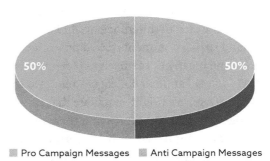

Pro Campaign Messages ▪ Anti Campaign Messages

FIGURE 5.2 Ineffective control of the message environment.

political campaign, result from an organized effort on behalf of another group to counter the campaign's persuasive goal, but they need not. Instead, they may come from the buzz generated from the campaign. In a clever experiment, communication scholars Clarissa David et al. (2006) explored how such an outcome could occur.

Prior to the experiment, participants completed items measuring **sensation seeking** (SS). Psychologist Marvin Zuckerman has long studied this personality trait (e.g., Zuckerman, 2007). He characterized high SS people (HSS) as easily bored. He finds them more open to new and varied experiences and to divergent ideas than their low SS (LSS) counterparts. Moreover, David and her colleagues report that HSS people tend to exhibit greater social dominance than their LSS counterparts (2006, p. 123). Thus when engaged in group interaction, we can expect them to speak more frequently on issues that interest them. David et al. (2006) also reported that those HSSs embrace more positive attitudes toward risky behavior, such as marijuana use, than do LSS.

David and her colleagues exposed their seventh- and 12th-grade student subjects to PSAs opposing marijuana use. They judged some of these PSAs as weak arguments and others as strong arguments. They assigned approximately one-half of the students to watch the weak PSAs and the other half to watch the strong PSAs. After exposure to the PSAs, approximately half of the students in both the weak PSA and strong PSA conditions completed outcome measures, such as attitude toward marijuana, beliefs about marijuana use, and intentions to use marijuana in the future (the no-chat group). The other half spent time chatting online with groups of other participants about the PSAs before completing the outcome measures (the chat group).

An analysis of the talk in the chat groups indicated that the HSS students talked more than their LSS student counterparts. Not surprisingly, the HSS students' comments tended to advocate the pro-marijuana position. Importantly, the messages shared in the chat rooms apparently affected others because more pro-marijuana attitudes, less anti-marijuana beliefs, less expected disapproval from authority figures from using marijuana, and more expected ostracism from peers for saying "no" to marijuana emerged for those in the chat groups than in the no-chat groups—results that held regardless of the strength of the PSAs. This last point requires careful evaluation. Little difference in the focal outcome measures occurred as a result of varying the strength of the PSAs, but the lack of difference might have resulted because the investigators classified weak and strong arguments based on subjects' perceptions of them rather than on properties of the messages themselves (review Chapter 2 to pursue this point).

David and her colleagues reported that adolescents tend to overestimate their peers' drug use. We might speculate that this judgmental error results from their drug-using peers frequently expressing their preferences and habits, whereas non-users remain silent about the issue. If so, the minority of students who use drugs would saturate the message environment with pro-drug comments and criticisms of those who argue against drug use. Consequently, students with negative attitudes toward marijuana, although a majority, can come to perceive themselves as a minority. We have long known that although minorities may exert some influence on majorities under special conditions, generally, minority groups exert little influence on majorities (Wood et al., 1994). But when a majority perceives (incorrectly) a minority as the majority, this generalization can reverse. In a sense, inaccurate perception of reality, rather than fact, becomes the new reality. This perceived reality, rather than fact, then drives attitudes and actions.

The late German political scientist Elisabeth Noelle-Neumann's spiral of silence framework provided an extended explanation of this phenomenon. Noelle-Neumann (1974) argued that we feel isolated when we perceive our self in the minority on some issue. This feeling of isolation results in us failing to express our opinion on such issues. Thus when we perceive ourselves as a member of a group composed of those taking a minority position, we express our opinion less often than when we perceive that others support our position. This state of affairs results in members of groups who perceive themselves as taking a majority position voicing that opinion more often, usually substantially more often, than members of groups who perceive themselves as taking minority positions on important issues. Thus the perceived majority, whether an actual majority, comes to dominate the message environment and exerts more influence on others' attitudes and actions.

Glynn et al. (1997) reviewed the extensive spiral of silence literature and generally found the results consistent with Noelle-Neumann's idea. In sum, the David et al. experiment demonstrates how negative buzz could thwart a persuasive message campaign, despite the fact that initial exposure to PSAs generated favorable persuasive outcomes. Noelle-Neumann's spiral of silence framework provides an explanation of one way that the negative buzz might operate.

A SUCCESSFUL CAMPAIGN: AN EXAMPLE OF POSITIVE BUZZ

In marked contrast to the negative buzz observed in David and her colleagues' experiment, other research in the areas of communication campaigns and the diffusion of innovations has discovered evidence of positive buzz. By the term diffusion in this context, we mean the spread of persuasive messages promoting an idea throughout a defined population of people.

A study of the diffusion of hybrid seed corn conducted by sociologists Bryce Ryan and Neal Gross (1943) provided an example of positive buzz. Prior to the early to middle part of the 20th century, farmers used *open* (or uncontrolled) pollination to grow their corn crops. In contrast, *hybrid* seed corn represents the results of a controlled pollination process. Farmers may use seed that agricultural scientists bred so as to ship better, produce greater yields, provide better resistance to disease, or a number of other advantages. When Ryan and Gross studied the diffusion of hybrid seed corn from 1928 to 1941 in a small Northwestern Iowa community, relatively few farmers had adopted this innovation, opting instead for the traditional open pollination method.

The innovation spread rapidly. In the North Central United States, for example, farmers did not have access to it until 1928, but by 1939, hybrid seed corn accounted for 75% of the area's corn acreage. Farmers' decision to adopt hybrid seed corn resulted from several sources of influence. Early on in the adoption process, salesmen provided most of the educational material about the innovation and proved most influential. Media, such as radio advertisements and the *Farm Journal*, also made the list of important sources of information. Later in the diffusion process, however, neighbors (i.e., fellow farmers from the area) generating positive buzz emerged as more influential. Notably, we would expect farmers to have perceived these neighbors as particularly credible sources of information and influence.

Even with all of these social forces involved, farmers adopted the innovation slowly. Typically, they had heard of the innovation 5–10 years before adopting it. Furthermore, immediate complete adoption rarely occurred. Typically, a farmer would experiment by planting part of his acreage in hybrid corn for 3 or 4 years before using it for all of their acreage. Put differently, partial adoption and increases in seed corn planting occurred with time and experience.

Individual differences in the time of adoption emerged as well. Some members of the farm community adopted relatively early. The early adopters tended to have more education and larger farms. The investigators also characterized them as more cosmopolite, as measured by the number of trips they made regularly to the nearest big city, in this case Des Moines, Iowa. Figure 5.3 depicts the nature of adoption over time. As typical of the diffusion process, few adopt early. At some point, a critical mass of users forms so that diffusion accelerates. Finally, the percentage adopting levels off as the innovation saturates the social system to which it has diffused. These dynamics give rise to the S-shaped curve that you can see in Figure 5.3. In Ryan and Gross's (1943) study, 99.2% of the farmers in the focal community had adopted hybrid seed corn by 1941.

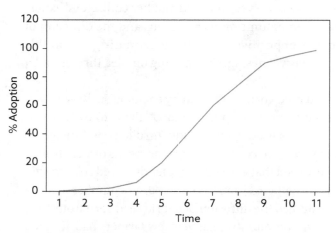

FIGURE 5.3   The diffusion curve.

A thorough analysis of the diffusion of hybrid seed corn must also include some comments about the product. Rogers (2003, pp., 15–16) argued that the success and speed of adoption depend on a number of characteristics of the innovation. First, as the **relative advantage** of the innovation increases, the speed and thoroughness of its diffusion increases. The relative advantage of an innovation refers to the extent to which it represents an improvement over what it replaced. Advantages such as increased yields and disease resistance made convincing farmers to begin using hybrid seed an easier task because advocates could generate stronger arguments for their position.

Second, the greater the **compatibility** of the innovation with the values, needs, and experiences of the target audience, the speedier and more thorough the diffusion of the innovation. Certainly, hybrid seed corn meets this criterion as well. The target audience would have desired the advantages of the innovation, and changing to hybrid seed corn would not have caused major disruption to the manner in which they went about planting and harvesting their corn. Once again, the compatibility of the innovation made convincing the farmers an easier task.

Third, the more **complex** the innovation, the slower the diffusion process, or, put positively, the greater the ease of adoption, the faster and more thorough the diffusion process. Adopting hybrid seed corn did require farmers to acquire new knowledge, but salesmen, extension agents, media, and neighbors contributed to making it easier to acquire the requisite knowledge. Consequently, the mild complexity involved in converting one's acreage to hybrid seed corn did not provide a serious barrier to convincing the farm community to adopt the innovation.

Fourth, **trialability** refers to the extent to which the adopter of an innovation can try it on a limited basis initially. The greater the trialability of an innovation, the more thorough the diffusion process. The Iowa farmers studied by Ryan and Gross provide an excellent example of the importance of this characteristic. Rarely did anyone adopt hybrid seed corn for all of their acreage. Instead, they experimented, using hybrid seeds with smaller plots of land and gradually increasing the amount of acreage planted in this manner over time. This feature of the innovation would also have contributed to convincing farmers to adopt the innovation because the change advocated appeared less risky to the farmers.

Fifth, **observability** refers to the extent to which others can see the results of adopting the innovation. Generally, the easier to observe the effects of successful innovations, the speedier and more thorough the diffusion of the innovation. Farmers could see the fields of their neighbor who had planted hybrid seed corn, and in the Ryan and Gross study sample, they noticed the difference in the quantity of the harvest. Once again, this property served to make it easier to convince farmers to adopt the innovation; one could point to the abundant crop of a neighboring farmer who used seed corn as evidence of its effectiveness.

OPINION LEADERS AND THE TWO-STEP FLOW

Although the Ryan and Gross study provides an example of positive buzz, it does not help us answer some of the questions important to the diffusion process. For example, it does not locate the sources of influence effectively (i.e., *which* neighbors convinced their fellow farmers to adopt the innovation?). Nor does it tell us *how* they went about it. To address these issues, we must turn to some complementary programs of diffusion research. Two important classic research programs addressed this issue.

In two very influential books, sociologist Paul Lazarsfeld and colleagues reported the results of studies examining how the mass media affected people's attitudes and behavior. In *The People's Choice*, Lazarsfeld et al. (1944) investigated the media's influence on voting behavior; in *Personal Influence*, Katz and Lazarsfeld (1955) probed the media's effect on food and other household purchases, fashion, and films. Their inquiries resulted in the addition of an important new concept to the social scientific vocabulary: the **two-step flow**.

Lazarsfeld and his colleagues found that the content contained in the media of the day, such as newspapers, magazines, and radio, had a direct effect on certain people they termed "opinion leaders" (the first step). In turn, these opinion leaders exerted personal influence on the remainder of the population (second step). Rogers (2003) described **opinion leadership** as the extent to which a member of a social system influences in a desired direction other members of that social system (pp. 37–38). An **opinion leader** (OL) refers to one who engages in opinion leadership frequently. Others have used alternative terms to describe OLs—for example, "molecular leaders" (Lazarsfeld et al., 1944), "influentials" (Keller & Berry, 2003), and "superdiffusers" (Boster et al., 2011).

Notably, OLs need not hold official positions of leadership, nor must they have a status, such as we assign to elites. An administrative assistant and soccer mom may function as an OL in community educational matters; a journeyman electrician and Lions Club member may function as an OL in the domain of local politics. Regardless of their status or the roles they fill, OLs tend to share three characteristics.

First, they know a lot of people so that we might refer to them as high in connection or, more simply, as **connectors**. Not only do they know many other people but also they know a diverse set of people. If we think of a social network, such as the small one depicted in Figure 5.4, we can obtain a better idea of connection. Each circle represents a person. Each line represents a connection between two people. The figure depicts two groups. The blue group contains five members, the orange group, four. In both groups, each member knows the other member. But C in the blue group and G in the orange group have a connection with each other. Because of C and G's information and social influence, such as persuasive messages, the blue

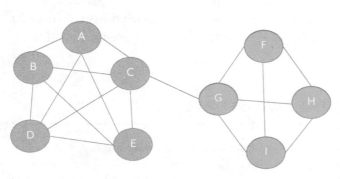

FIGURE 5.4   Connections among members of two groups.

group members (A, B, D, E) can get to the orange group members (F, H, I), and the reverse. Without this connection, it could not. We would characterize C and G as connectors. Without their relationship, unique information known by members of either the blue group, orange group, or both would remain unknown to the members of the other group.

Self-reports provide one of the ways of identifying connectors (see, Boster et al., 2011; Carpenter et al., 2015). For example, connectors agree with statements such as, "I'm often the link between friends in different groups," "I often find myself introducing people to each other," "I try to bring people I know together when I think they would find each other interesting," "I frequently find that I am the connection between people who would not otherwise know one another," and "The people I know often know each other because of me."

Research has shown that people's responses to items such as these do indeed allow us to identify connectors (Carpenter et al., 2015). In addition, research has clarified the profile of connectors and aided us in understanding why they might assume such a role. For instance, they tend to maintain an active presence of social media, such as Facebook (Carpenter et al., 2015). Furthermore, they tend to have less social anxiety than most of us (Boster et al., 2011). As a result, they find it easier to interact with others (even those who might be very different from them) than do most of us, which facilitates their ability to form connections.

Second, OLs tend to persuade others effectively. Consequently, we characterize them as **persuaders**. Persuaders engage in argument frequently; they know how to make their case in different ways so that they excel at audience adaptation, and they exhibit a reluctance to concede points when arguing with another person.

Boster et al. (2011) found that they tended to endorse statements such as, "I am good at thinking of multiple ways to explain my position on an issue," "When in a discussion, I'm able to make others see my side of the issue," "I am able to adapt my method of argument to persuade someone," "I can effortlessly offer multiple perspectives on an issue that supports my position," and "More often than not, I am able to convince others of my position during an argument." Carpenter et al. (2009) observed that persuaders proved more effective at generating arguments, produced more of them, and developed more themes in an argument production task. Boster et al. (2011) reported that those scoring high on the persuaders' scale scored higher on Infante and Rancer's (1982) argumentativeness scale as well, thereby demonstrating that responses to these items identify persuaders well.

Third, we can characterize OLs as **mavens**, or experts, in some specific domain. In this context, we refer to a domain as a relatively specific area of knowledge. So, for instance, some might know a lot about politics, and we would refer to them as "political mavens." Others might have a wealth of knowledge about healthy lifestyles or contemporary music or fashion. We would refer to them as "health mavens," "music mavens," and "fashion mavens," respectively.

Mavens like to talk about their areas of expertise; they like to share their knowledge with others, and others tend to seek them out for information. Boster et al. (2011) found that healthy lifestyle mavens tended to endorse statements such as, "When I know something about a healthy lifestyle topic, I feel it is important to share that information with others," "I like to be aware of the most up-to-date healthy lifestyle information so I can help others by sharing when it is relevant," "If someone asked me about a healthy lifestyle issue that I was unsure of, I would know how to help them find the answer," "Being knowledgeable enough about healthy lifestyles so that I could teach someone else is important to me," and "People often seek me out for answers when they have questions about a healthy lifestyle issue."

Boster et al. (2011) found that mavens tended to have higher value-relevant involvement for the issues falling within their domain of expertise. Boster et al. (2015) reported that mavens have more knowledge in their area of expertise, that others do seek them out for information concerning their areas of expertise, and that they provide useful information when asked. Thus responses to the Boster et al. (2011) items help us to identify mavens accurately.

Jeffrey A. Kelly (1991, 1992) applied the OL concept in a creative way in a program of research designed to change behavior in a prosocial direction (decreasing HIV infection). In the process of so doing, he found a way to exert some *control* over the buzz. He and his colleagues conducted these studies in the towns of Hattiesburg, Mississippi; Biloxi, Mississippi; and Monroe, Louisiana. At the time, these municipalities had populations ranging from approximately 50,000–75,000. A reasonably substantial distance (at least 75 miles) separated each of these cities from other cities of the same or larger size. Each city had one or two gay bars (with predominately male clientele), high self-reported rates of engaging in high-risk sex, and moderate HIV prevalence. Notably, these cities did not differ substantially demographically in risk characteristics, knowledge about HIV, or in any other important ways prior to Kelly's studies.

Kelly et al. (1991, 1992) employed bartenders to identify the OLs. Specifically, in the experimental group (intervention cities), his research team asked the bartenders to observe the interaction patterns among the patrons at the bars at which they worked and to identify the most popular men among them. Kelly's research team located most of them, and they recruited them as OLs, with the vast majority agreeing to participate. Those agreeing to participate received four 90 minute training sessions that addressed the nature of HIV, strategies for combating its spread, and social skill training in advocating safe sex practices. Subsequently, they went about trying to influence their peers to engage in safer sex practices. Control group cities did not receive this intervention (until later, see Kelly et al., 1992).

Kelly's research team administered surveys outside the bars before beginning the study. Then they repeated administering them some months later and then again after another lag of several months. They found that, compared with the control (no intervention) group, members of the experimental (intervention) group changed in the direction of engaging in safer sex (e.g., less unprotected intercourse, fewer sexual partners, and less anal intercourse). Moreover, Kelly and his colleagues reported evidence of normative change. Experimental/intervention group subjects said that they found it easier to insist that one's sexual partner engage in safe sex practices. Finally, the impressive effect sizes reported by Kelly's team provide a striking contrast with the more modest effects typically reported in more passive informational campaigns.

OPINION LEADERS ONLINE

Opinion leaders like influencing others about topics that interest them, and the Internet has given them a wide array of platforms for doing so, such as social network sites like Facebook, Twitter, and Instagram, as well as older but still relevant media, such as blogs, email, and message boards. We shall distinguish between two types of online opinion leaders: (1) those using identification and (2) those using persuasion.

Identification-Based Opinion Leaders

Recall that influence through identification occurs when one person forms an attitude or engages in action because they identify with a particular person on whom they want to model their behavior. Some celebrities directly inform their followers of which products they use via social network sites, sometimes after receiving a fee for that endorsement. In such cases, they rarely interact directly with their followers because the sheer number of messages they receive makes direct reply impractical. So they usually produce generic messages instead of adapting their arguments.

Consider, for example, a celebrity who posts pictures of herself drinking a new brand of alcoholic beverage. She does not present a logical argument for the merits of the beverage. She does not know how many of her followers have decided to try the new beverage. At most, she might have some automated sentiment analysis of the comments and a count of how many people indicated a positive response, such as a "like." We identify the social influence of such "influencers" as influence via identification, not persuasion.

Persuasion-Based Opinion Leaders

On the other hand, other online opinion leaders do use the various methods of persuasion discussed in this book. They might have a popular blog or podcast focused on a well-defined area. They too can have a wide reach, but they usually confine themselves to a topic area such as politics, fashion, or health. Part of their effectiveness lies in maintaining credibility through presenting themselves as high in expertise, trustworthiness, and goodwill. They establish their expertise both with credentials and by offering useful information and advice on their topic of choice. They establish their trustworthiness often by showing transparency about when they receive compensation and what form that takes. They establish goodwill by showing appreciation for their audience and providing helpful advice. Some evidence suggests that such opinion leaders must establish a trusting relationship with their followers to have a substantial effect on their followers' behavior (Dhanesh & Duthler, 2019).

Their direct interaction with their audience also distinguishes the persuasion-based opinion leader. They may have a large audience, but they do respond directly to questions. For example, on a social network site like Twitter, they can reply directly (Cha et al., 2010). If they keep a blog that allows comments, they can reply there as well (Li & Du, 2011). These direct interactions also provide the opportunity for further adaptation of their message to particular concerns. A political blogger might address someone's specific concerns regarding a detail about a health-care policy just as a baking blogger might suggest to a reader an ingredient substitution for that reader's allergy. Online opinion leaders who do not rely on identification tend to use the traditional persuasion tools of establishing credibility and adapting messages to particular targets.

Two-Step Flow Online

The Internet has also provided people with more access to more information than at any point in history. If we can look up information on literally any topic, why would we still turn to opinion leaders? In the traditional two-step flow described by Katz and Lazarsfeld (1955), the opinion leaders read mass media sources, such as newspapers and magazines, that their followers did not. But now, we can reach all of the information we used to get from opinion leaders by a simple Google search.

Ironically, the enormous amount of information we can access in some ways makes us more reliant on opinion leaders than ever. For example, if you wanted to learn how to start cooking healthier food, you could try googling "healthy recipes" and then face an unmanageable number of results (Chris actually got 1.9 billion hits from trying that search term). Instead, you might turn to a friend who could point you to some helpful websites to get you started and offer some advice on easy-to-make dishes.

In this way, opinion leaders help us deal with information overload, a phenomenon in which having too much information actually makes it harder to make decisions because we cannot digest all of the available information in an efficient way (Jacoby, 1975). Most of us do not wish to spend our time deeply investigating consumer products, lifestyle choices, and every political candidate. So we will likely continue to rely on opinion leaders, despite the access we hypothetically have to more information than ever before.

THINKING CRITICALLY ABOUT OLs AND THE TWO-STEP FLOW

Kelly applied his intervention to relatively small, stable communities in medium-sized cities. Patrons of these bars had few feasible alternative social options. Hence they tended to congregate in a few bars. Consider a larger population, say, all residents of a city of one million inhabitants. Boster and colleagues have argued that OLs (superdiffusers/influential) comprise approximately 5% of the population. Keller and Berry (2003) suggested that OLs comprise a slightly larger percentage, but using the 5% figure as a conservative estimate, a population of one million would contain 50,000 OLs. Imagine trying to identify all of them! Identifying even a sample of 10% of them would require finding 5,000 people. Now imagine trying to enlist their aid in spreading an idea! Or training them. Such a strategy lacks feasibility.

Reacting to what he sees as the overly simple two-step flow hypothesis, sociologist Elihu Katz, Paul Lazarsfeld's coauthor of the book *Personal Influence*, has called for retiring the ideas of OLs and the two-step flow hypothesis (Katz & Fialkoff, 2017). Katz pointed to the difficulty of identifying OLs, and he also questioned if OLs have the ability to influence others as much as the concept and the hypothesis suggest. Of course, if an investigator misidentifies OLs, then we would not be surprised to find the misidentified OLs—not OLs after all—ineffective at influencing others. In such a case, the campaign would fail even if the two-step flow hypothesis provided an accurate model of the manner in which influence diffuses through a community. Nevertheless, even the staunchest defender of these ideas must grant that in a relatively large social system, identifying OLs will provide a daunting challenge, and investigators will have difficulty demonstrating conclusively that OLs actually served to mediate the effect of various media on the community.

Katz and Fialkoff (2017) raised another important point about the two-step flow, however. They suggested that the flow of influence might involve *more than or less than* two steps. In their own words,

> "The concept is seeking retirement not because the connection between person and media is incorrect, but rather because it involves far more than two steps; it takes a network! Or, perhaps, only one step will suffice, given the contemporary tailoring of messages." (p. 87)

Regarding the one-step suggestion and hearkening back to our discussion of tailoring in Chapter 3, one well-constructed, personalized message from only one non-OL source might have sufficient strength to change attitudes. The suggestion that persuasion would require a network requires additional exploration. Psychologist Bibb Latane's (1981) concept of social impact provides one fruitful way of doing so.

Latane asserted that three factors determine how others affect us: strength, immediacy, and number. The strength of social influence attempts may depend on many factors, among them Latane listed the power and the importance of the influencing agent

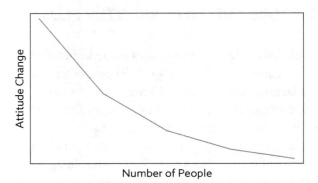

FIGURE 5.5   Diminishing effects of additional persuaders.

to the target. We might add more familiar concepts, such as source credibility or message quality, to this list. **Immediacy** might include spatial and temporal proximity but also the presence or absence of barriers, physical or nonphysical, that separate people and thereby prevent them from communicating with one another. **Number** refers to the number of different people trying to influence a target person.

According to Latane, social impact increases with increasing strength and increasing immediacy. With respect to number, he expected that social impact increases as the number of influencing agents increases as well but not in a simple additive or linear manner. Instead, he argued that each new source has less impact than the previous one. Put differently, additional sources have diminishing social influence returns. Figure 5.5 depicts this relationship graphically.

Applying Latane's idea to Katz and Fialkoff's critique of OLs and the two-step flow, it may take persuasive messages from several members of our social network to change our attitudes, behavior, or both. Put simply, numbers matter, both the number of sources and the number of unique arguments (Harkins & Petty, 1981).

MINORITY INFLUENCE

The large body of research examining minority influence reinforces the point that numbers matter, as it indicates that those holding minority positions face a daunting challenge when attempting to convince those holding majority positions to change their attitudes (e.g., Wood et al., 1994). As a way of redressing what he saw as an omission in social influence research, psychologist Serge Moscovici initiated a line of inquiry (see Moscovici & Zavalloni, 1969) designed to examine how minorities might resist influence from majorities, as well as convincing them to adopt the minority point of view. At that time, many experiments emphasized how majorities influenced minorities. But Moscovici pointed out that for social change to occur, minorities must somehow influence those holding majority positions. And social change does occur. For example, in the United States, civil rights movements have secured rights previously denied to a number of minority groups. Environmental groups who once held minority positions have influenced public opinion in a substantial way. And attending to a broader swath of history, medical innovations that have transformed medical practice have arisen from a minority of scientists arguing for change in medical theory, diagnosis, and treatment

(Barry, 2018). For these changes and others to have occurred, minorities must have influenced majorities.

To understand this line of research, we must clarify what we mean by "majority" and "minority." The most common way to think of these terms involves the number of people holding various views. For example, Gallup polling data indicate that substantially fewer than 50% of U.S. residents supported gay marriage in 1987. Indeed, well more than 50% of those polled indicated that they opposed gay marriage in 1987. Thus, not supporting gay marriage would have constituted the majority position at that time. By 2019, those percentages had reversed. Those supporting gay marriage now constitute the majority, well more than 50% of the population, so that substantial social change has occurred.

Moscovici and others focused on understanding how minority groups can effect such changes, and from these programs of research, several answers emerged. Minority members must have some support for their position; at least one other person must agree with them. They must agree with each other, presenting a solid front, and they must remain consistent in advocating this common position. Their effectiveness may also depend on their flexibility. Put differently, they may have to accept partial, rather than total, majority agreement (Gardikiotis, 2011; Wood et al., 1994).

Typically, majority group members have several ways of influencing minority group members (e.g., compliance, persuasion, and, perhaps, even obedience and identification). Minority group members, however, find themselves limited. Not having the numbers necessary to exert compliance pressures, and generally not having the structural power to exert obedience pressures, they must rely on persuasion. They do have one persuasive advantage, however. They tend to understand the majority position better than the majority understands their position (Robinson & Keltner, 1996). Thus minority group members find themselves better positioned to present high-quality arguments critical of the majority position than majority members can of the minority position. But the results of minority persuasion may differ from what we have come to expect. They may not appear immediately but instead only after a delay or time lag. Moreover, they may arise indirectly, affecting related attitudes rather than the target attitude (Alvaro & Crano, 2017; Gardikiotis, 2011; Wood et al., 1994). Put another way, minority persuasive efforts may produce displacement effects.

Conclusion

So, we return to the questions with which we started this chapter. Likely not all persuasive messages generate a substantial amount of buzz; perhaps even the majority of them, or even the vast majority of them, do not. But as the examples in this chapter illustrate, some do. And the buzz generated in these examples has implications for shaping, reinforcing, or modifying our attitudes, beliefs, and behaviors about important matters, such as drug use and safe sex practices. We also know that the buzz may work to counteract our persuasive goals (negative buzz) or to promote them (positive buzz). The concept of the OL and the two-step flow model may describe how the buzz spreads in some cases but not in all of them. In some cases, we might change our minds only after multiple members of our social network, some of whom may merit the label OL and others not, transmit messages with the intent of changing us. In yet other cases, a single message, transmitted by an OL or someone not an OL, might suffice to change our attitudes.

But how much buzz might we expect a persuasive message, particularly one released as part of a communication campaign, to generate? The existing body of knowledge does not address this issue as directly or as thoroughly as we might like. Nevertheless, given what we know about persuasion, we can venture some informed guesses. For instance, we can expect highly controversial issues to generate more buzz than less controversial issues. In the United States, issues such as abortion have long proved contentious, construction standards for mobile homes much less so. Many people have fully formed, strong attitudes about the legalization of abortion. Many fewer have either strong or fully formed attitudes about construction standards for mobile homes. Consequently, they tend to speak out, either counterarguing with others who disagree with them or supporting those who agree with them, when encountering messages advocating either promoting abortion rights or promoting the denial of abortion rights.

And who might we expect to speak most frequently? We can advance another educated guess that those most highly involved will voice their opinion and argue in support of it more so than will those less involved. We especially expect to find that those whose lives the policy effects in important ways (outcome-relevant involvement) have more motivation to speak on the issue. Similarly, we expect that those for whom the issue connects closely with their core values (value-relevant involvement) to have more motivation to speak. Furthermore, given what we know about Noelle-Neumann's concept of the spiral of silence, we expect to observe a tendency for those who perceive themselves as part of majority opinion on the issue to speak more frequently than those who perceive themselves as part of minority opinion.

With whom might we expect them to speak? Our informed guesses suggest people might approach those they know more often than those they do not know, those with whom they come into contact frequently more often than those with whom they come into contact infrequently, those they expect to agree with them, and those who might disagree or be neutral on the controversial issue but who they suspect they can per-suade. Notably, the Internet changes the complexion of some of these claims. It allows us the possibility of "knowing" more people and having contact with them on various platforms that do not require face-to-face or telephone contact. And a shrewd exam-ination of their posts provides a means of ascertaining their positions on issues, as well as making an estimate of the difficulty persuading them.

We can anticipate that when they speak, they will attempt to modify the attitudes of those with whom they disagree, reinforce the attitudes of those with whom they agree, shape the attitudes of those lacking attitudes on the issues, and defend their own attitudinal positions. But what effect they might have will depend on matters touched on in previous chapters, such as their persuasive skill, the susceptibility of their persuasive targets to their messages, and the mix of other persuasive arguments and counterarguments circulating in the social environment.

So controlling the buzz provides a daunting challenge. The small effect of campaigns reported by Snyder and Hamilton (2002) may result from negative buzz blunting the effect of many campaign messages, the process observed in the David et al. (2006) experiment. As Kelly et al. (1991, 1992) demonstrated, identifying, training, and encouraging OLs to reinforce persuasive campaign messages may reduce negative buzz, as well as facilitate the campaign messages. Nevertheless, we have far to go to develop the social technology to control the buzz.

6

How Can We Maintain Attitude Change?

The same man, in divers times, differs from himselfe; and one time praiseth, that is, calleth Good, what another time he dispraiseth, and calleth Evil.

—Thomas Hobbes, *Leviathan*

No, Time, thou shalt not boast that I do change

—William Shakespeare, *Sonnet 123*

MANY UNIVERSITIES HAVE INSTITUTED MANDATORY workshops for first-year students designed to change their attitudes about sexual consent in hopes of reducing the frequency of sexual assaults. When researchers evaluate the effectiveness of these workshops, they find that attitudes and beliefs change in the desired directions such that their attitudes and beliefs shortly before the workshop have changed in the desired direction by the end of the workshop. That sounds like success, right? The bad news is that within a year, the attitudes and beliefs of the students who participated in the workshop tend to drift back to the baseline levels: the attitudes they had before the workshop.

A meta-analysis by the psychologists Stephen Flores and Mark Hartlaub (1998) examined the effects of 15 of these interventions. They found that immediately after the workshop, or class, attitudes and beliefs had improved at a rate indicating that for every 6.61 who experienced the workshop, one would show a positive outcome. Unfortunately, 4–6 weeks later, the effect fell to the point where only one person in 31.1 likely retained a positive outcome relative to a control group.

Why did the attitudes of the people in the workshop mostly return to their baseline after about a month? You can probably guess some of the reasons. Perhaps the students forgot what they learned. Perhaps they had conversations with their friends that contradicted what they learned. Perhaps they investigated the matter and found information that contradicted what they had learned. Or perhaps they just thought about the matter some more and remembered why they had the attitude they had in the first place. These processes all exemplify attitude decay.

Attitude decay refers to the process by which people's attitudes return to their original pre-message level after a period of time has elapsed. Establishing the phenomenon requires that an audience receive a persuasive message that causes the audience to change their attitudes in the direction advocated in the message. Then over time, the audience's attitudes return to the same position the attitudes occupied before the message.

You may readily recognize the importance of this issue. In most contexts, when we persuade the audience, we want them to stay persuaded. Attitude decay represents a problem for the kind of anti-sexual-assault workshops we just discussed and other kinds of behavioral interventions to improve the health and safety of the public. Politicians who give speeches to large crowds hope that the persuasion from that speech will retain its effect until Election Day and for every subsequent Election Day. Similarly, an advertiser who has written a clever ad for dish soap wants the audience for that ad to retain a positive attitude toward that brand for the foreseeable future in hopes that the audience will then buy that brand of dish soap repeatedly. Yet research suggests that in many contexts, such persuasion attempts may have moderate short-term effects but minimal long-term effects.

In this chapter, we examine the extent to which attitudes decay occurs. Then we discuss the various causes of attitude decay using the hierarchical model of attitudes from John Hunter and his colleagues (1976). Next, we distinguish attitude decay from related concepts of nonattitudes and the sleeper effect. Finally, we discuss some proposals for preventing attitude decay or, put positively, of maintaining attitude change.

THE EXTENT OF ATTITUDE DECAY

Given the importance of this issue, you might expect that social and behavioral scientists have produced excellent estimates of how quickly attitudes tend to decay. Unfortunately, we do not possess many such estimates. A few particularly suggestive studies exist, however. For example, political scientist Alan Gerber and his colleagues (2011) conducted a large-scale field study on the effects of political advertising. Specifically, their study concerned the television ads for the reelection of the governor of Texas in some parts of the state and not others. The ads ran in January before the November election. During the week that the ads appeared, the attitudes of the audiences exposed to them shifted in favor of the governor. A week later, that effect decreased, and within 3 weeks, they may as well not have run ads at all because the audience's attitudes had returned to baseline. A follow-up study by the political scientist Seth Hill and his colleagues (2013) estimated that the effects of political ads decayed so fast and so substantially that the advertisements appearing on television the day before the election had a greater effect on the audience's votes than all of the ads appearing in the previous months.

On the other hand, researchers have found several excellent examples of long-term stability. Perhaps the most famous among social scientists is the Bennington College Study (Alwin et al., 1991). In the autumn of 1935, the young social psychologist, Theodore Newcomb, began measuring the attitudes of the female students at Bennington College. He found that the longer they stayed, the more liberal their attitudes. Thus an initial attitude change occurred. Newcomb followed up again in 1960 and then, with Alwin and Cohen, again in 1984 (sadly, Newcomb passed away before completing the final report). The researchers found that the increase in liberal attitudes that occurred in the 1930s generally remained stable throughout the Bennington women's lives. Similarly, a panel study of young activists with liberal attitudes in 1965 generally remained so in 1984 (Marwell et al., 1987).

The closest we have to a meta-analysis to estimate average decay effects comes from a sleeper effect meta-analysis (Kumkale & Albarracín, 2004), of which we shall have more to say shortly. The meta-analysis looked at 72 studies that included a message from a credible source with attitudes measured directly after the message and again an average of 2 weeks later. They found that, on average, attitudes declined such that one person in 15.7 would likely have shown a decline in their attitudes during that time period. So clearly, attitudes decay sometimes and not at others. The research tends to substantiate the observation of Watts and McGuire (1964) that persuasive effects do not decay at the same rate. Next, we shall turn to a discussion of why attitudes decay.

WHY ATTITUDES DECAY

Attitudes do not exist as separate, unconnected units like books sitting on a shelf. Rather, more like people, they connect with each other with varying degrees of strength and structure. Hunter et al. (1976) provided a particularly useful model of attitude structure called the hierarchical model of attitudes. This model helps us understand not only attitude structure but also why attitudes might decay.

Attitude Hierarchies

Large businesses often organize the people who work there in a hierarchy with a small number of bosses at the top, a number of middle managers who report to them, and a large mass of employees who report to the middle managers. Similarly, our attitudes have a structure. For those with a hierarchical structure, a small number of abstract values stand at the top of the hierarchy. Values such as safety, freedom, and equality often rest at the top. Underneath them we find abstract attitudes. For example, you probably have a general value of companionship. Companionship might have a number of less abstract (or more concrete) attitudes underneath, such as "human friends" and "animal pets." Underneath "animal pets" you might have "cats," "dogs," "fish," and, for some of you, "snakes." Underneath cats you might have your attitude toward your pet cat. You can see how this hierarchy looks in Figure 6.1.

Consider how the hierarchy looks from the opposite direction. You might have a negative attitude toward smoking marijuana. Above that attitude might lie a more general negative attitude toward intoxicating drugs. Above that attitude might be a negative attitude toward risky behavior. Hunter and his colleagues argued that these hierarchies tend toward internal consistency. Their model assumes that the pressure generally flows downward so that more abstract attitudes keep the more specific attitudes in line the way the shift manager makes sure the guy making the pizza wastes a minimum of cheese. The model describes this downward pressure with the concept of **internal messages**. Internal messages refer to the thoughts that arise from our motivation toward internal consistency between our values and our attitudes.

External messages, on the other hand, come from outside the person. Frequently, they target the lower level attitudes. Suppose you hear a friend describe a positive experience with smoking marijuana. That external message might temporarily change your attitude toward smoking marijuana such that you start to evaluate it less negatively. But the model predicts that over time, your more abstract attitudes related to smoking marijuana remain unchanged (i.e., your attitude toward using intoxicating drugs). Hunter et al. (1976) asserted

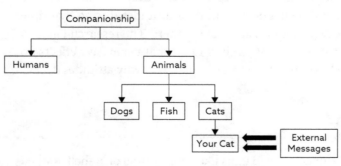

FIGURE 6.1 **An example of an attitude hierarchy.**

that they exert influence on your marijuana attitude so that it snaps back to the original position.

Thus the model offers an explanation of attitude decay. External messages that attempt to modify relatively concrete attitudes result in initial attitude shifts toward the message. But the internal messages demanding consistency with the hierarchy above the specific attitude eventually bring the specific attitude back into line with the rest. The model posits a need for internal consistency. But, importantly, the concept of downward pressure also suggests a means of avoiding attitude decay: changing values.

Changing Values

Persuasion researchers have conducted very few studies on changing values. But the social psychologist Milton Rokeach (1973) conducted some suggestive studies. As he noted, "The reason attitude changes are typically short-lived is that the more central values underlying them have been left intact" (p. 217). Rokeach also thought of values as more abstract than attitudes, but he also thought of one's self-concept as even more abstract than one's values. Therefore, he suggested that you can create a change in someone's values by showing that person that one of their values contradicts an important aspect of their self-concept.

Rokeach conducted a series of studies with undergraduate students in which he led them to perceive themselves as acting selfishly if they valued their own personal freedom over other people's equal rights. That intervention led people to value equality more highly. But over time, that change in value also changed attitudes, which then remained stable, even after a year had passed. Unfortunately, researchers have not followed up on Rokeach's method, and the possibility of changing values remains underexplored.

External Messages

The hierarchical model's inclusion of external messages helps explain attitude decay. In addition to internal messages bringing the temporarily changed attitude back in line, the attitude also receives other external messages. The social psychologist Leon Festinger (1964) noted that we should expect attitude decay to occur in the absence of changes in the kinds of external messages the audience receives after the initial change. As Festinger explained, "The world he encounters remains the same, his experiences remain the same, and so his opinion will tend to revert" (p. 416). We shall look at external messages we receive from the mass media and interpersonal sources.

If you watch a football game on television, you might see a commercial for a truck from one automotive company and conclude that the truck is the best available. But then you see a commercial for another truck from a different company, and you switch your allegiance. But then after the third quarter, you see a commercial for yet another truck and conclude that truck possesses superior qualities to the rest. Marketing researcher Michael Baumgardner and his colleagues (1983) argued that although the typical research study focuses on only one message, the typical mass media environment includes many persuasive messages. When they attempted to mimic that kind of television advertising environment, they found that attitudes could change and decay within minutes. So perhaps we should not expect one mass media message to produce stable attitudes when any changed attitude will soon encounter additional media messages of approximately equal strength.

As very social (and cultural) animals, we tend to interact with other humans frequently, and interactions with those others means additional exposure to external messages that may influence our recently changed attitude. In their classic work on persuasion, Hovland et al. (1953) argued that after you encounter a persuasive message, you might talk about it with your friends and family. At which point, you would receive information about whether your new attitude falls within the latitude of the accepted norms of your social network. If you do not receive social support for your new attitude position, you may revert to your old one. In an influential review on the attitude decay problem, social psychologists Thomas Cook and Brian Flay (1978) explained that attitude "persistence will be more likely if the postmessage environment supports a newly changed attitude, or is indifferent to it, as opposed to when it contradicts the attitude" (p. 44). Your postmessage environment includes conversations you have with friends. For those of you who live in residence halls on campus, you may have had conversations with roommates about politics. Political scientist Casey Klofstad (2007) found that increasing the extent to which people talked to their roommates about politics led to increasing their interest in politics and their political activity.

Conversations with peers can similarly affect attitude decay. The David et al. (2006) experiment discussed in the preceding chapter demonstrates this point by showing that junior high and high school students' changed their attitudes in an anti-marijuana direction after exposure to anti-marijuana public service announcements. But after discussions in which pro-marijuana buzz dominated the conversation, their attitudes decayed toward a more pro-marijuana position.

In general, our social networks generate a powerful source of external messages. Although mass media and other influences may try to change our attitudes, if we have a regular stream of external messages coming from our peers, those changes from mass media sources likely decay rapidly. Political scientist Lindsey Levitan and psychologist Penny Visser (2009) asked 99 students in their first week of classes about their attitudes toward then-president George W. Bush, as well as affirmative action policies. Two months later, they asked them the same questions and asked their subjects to estimate the attitudes on that topic for five of their friends. Those who had friends with a wider variety of opinions tended to show more attitude change between the first and second measurements of their attitudes, thus showing attitude instability. Although this study did not include a specific persuasive message, it does suggest the influence of our peers.

As social creatures who encounter persuasive messages by chance from our social networks, humans also sometimes deliberately seek out information.

Information Seeking

People might also seek out external messages after a change in attitude. Health communication researchers often study the conditions under which people try to learn more about potential health issues and methods of preventing them. One model, the risk information seeking and processing model (Griffin et al., 2013) recognizes that although people motivated to seek information about a health topic would ideally attempt to simply find accurate information, some might not. Instead, when they feel strongly motivated to maintain an existing attitude, they might engage in biased information seeking and try to find information that reassures them that they do not need to change their attitude. Suppose you drink a great deal of coffee on a daily basis. Then you see a news report on cable news that drinking coffee causes increased risks to your health. Would you then seek information that confirms your existing positive attitude to feel better about your coffee habit? Many would.

In one study, a group of health communication researchers in the Netherlands led by Meppelink et al. (2019) measured their subjects' beliefs about the value of vaccines for children. They then presented their subjects with 10 headlines, allegedly search results for childhood vaccines. Five had pro-vaccine headlines and five anti-vaccine. As you might expect, people most often selected news headlines consistent with their preexisting beliefs. Scholars use the term confirmation bias to describe this tendency for people to look for information that confirms what they already believe.

Although we have not found empirical evidence consistent with the connection between confirmation bias and attitude decay, information seeking could result from downward pressure exerted by our values. If we change our attitudes on a particular issue, the downward pressure from our higher order values might motivate both a return to our original position and biased information seeking to help justify that return. Suppose Varda opposes taxes in general, but then a friend convinces Varda that a local school needs a tax increase for needed repairs. Our hypothetical anti-tax Varda might leave this conversation feeling uncomfortable about this new positive attitude toward a particular tax. So she might go out and look for information that helps her feel better about deciding to return to her original position of opposition to the new tax for the school. In such a scenario, the attitude would initially change but then quickly decay because of finding information that successfully allowed her to return to her original position.

Genetic Basis for Attitude Stability

In addition to the aforementioned causes, some attitudes, when formed, remain stable because of genetic causes. Values usually sit at the top of the hierarchies described in the hierarchical model of attitudes. But from where do values come? Surprisingly, our genetics appear as one nontrivial source of some of our values. Values then affect our specific attitudes (Funk, 2011). Some research on twins from the political scientist Aleksander Ksiazkiewicz and his colleagues (2020) show that one can predict the stability of some attitudes based on the extent to which those attitudes have a genetic component. They looked at identical (MZ) and fraternal (DZ) twins because identical twins have mostly identical genes with each other, and fraternal twins have only around 50%. They looked at samples of twins in the United States and Denmark and examined the extent to which the twins in those samples shared similar attitudes. Generally, if identical twins show a stronger concordance with each other's attitudes than fraternal twins, then that counts as evidence that the attitude has a genetic component. The researchers found that attitudes with a genetic component sometimes showed greater stability between measurements taken several years apart.

The evidence indirectly suggests that some of people's values stem from genetic influences. At some point in people's lives, these values help shape their attitudes toward various attitude objects. In the case of the Ksiazkiewicz et al. (2020) study, these attitudes involved social and economic policies. In a series of studies by social psychologist Abraham Tesser (1993), the potentially heritable attitudes covered a wide variety of attitude objects and ranged from attitudes with a higher heritability estimate (e.g., the death penalty and jazz) to those with a lower heritability estimate (e.g., flogging and the coeducation of women and men). Once these values find expression in attitudes toward particular attitude objects, the connection to a strong value tends to produce attitudes that show little decay over time.

Next, we want to discuss two related issues that illustrate another pair of options for how attitudes might change over time. One concerns nonattitudes and the other focuses on the possibility that attitudes might actually change *after* a time lag.

NONATTITUDES

Although we have so far focused on situations in which an attitude initially changes and then reverts back to the original, political scientist Philip Converse (1964; 1974) suggested that some instability in attitudes occurs because people do not actually have attitudes. After analyzing several years of attitude research on public policies he concluded, "There is first a 'hard core' of opinion on a given issue, which is well crystallized and perfectly stable over time. For the remainder of the population, response sequences over time are statistically random" (1964, p. 242). Converse found that people's political alignment in terms of which political party they preferred remained fairly stable. But for certain attitude topics that did not produce a great deal of public discussion and did not include any major public events, many people do not actually have an attitude, even though they report one when surveyed. If you examine certain examples of their attitudes across time, they seem to just bounce around randomly like numbered balls in a Bingo cage. The term "**nonattitude**" refers to attitudes people report that when examined over time do not show any consistency.

Public opinion researchers disagree about the extent to which people possess non-attitudes versus attitudes on various topics. But for some topics, Taylor (1983) estimated that as much as 80% of the public possesses nonattitudes. Sean Freeder et al. (2018) confirmed that for some topics, 80% of the public may possess nonattitudes. They extended their inquiry and found that people who accurately reported which parties held which political positions tended to show a lower likelihood of having nonattitudes. It appears that when people have a clearer idea of what attitudes tend to cluster together, they produce more stable responses to attitude surveys (i.e., they have fewer nonattitudes).

Nonattitudes, however, differ from attitude decay. With nonattitudes, people appear to possess little reason to prefer one position or another on a topic. With attitude decay, their position changes temporarily but then changes back and likely remains. Consider a 10-point scale to measure the extent to which you like hot cocoa, with higher scores indicating more affection for the beverage. Someone who lives in Michigan might start the autumn months by reporting a 7 and then hear about the dangers of consuming too many sugary drinks in November and change to a 5. But by December, his friends would offer him hot cocoa after going sledding; his affection for warm drinks in general would exert pressure, and, eventually, his attitude would return to a 7. Any measurement after that would continue to produce a score of 7. But consider someone born and raised in Arizona. He might not have ever had hot cocoa and did not really have much basis for evaluating it. If you asked him in October, he might report an opinion of 6; in November, he might say 8; in December, he might say 5; in January, he might say 7; and so on. You can see the difference between the attitude decay of our Michigander friend and the nonattitude of our Arizonan friend in Figure 6.2. You might expect continued bouncing around over the next year for our Arizonan friend unless he developed a strong curiosity about this hot cocoa beverage about which survey researchers keep asking him. At that point, he might come to have a firmer attitude in favor or against. So much for nonattitudes. Our next topic illustrates a quote that Frank likes from the great physicist Niels Bohr: "The opposite of one profound truth may very well be another profound truth."

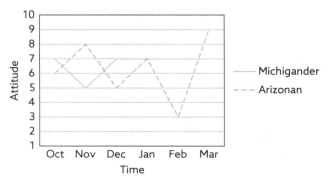

FIGURE 6.2   An example of the difference between attitude decay response and a nonattitudinal response.

THE SLEEPER EFFECT

In their review of attitude decay effects, Cook and Flay (1978) described four potential results of persuasion attempts. With **total persistence (maintenance)**, the attitude changes and remains in its new position. With **partial persistence**, the attitude changes and then decays somewhat but remains closer to the position advocated in the message than before message exposure. With **total attitude decay**, the audience's attitude returns to the pre-message exposure position; the persuasion attempt might as well not have happened. A fourth possibility also exists called **the sleeper effect**, in which the attitude does not change immediately after message exposure, but after a period of time, the audience adopts an attitude closer to the message position than they had immediately after message exposure. In other words, the persuasive effect of the message emerges, or gets stronger, over time rather than decaying or remaining stable. Figure 6.3 shows maintenance, total decay, and the sleeper effect illustrated graphically.

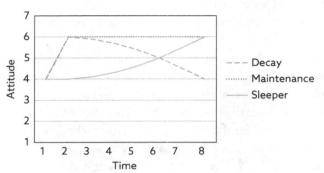

FIGURE 6.3 A graphic depiction of the differences among attitude decay, attitude maintenance, and the sleeper effect.

Like so many of our ideas about persuasion, this concept came from the Yale School of Persuasion. Hovland et al. (1949) reported on a study conducted with American soldiers during WWII, specifically in April of 1943. They showed one-half of their subjects a film about the United Kingdom's fight against Nazi Germany before the United States joined the war. They measured a variety of attitudes and beliefs before and after the film to note the effect of the film on the subjects. For another group, they took the same measures at the same time but did not show the film. The investigators had an interest in short- and long-term effects. So for some, they measured their attitudes again 1 week after the film and 9 weeks later for others. They wanted to determine whether an attitude decay effect occurred. For some of the attitude and belief items, they found decay such that the attitudes of those who responded to the attitude survey 9 weeks after the film showed less support for the position advocated in the film than did those who reported 1 week later. Yet for a number of items, a positive change emerged such that 9 weeks after the film, the attitudes and beliefs of the subjects showed greater agreement with the film than those who had seen the film only a week before. They gave this phenomenon the label the "sleeper effect." They also proposed an explanation that scholars continue to explore.

Hovland and his colleagues thought that the soldiers might be skeptical of the trustworthiness of a film that the government told them to watch. But over time, the soldiers in the study might forget *where* they had heard the information in the film but remember *what* they had heard. Have you ever said to someone, "I don't remember where I heard it, but I heard that…?" At which point, you repeat some interesting bit of information that supports your attitude without knowing the source of that information. Most of the research on this phenomenon has focused on this forgetting the source explanation.

We mentioned the sleeper effect meta-analysis by Kumkale and Albarracín (2004) near the beginning of this chapter when we discussed the extent of attitude decay. We provided their estimate of the extent to which attitudes decay when the message has a trustworthy source. But to detect a sleeper effect, you must also have a condition in which the source clearly appears untrustworthy. In their meta-analysis, they found the small average decay effect for trustworthy message sources, but they found a small average sleeper effect for untrustworthy message sources. In addition, the average study found a small increase in the extent to which subjects' attitudes conformed to the persuasive message recommendations for attitudes measured at a later time.

Yet if we have learned anything so far, we have learned that some attitude change decays. The possibility remains that after a certain period of time has elapsed, even the positive change from the sleeper effect could also decay, and attitudes would return to baseline levels. Theoretically, we might find a Goldilocks amount of time for which the sleeper effect increases conformity with message recommendations, but perhaps some time later those attitudes would still decay.

POTENTIAL SOLUTIONS

Now that we have something of a handle on attitude decay, nonattitudes, and the sleeper effect, we shall turn our attention to ideas concerning how to prevent attitude decay. These ideas come in two forms: (1) more messages and (2) better messages. We shall address the former and then the latter.

Multiple Messages

Have you ever wondered why you keep seeing the same advertisements over and over again? Have you reached the point where you can sing along with the video advertisements you have seen repeatedly or recite the lines in the ad along with the spokespeople? Well, the advertisers do it intentionally, hoping to keep your attitudes toward their products and services positive by using repetition. And some evidence suggests that the strategy works.

For example, psychologists Homer Johnson and Thomas Watkins (1971) exposed their subjects to a persuasive message that argued that a person should take a skin test for tuberculosis (TB) instead of the traditional chest X-ray. You may wonder how this suggestion could possibly present a tough sell. At the time, medical researchers had only recently introduced the skin TB test with which many of you grew up. So after years of public health officials telling people that they could only accurately detect TB with annual chest X-rays, the audience likely expressed skepticism. The researchers attributed the message to a credible doctor and then they heard the message either one time or five times in a row with a 20-second break between each repetition. Both groups showed attitudes consistent with message recommendations. But after 4 weeks had elapsed, the one-time exposure group showed substantial decay, whereas the five-time repetition group showed minimal decay. Repetition seemed to reduce decay. The authors did, however, describe an unpublished study in which a similar induction failed to prevent decay, but the second measure of attitudes took place 2½ months after message exposure. So this method may not prevent decay indefinitely. Nevertheless, one more part of this study merits discussion. They also used a comparison group that heard the message one or five times, but in this case, they attributed the message to a quack doctor who had previously served prison time for fraud. In this case, the induction did not prevent decay because the attitude did not change much initially.

Perhaps you responded negatively to the idea of hearing the same message over and over. Perhaps that got you wondering, what about those commercials for the same product that vary the pitch somewhat? Marketing professor Curtis Haugtvedt and his colleagues (1994) wondered the same thing. They identified three different kinds of message repetition. You can simply repeat the exact same message. You can have three different versions, varying some cosmetic details, such as a different spokesperson. You can also have three different versions that present three completely different arguments in favor of the products. They assigned one-fourth of their subjects to each of those three options and the other one-fourth to read only one message. They embedded these print advertisements for a pen in a series of comic strips that they claimed represented a potential television cartoon series. They measured the subjects' attitudes toward the pen advertised immediately after the end of the message exposures and again 1 week later. They found substantial decay in the attitudes of the subjects who only heard the pen advertised once. They found minimal decay in all three repetition conditions such that all three types of repetition seemed to have had a similar effect.

So much for lab studies. But what about actual behavior change interventions? A few studies have tested what those who design persuasive campaigns call "booster messages." Some health interventions involve a lengthy series of lessons or workshops. Then after a period of time has elapsed, the investigators expose the original audience to shorter versions of the intervention in hopes of preventing attitude decay. They call the second and shorter part of the intervention the booster message.

One group of researchers targeted their intervention at seventh graders in hopes of discouraging them from using alcohol, tobacco, and marijuana. A team led by Longshore et al. (2006) evaluated the effectiveness of this new intervention. The seventh graders received the new program and showed the expected positive effect on the students' anti-alcohol/tobacco/marijuana attitudes and beliefs. But then some members of the same group received the booster sessions at the beginning of ninth grade. The researchers examined the effects of the campaign at the end of ninth grade. They found decay in the group that did not receive the booster session. But they found that the members of the group who received the booster session only saw lower marijuana use if they had also seen antidrug advertisements on television recently. So the booster session by itself did not work, but it did succeed when combined with the ongoing television campaign, ensuring multiple exposures to anti-drug messages. To keep campaign effects going, they seem to require more messages.

But other work suggests that we might consider the dangers of overexposure to a persuasive campaign. Communication scholar Jiyeon So and colleagues (2017) conceptualized and developed a measure of **message fatigue**, which they conceptualized as "the phenomenon of feeling tired of receiving similar messages" (p. 5). They suggested that sometimes, over a long period of time, people grow tired of seeing the same kinds of messages and feel annoyed when they encounter such messages. They found the extent to which their subjects felt message fatigue correlated positively with avoiding messages on the topic and negatively with trying to learn more about the topic. Unfortunately, scholars have yet to identify that Goldilocks amount of repetition in persuasive messages such that the audience encounters the right number of messages over the right amount of time so that attitudes persist without producing message fatigue.

Discussion Instead of Persuasion

Most of the persuasion research we have discussed employed a single carefully constructed message that researchers exposed some subjects to and not others. But some classic and contemporary research suggests that rather than telling people what to believe, we might be better off getting them into a guided discussion about the issue.

As mentioned in Chapter 5, during WWII, the U.S. government wanted to send as much of the available meat to the soldiers as it could so that the soldiers fighting the war would have sufficient amounts of protein, iron, and other nutrients in their diets. Our vegetarian and vegan readers may take issue with the necessity of meat for a healthy diet, but the prevailing ideas at the time suggested meat as the cornerstone of a robust constitution. But the government wanted the people in the United States to get protein and iron too. So the government funded experiments concerning different methods of convincing Americans to eat other less desirable parts of animals, such as hearts and kidneys.

Lewin (1947) first established who decided what went on the dinner table in their Iowa sample. They found that, in nuclear families, the wife nearly always made such choices, although she would take input from the other members of the household. Next, they gathered women together for a session about eating these less tasty cuts of meat. Some of them heard a lecture about the nutritional and patriotic merits of eating these meats, as well as recipes for preparing them. After 2 weeks, only a small percentage of these women had prepared and eaten one of these alternative meat choices. The other women in the study heard a researcher describe briefly the problem of encouraging women to serve these nonstandard cuts of meat for the war effort and then asked them to have a discussion about how best to convince other women to serve these unconventional cuts of meat. Within 2 weeks, approximately one-third of them had done so. Importantly, subsequent studies replicated this pattern of results (Radke & Caso, 1948).

The inclusion of a discussion may have generally positive consequences for persuasion attempts. A meta-analysis of interventions targeted at convincing young people to avoid alcohol/tobacco/illegal drugs shows that such interventions tend to show longer lasting positive effects when the intervention uses group discussions instead of lectures (Derzon & Lipsey, 2002). There exists a disadvantage to using a group discussion instead of a one-shot message: it does not scale up easily. A group discussion cannot occur in a size larger than a group. You can broadcast a carefully prepared single message to millions of people, but you cannot have a group discussion with millions of people. Ideally, we seek a method of producing messages that produce long-term attitude change more efficiently.

Sticky Messages

A few years ago, Frank read a book about "sticky messages" by Chip Heath and Dan Heath (2007). They wanted to understand the same problem we have discussed in this chapter: attitude decay. They noted that people receive plenty of persuasive messages and that most do not "stick"; that is to say, the messages do not linger in people's memories and therefore do not produce enduring attitude change. They suggested that for a message to produce enduring attitude change, the message must possess six characteristics.

Heath and Heath proposed that if a message had these six characteristics, it would have the overall attribute of "stickiness." They argued that sticky messages produce enduring change because the audience remembers them better. We saw that if people continue to receive messages over time, they maintain their initial changes in attitude. But what if people essentially continued to recall the message whenever they found themselves in a relevant context? Suppose a young person saw a particularly compelling anti-meth advertisement such that whenever someone offered them the chance to use that particular illegal drug, they remembered the message and refused. Heath and Heath thought that scenario produces the long-lasting attitude change we have sought in this chapter.

The six message characteristics form the acronym "SUCCES." That name lacks the final "S" for the full word "success," but it is close enough to stick. The first S stands for simplicity. You want a short message that distills the basic idea into one catchy saying. The U stands for **unexpectedness**. The researchers argued that the message needs to surprise the audience and thus grab their attention. If the audience does not notice the message, that message has a low likelihood of sticking in their memory. The first C stands for **concreteness**. In this case, they expect the audience to understand and remember a message that refers to detailed and specific situations. They favorably mention fables, such as "The Boy Who Cried Wolf," as providing a clear set of details to teach the message content to the audience. The second C stands for **credibility**. Most discussions of credibility focus on the credibility of the speaker. Heath and Heath focus on the credibility of the message itself (i.e., the perceived trustworthiness of the information in the message). They argue that the audience will perceive message content as highly probable in a highly credible message and thereby trust the information to a greater extent. They suggested that specific details add to the credibility of a message. The single E stands for **emotional**. By emotion they really mean giving people a reason to care about the outcome endorsed in the message recommendation. They claim that people better remember such messages. The final S stands for **stories**. They note that people retain stories, or narratives, better than a list of dry facts.

So Frank and his colleagues (2018) set out to test Heath and Heath's claims. They attempted to persuade undergraduate students to wear sunscreen more frequently. In both conditions, the students read a story about the importance of wearing sunscreen. But in the sticky message condition, the message met the six SUCCES criteria to a greater extent than in the control condition. They found that, initially, both messages changed students' attitudes in a positive direction. But 10 days later, they found the students in the sticky condition showed less attitude decay than those in the control group.

Encouraged by these findings, Frank and some colleagues conducted a follow-up study. This time, they compared a message containing all six components to a control message containing none. They replicated the previous study and added measurements of the extent to which the subjects perceived five of the six criteria (five of the criteria involve a matter of degree, whereas a message either includes a narrative or not, so the stories criterion lacked a measure). They found that only perceived simplicity had a direct effect on attitudes. Furthermore, perceived simplicity affected attitudes above and beyond the effect of learning the message. The main idea of sticky messages concerned the extent to which the audience learns the message, and yet simplicity had an effect aside from how well the audience learned the message. In addition, message learning did not seem to explain the effectiveness of the sticky message in general. Frank's study produced one of those interesting cases where we end up with more questions than answers. Hopefully, future research will help us understand which aspects of sticky messages prevent attitude decay. Perhaps you will conduct a study to help us figure it out.

Conclusion

Sometimes attitude change lasts a lifetime (e.g., the liberal attitudes of the women of Bennington College), and sometimes it fails to last 5 minutes (e.g., many television commercials). Unfortunately, most reviews of this problem start by lamenting the dearth of research in this area. You may be wondering why such an important question has not received more attention. The difficulty of studying the question remains one important barrier.

Attitude decay studies necessitate the measurement of attitudes at multiple time points. Traditional persuasion studies often conduct all of the measurements within a single session. Investigators face sufficient difficulties getting a group of people to participate in a study once. Getting the same group to participate multiple times presents even more difficulties. Think of an occasion where you tried to get a large group of people to agree on a single date for an event. Imagine trying to get the exact same group together exactly 3 weeks later. Therein lies the difficulty with this line of research.

But the difficulty with the research does not mean that we can ignore it. Until scholars find solutions to the problem of attitude decay, we remain haunted by the possibility that all of our persuasion research on temporary attitude change does not provide us with useful information about long-term attitude change. As Cook and Flay (1978) noted in their influential review of the attitude decay problem, "doubt has to be raised about whether many past persuasion studies really resulted in a change in 'attitude,' and whether it might not be more accurate to label the observed change as 'a temporary accommodation to new information.'" Hopefully, we study attitude change, but perhaps we sometimes merely study fleeting changes.

7

Can a Persuasive Message Be Counterproductive?

Criteria for a CME

Social Judgment Theory
Classic Experiment
A Contemporary Experiment Examining Insult
Audience-Centered Versus Source-Centered Views of CMEs

Some Suggestions for Avoiding Snatching Defeat From the Jaws of Victory

Primum Non Nocere

("First to do no harm," principle of bioethics)

T HOSE SEEKING TO INFLUENCE OTHERS expect that their persuasive messages result in their audience agreeing with them more than they did prior to message exposure. Nevertheless, audiences might shift their attitudes away from, rather than toward, the position advocated in a persuasive message. Some scholars refer to such an outcome as a "boomerang effect." Because of the ambiguity of this term, we prefer, and will use, the phrase counterproductive message effect (CME).

The quotation that forms the subtitle to this chapter cites an often quoted principle of medical ethics. Medical school professors counsel their students to make a priority of avoiding doing harm to their patients. Physicians may not find the correct diagnosis for an illness, or may not design an effective treatment for it, or both. Nevertheless, they can avoid making incorrect diagnoses, employing treatments that make the condition worse, or both. Influence agents might profitably adopt the same attitude. Even if unable to persuade an audience or person, we want to avoid exposing them to persuasive messages that result in them agreeing with us less after message exposure than they did prior to message exposure. In this chapter, we examine the frequency of such CMEs, their consistency, the conditions under which they might occur, and some explanation for them.

Figures 7.1–7.4 depict four possible outcomes of persuasion attempts. Each of these figures represents attitudes as arrayed on a continuum ranging from anti (negative or opposing) to pro (positive or favoring). For example, "anti" might mean opposing legalized abortion, capital punishment, or deficit spending, whereas "pro" might mean having favorable attitudes toward legalized abortion, capital punishment, or deficit spending. The zero point on each of these figures represents neutrality, neither opposing nor favoring the focal attitude object. M represents the attitudinal position advocated in the message. In each of the figures, M marks a position opposing, and fairly strongly so, the attitude object. A_0 depicts the initial attitude of a hypothetical audience member (i.e., the attitude of that audience member prior to message exposure). A_1 depicts that audience member's attitude after exposure to the persuasive message.

Figure 7.1 illustrates an outcome that those seeking to influence others want to achieve. Notice that the hypothetical audience member has a moderately positive attitude before message exposure and a more negative attitude after message exposure. Thus this audience member changed in the direction advocated in the persuasive message. Hence, in this case, the persuasive effort exhibited a **successful persuasion attempt**, perhaps not as much as the influencing agent would like—after all, the hypothetical audience member still has a positive attitude after message exposure—but successful nonetheless.

FIGURE 7.1   Effective persuasion: Attitude change in the direction of the position advocated in the persuasive message.

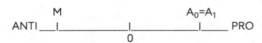

FIGURE 7.2   Ineffective: No attitude change induced by the persuasive message.

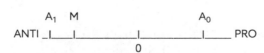

FIGURE 7.3   Overshoot: Attitude change exceeding the position advocated in the persuasive message.

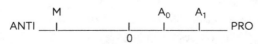

FIGURE 7.4   A CME: Attitude change in the direction away from the position advocated in the persuasive message.

Figure 7.2 illustrates the result of an **ineffective persuasion attempt**. Our hypothetical audience member has the same attitude after message exposure as before message exposure. Therefore, no change has occurred, but no harm has occurred either. In a sense, Figure 7.2 represents a wasted persuasive effort.

Figure 7.3 illustrates the result of a hypereffective persuasion attempt. The hypothetical audience member's attitude changes so much that it goes beyond the position recommended in the message. We can refer to this outcome as **overshoot**. We know of no empirical evidence of overshoot, but we cannot dismiss the possibility that it will (or has) occur (occurred).

Figure 7.4 illustrates a fourth and final outcome. In this depiction, the audience member's attitude moves away from the position advocated in the message. The message advocated that our hypothetical audience member adopts a less favorable attitude toward the focal issue, yet after message exposure, our hypothetical audience member adopted a more positive one. Therefore, Figure 7.4 depicts a CME. From the standpoint of influencing agents, they have done harm to their cause. For instance, imagine that you tried to convince a group of people at high risk of colorectal cancer to have a more positive attitude toward getting a regular colonoscopy but that after your persuasive message, they reported less favorability toward colonoscopies than before exposure to your message. Certainly, you (and others) would view your persuasion attempt as counterproductive.

CRITERIA FOR A CME

To label Figure 7.4 a CME does require some elaboration beyond what this figure depicts. To simplify our analysis, let us constrain it and consider a *single persuasion experiment*. And narrowing the question a bit more, let us restrict our thinking to attitude modification rather than to attitude shaping or attitude reinforcement.

First, a rather obvious criterion necessary to conclude that a CME occurred involves the *number of people* affected. In an experiment with a sample of 100 people, if only one person changed in the direction advocated in the message and the other 99 did not change, we would not likely label that persuasion effort successful. Instead, we would focus on some statistical summary measure of average change for the entire sample. Most often, scholars use the mean, the arithmetic average, for that purpose. In contrast, some have used other summary measures, such as the percentage of people in the sample who change in the direction advocated in the message.

Similarly, if only one person changed in the direction opposite that advocated in the persuasive message and 99 did not, we would not likely label that persuasion effort a CME. Instead, we would require substantial average change away from the position advocated in the persuasive message or a substantial percentage of the audience changing in the direction opposite that advocated in the persuasive message.

Second, people must have an *attitude toward the focal object or issue* of the persuasion attempt. In the absence of an attitude toward the focal object, we could not talk meaningfully about attitude modification. Instead, we would speak of attitude shaping. So studying attitudes toward hydroponically grown vegetables would likely not fit this criterion because most of us have not formed an attitude toward this issue, whereas attitudes toward the safety of our food and drinking water would fit this criterion because most of us have formed attitudes on these issues.

Third, we must *measure the modification in attitude*. To do so demands that we obtain a measure of attitude prior to exposing the audience to the persuasive message and then do so after message exposure as well. The difference between these two measurements, post-test score minus pretest score or post-test percentage changing in the opposite direction of the message recommendation less the pretest percentage changing in the opposite direction, then serves to quantify the extent to which audience members modified their attitude.

Fourth, the audience members must *perceive the persuasive message as advocating the position that it claims to advocate.* To claim that audience members moved their attitudes toward the position advocated in the message, the definition of a productive message effect, we must know something about their perception of the position advocated in the message. Similarly, to claim that the audience moved their attitudes away from the position advocated in the message, the definition of a CME, we must know what position the audience perceived the message advocated. In Figure 7.5, we see that the speaker intends to send a persuasive message, M_I, advocating a negative position on the focal topic. Although the investigator may have designed the message with this intent, suppose that the audience members judge that M_I advocates a neutral attitude toward the focal topic, M_P. In Figure 7.5, an audience member's attitude becomes more positive after message exposure. It moves away from M_I, but it moves toward M_P. This scenario does not represent a CME *because the audience moves toward the position that they think the message advocates.* Instead, it illustrates a failure on the part of the source of the message to communicate clearly and unambiguously the position that she wishes to advocate.

You may find it difficult to imagine such a situation. But consider a speaker who attempts to convince an audience that the United States should reduce fossil fuel consumption substantially in the next decade but that a substantial proportion of audience members come away from the speech with the impression that the speaker has presented a balanced message, perhaps describing both arguments for and against fossil fuel use. Such a possibility could occur, particularly if the premises of the speech's arguments contained substantial ambiguity, lacked clarity, or both, or if the speaker left the conclusions to the arguments implicit, or if the speaker did present both pro and con arguments with the expectation that the audience would understand that the anti-fossil-fuel arguments contained better arguments and better evidence than the pro-fossil-fuel arguments.

A fifth criterion requires that a subset of the sample *receive exposure to the focal persuasive message.* Without this criterion, we could not judge the success or failure of the persuasive message. Generally, we refer to those exposed to the focal persuasive message as participating in the *experimental condition.*

Sixth, and less obviously, we require some type of *control group* with which to contrast the responses of those in the experimental group. The control participants

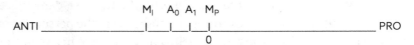

FIGURE 7.5 A CME resulting from misperceiving the position advocated in the message.

do not receive the focal message. Instead, the investigators may not expose them to a persuasive message (*no treatment control*), or may assign them to read (or watch or listen to) a message irrelevant to the topic in question (*irrelevant message control*), or present them with an alternative message relevant to the topic in question (*alternative message control*). To clarify the point, consider the following example.

Suppose that we want to perform an experiment examining the impact of inserting fear-arousing material into a persuasive message. Based on an extensive review of past research, we find reason to believe that the more fear-arousing material we insert into our persuasive message, the greater its effectiveness. To test this hypothesis, we locate 200 subjects willing to participate in our experiment. Consistent with the advice we receive from methodological experts, we randomly assign 100 of them to the experimental condition and the other 100 to the control condition. First, we measure their attitude toward wearing bicycle helmets when riding one's bicycle. Next, all 200 of the participants receive a message advocating the use of bicycle helmets when riding a bicycle. The experimental condition participants receive the focal message. It includes severe warnings about the dangers of failing to wear a helmet when riding one's bicycle. It also includes color pictures of people who did not wear a helmet and who experienced traumatic head injuries from car-bicycle crashes (*high-fear condition*). The control condition participants' message also warns about the dangers, but these warnings lack the severity of those in the high-fear condition. Moreover, they do not receive exposure to the gory pictures of traumatic head injury patients. We shall label this alternative message control group *the low-fear condition*. Alternatively, the investigator might have control participants engage in some other tasks, such as filling out personality questionnaires. We would characterize such a control group as a no treatment control. Or the investigator might have the control participants read an irrelevant persuasive message, perhaps one about proper toothbrushing techniques. Finally, all subjects again complete the measure of attitude toward wearing a bicycle helmet when riding one's bicycle.

Seventh, to the extent that the focal message produced a CME, those in the experimental group would, on average, *change in the direction opposite of the position advocated in that message*. So in the example provided in the preceding paragraph, after message exposure, we would find that our experimental condition participants have, on average, less favorable attitudes toward wearing bicycle helmets when they ride their bicycles than they did prior to message exposure.

Eighth, and finally, we would also find that, on average, *those in the experimental condition changed more in the direction opposite that advocated in the persuasive message than did those in the control condition*. This criterion highlights the very important role that control groups play in interpreting the results of persuasion experiments. For example, change in the experimental group could result from changes in historical circumstances. Perhaps during the experiment, a celebrity bicycle accident resulted in a rash of media stories and social media posts arguing that bicycle helmets did not prevent traumatic head injuries but gave people the false impression that they did, and perhaps the change observed in the experimental condition resulted from this event. If so, change would also occur in the control condition because these participants would have heard these stories and seen the posts also. But if change in the direction advocated by the persuasive message for experimental condition participants exceeded (in the direction opposite that advocated) that of control group participants, then we can dismiss that possibility and draw the inference that the persuasive message produced a CME of some magnitude.

Table 7.1 summarizes these eight criteria. The evidence required to draw the conclusion that a *single* experiment produced a CME must meet them. Notably, the evidence from a single experiment required to draw the conclusion that the persuasive message produced a *productive message effect* shares the first six of these criteria. The seventh criterion, however, would require that the audience's attitude change in the direction of the position advocated in the persuasive message. The eighth criterion would then require that this amount of change exceed that observed in a control group.

But these criteria pertain only to a *single experiment*. Given the vast volume of persuasion experiments performed each year, one would expect by chance alone to find some CMEs. To have confidence that any observed CME resulted from systematic factors rather than chance, we would have to observe a CME emerging consistently under certain specific conditions. Put differently, the strongest evidence of a CME would come from a thorough meta-analytic review that demonstrated that certain features of the persuasive message produce a consistent CME. No such meta-analysis yet exists, but we can look to a particular persuasion theory for a clue as to at least one of the conditions that might generate a CME. We turn to that matter next.

TABLE 7.1 Message Effect Criteria

	Productive	Counterproductive
Number of People	Mean attitude change in the sample	Mean attitude change in the sample
Attitude Topic	Must have one, attitude modification	Must have one, attitude modification
Measurement	Attitude change	Attitude change
Perceive the Position Advocated in the Message	Must perceive it accurately	Must perceive it accurately
Experimental Condition	Must have one	Must have one
Control Condition	Must have one	Must have one
Observed Change: Experimental Condition	Toward the position advocated in the message	Away from the position advocated in the message
Relative Change	More change toward the message in the experimental group than in the control group	More change away from the message in the experimental group than in the control group

SOCIAL JUDGMENT THEORY

Social judgment theory resulted from the collaboration of two famous psychologists, Carl Hovland and Muzafer Sherif (e.g., see Hovland et al., 1957). They began by partitioning attitude continua, such as the ones depicted in Figures 7.1–7.4, into different regions or, as they termed them, latitudes. Figure 7.6 provides the example that we shall consider first. In this figure, LOA refers to the latitude of acceptance, LOR refers to the latitude of rejection, and LON refers to the latitude of noncommitment.

Your LOA includes your own attitude on an issue plus all of the other attitudinal positions on that issue that you find reasonable or at least tolerable. Put another way, you might see yourself as possibly adopting these positions at some point in your life. Your LOR includes those attitudinal positions that you find unacceptable, unreasonable, and perhaps intolerable. You could never see yourself as willing to adopt such positions. The LON includes those positions that fall into neither of the other two categories. Hovland and Sherif do not clearly define this latitude. To speculate, you might lack certainty as to the acceptability of those positions that fall into the LON.

In Figure 7.6, those attitudes comprising the LOA fall toward the middle of the attitude continuum. A person with an attitude toward fossil fuels such as this one finds the moderate position on the issue the most favorable. Such a person might approve of the use of both fossil fuels and other energy sources, perhaps preferring an approximately equal mix of the two. Two parts of the attitude continuum receive the label LOR. They both fall at the extreme ends of the attitude continuum. A person with this attitude toward fossil fuels rejects extreme positions, such as using them exclusively or not using them at all. Two parts of the attitude continuum also receive the label LON. In this example, moderately positive and moderately negative attitudes comprise these parts of the attitude continuum. Perhaps our hypothetical subject has not yet decided on the acceptability of such positions.

Figure 7.7 shows what the partitioned attitude continuum might look like for someone who strongly favors the use of fossil fuels. The LOA appears at the far right of the continuum. Also, notice the narrowness of the continuum. A large LOR ranges from all moderately positive positions and includes all of the negative side of the continuum. A modest LON encompasses some of the moderately positive positions. Such a person finds only a narrow range of positive positions acceptable and rejects almost all but these positions.

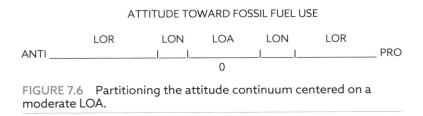

FIGURE 7.6 Partitioning the attitude continuum centered on a moderate LOA.

ATTITUDE TOWARD FOSSIL FUEL USE

```
                        LOR                              LON    LOA
ANTI _____ |_____|____ PRO
                         0
```

FIGURE 7.7 Partitioning the attitude continuum centered on an extreme pro-fossil-fuel LOA.

ATTITUDE TOWARD FOSSIL FUEL USE

```
        LOA  LON                    LOR
ANTI ____|____|_____ PRO
                         0
```

FIGURE 7.8 Partitioning the attitude continuum centered on an extreme anti-fossil-fuel LOA.

Figure 7.8 provides an example of someone with a strong anti-fossil-fuel attitude. A narrow LOA appears at the far left of the continuum. A wide LOR encloses most of the remainder of the continuum. This person finds only a narrow range of negative positions acceptable and rejects almost all other positions.

One's attitude toward an issue determines the location of the LOA on the attitude continuum and to a considerable extent the location of the LOR as well. Nevertheless, these examples point to another important property of these latitudes: their width. Notice that for the examples of extreme attitudes, Figures 7.7 and 7.8, the LOR looms large across the attitude continuum. In contrast, these figures have smaller LOAs. Hovland et al. (1957; see also Hovland & Sherif, 1952; Sherif & Hovland, 1953) suggested that ego-involvement determines the width of these intervals.

Contemporary scholars refer to this concept as value-relevant involvement. Cho and Boster (2005) described an issue as having high value-relevant involvement or ego-involvement to the extent that "it helps people sustain their sense of self-identity" (p. 237). Similarly, Johnson and Eagly (1989) defined value-relevant involvement as "the psychological state that is created by the activation of attitudes that are linked to important values" (p. 290). These definitions converge because our values largely define our sense of self.

Hovland and Sherif (1957; Hovland & Sherif, 1952; Sherif & Hovland, 1953) suggested that as ego-involvement increases, the LOA (and perhaps the LON) shrinks, and the LOR expands. Thus they posit that those people with a heavy psychological investment in an issue judge few attitudinal positions acceptable and many as unacceptable. Conversely, those with a lighter psychological investment judge more positions acceptable and fewer unacceptable.

Hunter et al. (1984) suggested another determinant of the width of these latitudes. They argue that we view persuasive messages advocating positions that fall into the LOA as accurate and unbiased, whereas we view persuasive messages advocating positions that fall into the LOR as inaccurate and biased (see pp. 60-ff). Because accuracy and bias largely define the credibility of the speaker, it follows that we will view those who advocate positions that fall into the LOA as highly credible and those who advocate

TABLE 7.2   A Summary of Social Judgment Theory Predictions

	Perceptual Effect	Judgmental Effect	Persuasion Effect
LOA	Assimilate	Accurate, unbiased	Change toward the message
LON	Neither assimilate nor contrast	Unknown	No change
LOR	Contrast	Inaccurate, biased	No change; change away from the message

positions that fall into the LOR as low in credibility. Over time, we come to associate our pre-persuasive message judgment of the credibility of the source with accuracy and a lack of bias. Subsequently, we come to expect that these highly credible sources will advocate accurate and unbiased positions. Consequently, Hunter et al. (1984) claimed that the LOA expands for high credibility sources and shrinks for low credibility sources.

As we hinted in the preceding paragraphs, social judgment theory makes claims not only about persuasion but also about perceptual and judgment effects. For each of these three outcomes, the LOA, LOR, and LON play an important role. Table 7.2 provides a summary of these social judgment theory predictions.

As Table 7.2 indicates, when a persuasive message falls into our LOA we assimilate it. In the jargon of social judgment theory, **assimilate** means to perceive that it advocates a position closer to our own than it really does. In addition, we judge it as accurate and unbiased. And the message affects us; we change our attitude in the direction of the position that we perceive the message advocates.

But when a persuasive message falls into our LON, we respond to it differently. Although social judgment theorists do not discuss the LON in detail, we can infer from their treatment of the LOA and LOR that when a message falls into our LON, we perceive it accurately. The accuracy and bias with which we judge it remain unknown. And the persuasive message produces no change.

Finally, when a persuasive message falls into our LOR, we respond to it *very* differently. Perceptually, we **contrast** it. In the jargon of social judgment theory, to contrast means to perceive that it advocates a position further away, or more different, from our own than it really does. Furthermore, we judge the message as inaccurate and biased. And, finally, either we do not change, or we change in the direction opposite of that advocated: a CME/boomerang effect.

Thus social judgment theory predicts either no change or a CME when we listen to a message so discrepant from our own position that it falls into our LOR. But as both Kiesler et al. (1969) and Hunter et al. (1984) have pointed out, the prediction of a CME does not derive from the postulates of the theory. Instead, it appears that they made this prediction based on the results of at least one of their experiments. In the next section, we shall review two classic experiments often cited as evidence of CMEs.

Classic Experiment

The Hovland, Harvey, and Sherif and the Abelson and Miller Experiments. Hovland et al. asserted that CMEs most likely occur when the audience has high ego-involvement and when the persuasive message falls into their LOR. In a 1957 experiment, they attempted to create these conditions. The topic upon which they attempted to change audience attitudes involved the "wet-dry" controversy in Oklahoma. The "wets" wanted to see alcohol sales permitted. The "drys" did not, and the law at the time favored their position; Oklahomans lived in a dry state. Although a referendum held shortly before the experiment began upheld the prohibition law, the narrow margin of victory indicated that a substantial amount of controversy surrounded this issue.

Hovland et al. assembled three different audiences. One audience included those holding a strong "pro-dry" position. This audience included members of the Women's Christian Temperance Union, members of the Salvation Army, students preparing for the ministry, and students attending denominational colleges. A second audience consisted of those adopting a strong "pro-wet" position. The experimenters and their colleagues found persons advocating the "pro-wet" position primarily from among their personal acquaintances. A third "unselected" group consisted of those taking a more moderate position on the wet-dry issue. College students from Oklahoma provided the participants for this group.

The investigators asked their participants to complete some questionnaire items, including nine items designed to indicate their position on the wet-dry issue. For each item, participants responded either "yes" or "no." We reproduce those nine items in Table 7.3. As the table indicates, the statements range from those espousing an extremely pro-dry position (A) to those espousing an extremely pro-wet position (I), with the fifth and middle statement (E) advocating neutrality. Hovland et al. instructed their participants to select that statement most agreeable to them, to note other unobjectionable statements, to select that statement most objectionable, and to note other objectionable statements.

The investigators prepared three 15-minute persuasive messages, each attributed to an anonymous source. One advocated an extreme pro-dry position, a second an extreme pro-wet position, and a third a moderately wet position. Some of the pro-wet and some of the unselected subjects received the pro-dry message. Some of the pro-dry and other unselected subjects received the pro-wet message. And some from all three groups received the moderately wet message. After message exposure, subjects again completed the attitude measure so that the investigators could obtain a measure of attitude change by subtracting the initial, or pretest, score from the subsequent, or post-test, score.

We might expect that the pro-dry message would produce a CME among the extremely pro-wet respondents. We might also expect that the pro-wet message would produce a CME among the extremely pro-dry respondents. And both pro-wet and pro-dry respondents might change in a direction opposite of that advocated in the moderately wet message or perhaps simply not change their initial attitude.

The results of the experiment indicated that the investigators obtained the predicted social judgment theory perceptual and judgment effects. The wets judged the pro-wet message the least biased; the drys judged the pro-dry message least biased; the moderates judged the moderate message as least biased. Furthermore, both the drys and

TABLE 7.3   Hovland et al.'s (1957) Attitude Items

(A) Since alcohol is the curse of mankind, the sale and use of alcohol, including light beer, should be completely abolished.

(B) Since alcohol is the main cause of corruption in public life, lawlessness, and immoral acts, its sale and use should be prohibited.

(C) Since it is hard to stop at a reasonable moderation point in the use of alcohol, it is safer to discourage its use.

(D) Alcohol should not be sold or used except as a remedy for snakebites, cramps, colds, fainting, and other aches and pains.

(E) The arguments in favor and against the sale and use of alcohol are nearly equal.

(F) The sale of alcohol should be so regulated that it is available in limited quantities for special occasions.

(G) The sale and use of alcohol should be permitted with proper state controls so that the revenue from taxation may be used for the betterment of schools, highways, and other state institutions.

(H) Since prohibition is a major cause of corruption in public life, lawlessness, immoral acts, and juvenile delinquency, the sale and use of alcohol should be legalized.

(I) It has become evident that man cannot get along without alcohol; therefore, there should be no restriction whatsoever on its sale and use.

the wets appeared to contrast the moderate message, as expected. The attitude change data, however, failed to produce a CME. For example, the mean attitude change for the drys exposed to the pro-wet message did not differ substantially from 0, or no change (−0.05, see Table 7.2, Hovland et al., 1957, p. 49), and the mean attitude change for the wets exposed to the pro-dry message exhibited the same pattern. Had a CME occurred, we would have observed substantial change away from the position advocated in the message, but that outcome did not emerge. Thus a careful reading of this classic study, often cited as producing evidence of a CME, shows that it did not provide such evidence.

In contrast to social judgment theory generally, and to Hovland et al. (1957) particularly, Abelson and Miller (1967) hypothesized that CMEs would result if the source of a persuasive message insulted the audience. They suggest two reasons for believing that insult would produce such an effect. First, they offer a social equity explanation. As Abelson and Miller put it,

> "Participation in a communication situation represents a social 'investment' ...,
> a willingness to expose one's views to challenge, in return for which a certain
> level of social 'reward' in the form of social acceptance or approval is considered
> appropriate. If social equity is violated by virtue of gratuitous insults from the
> other party, the victim attempts to redress the inequity in some fashion, very
> possibly by 'withdrawing his investment' and adopting a more extreme version
> of his original position. It is as though the victim says, 'I'll show you. If you're

going to insult me when I give you a chance to change my opinions, I not only won't change them, I'll make them more objectionable to you'" (p. 323).

Of a second possible explanation, the imagined supporter explanation, Abelson and Miller wrote,

> "The 'imagined supporter' mechanism involves a completely different kind of explanation. In giving his insults during persuasive argument, the attacker conveys the impression that people arguing his particular side of the issue are obnoxious individuals. The victim, harassed and confronted with an obviously bad opinion model, may cast about in his memory for a good opinion model, a reference person whose views may be adopted the more effectively to ward off hostile arguments. The chances are that his 'imagined supporter' will be someone whose views are well crystallized and highly polarized, i.e., someone probably more extreme in his opinions than the victim himself. It is as though the victim says, 'Well, if a lout like you has those opinions, they can't be right. The good people I know don't believe those things at all. In fact, I can recall someone proving the exact opposite'" (1967, p. 324).

To test this idea, they staged interviews about employment discrimination against Black Americans with people in Washington Square Park in New York City. At this time, this topic had high salience for the participants, as demonstrations opposing employment discrimination against Black Americans had occurred recently.

Subjects first responded to an item assessing their attitude toward the demonstrations that had occurred (Abelson and Miller included only those subjects who reported supporting the demonstrations)—the pretest attitude measure. While the subject responded to the pretest attitude measure, the interviewer asked if others standing nearby would also give their opinion on the issue. A confederate of the experimenter agreed to do so. The interviewer then asked a series of six questions to both the participant and the confederate. For one-half of these questions, the participant answered first; for the other half of the questions, the confederate answered first. The confederate's responses always indicated opposition to the demonstrations. As the participant and confederate responded to the questions, the interviewer asked them if they agreed or disagreed with what the other had said. After the six questions, the interviewer again asked them to respond to the item assessing their attitude toward the demonstrations—the post-test attitude measure.

Abelson and Miller varied insult by the manner in which the confederate responded to the six questions. Those subjects in the *insult condition* heard the confederate preface his answer by insulting them (e.g., "That's ridiculous," "That's just the sort of thing you'd expect to hear in this park," "That's obviously wrong," "That's terribly confused," and "No one really believes that"). Those in the *neutral remarks* condition heard the confederate preface his remarks with statements to the effect that he had heard this opinion expressed before, that he had listened carefully, or that he found the subject's comments interesting. In the *control conditions*, the confederate admitted not to have much knowledge of the demonstrations but agreed to read comments that others had made—the same anti-demonstration remarks expressed in the insult and neutral remarks, except that they did not include the prefaced insults/neutral comments.

As with the Hovland et al. experiment, Abelson and Miller claimed evidence of CMEs, but their results did match their claims (Abelson and Miller, 1967, Table 3, p. 329). Although they obtain negative change when the confederate insulted the subject, it did not differ substantially from the change (negative but not substantially so) found in the neutral remarks condition, thus failing to meet the eighth criterion for a CME, nor did the change in the neutral remarks condition differ substantially from that found in the control conditions. Finally, change in the insult condition differed (more negative) from the control conditions but only when Abelson and Miller used an exceptionally liberal statistical test. In sum, these results hardly provide a ringing endorsement for CMEs.

A Contemporary Experiment Examining Insult

Relatively recently, Kim et al. (2017) replicated and expanded Abelson and Miller's (1967) experiment. Student subjects in the experimental conditions read a message advocating banning student cell phones from classrooms at the students' university. The study also included a control condition in which the subjects read a message on a topic irrelevant to cell phone use in classrooms.

Kim et al. varied three parameters. First, as did Abelson and Miller, they varied the presence/absence of insults. For some, the persuasive message included insults, whereas others read the persuasive message excluding the insults. Notably, Kim et al. employed stronger insults than did Abelson and Miller. Specifically, they labeled those who bring cell phones to class as "inconsiderate and rude." And they asserted that "only obnoxious idiots bring cell phones to class."

Second, they varied argument quality with subjects assigned randomly to read either a low-quality or a high-quality argument. The high-quality argument consisted of logically valid arguments with strong evidence supporting the premises of the arguments. The low-quality argument included logical errors and lacked high-quality evidence.

Third, they included a threat induction. Those exposed to the high threat message read that "there are many good reasons to ban cell phones in classrooms" and later "cell phones must be banned from classrooms and this ban must be strictly enforced." The low threat message did not include these two statements.

Kim et al. expected each of these message variations to affect the persuasiveness of the message. Specifically, they expected those exposed to the insult version of the message to change their attitude less than those who received the no insult version, those who read the low-quality arguments version of the message to change their attitude less than those who read the high-quality arguments version, and those who read the version including threats to change their attitude less than those who read the no threat version.

In addition, they expected to obtain these results for the same reason—namely, because they thought each of these message inductions would affect reactance. In 1966, psychologist Jack Brehm published *A Theory of Psychological Reactance*, and in 1981, he coauthored a second volume on the topic with Sharon Brehm entitled *Psychological Reactance: A Theory of Freedom and Control*. In the 1966 volume, Brehm defined free behaviors as "acts that are realistically possible" (p. 3) and then described reactance in the following way, "*Given that a person has a set of free behaviors, he will experience reactance whenever any one of those behaviors is eliminated or threatened with elimination*" (p. 4). Brehm thought that when we experienced reactance, we would respond in ways designed to restore our behavioral freedom. Pertinent to the study of persuasion, that claim implies that when a persuasive message threatens an audience's behavioral freedom, members of that audience will attempt to restore their behavioral freedom by resisting the persuasive appeal *or perhaps by changing in the direction opposite of that advocated in the message*. Therefore, he thought that reactance *might* lead to a CME.

Kim et al. thought of reactance somewhat differently than did Brehm. Building on the research of communication scholars Jim Dillard and L. J. Shen, they conceived of reactance as having two components: (1) anger and (2) negative thoughts. So, for Kim et al., as for Dillard and Shen (2005), when we experience reactance in response to exposure to a persuasive message, it means that the message content angers us, and it results in our counterarguing with the message or perhaps derogating the source of the message.

Kim et al. (2017) believed that the presence of threats would result in more reactance than the absence of threats. They expected that threats would anger their audience and that those threats would stimulate the audience to think of reasons why cell phones should *not* be banned from the classroom. Moreover, they believed that weak arguments would result in more reactance than strong arguments because their audience would notice the fallacies and lack of supporting evidence in the weak arguments and that those perceptions would also stimulate counterarguing with the message. In addition, they expected weak arguments to anger the audience. In the authors' words, "Poor arguments beside those involving ad hominem attack may evoke anger, along with negative thoughts particularly when delivered to a relatively well-educated audience who would consider it as an insult to their intelligence" (p. 933). Continuing they added, "Embedded in the process of education is the assumption that the source as a teacher is intellectually superior to the learners or message recipients. When the source/teacher violates the assumption by attempting persuasion with low-quality arguments, anger may arise in the audience/students, deeming the attempt as an insult to their intelligence ('*how dare you expect to persuade me with such a stupid argument?*') or an unjustifiable hoax ('*why are you wasting my time?*')" (p. 937). Furthermore, they believed that the presence of insults would produce more reactance in the audience than would the absence of insults. Because insults constitute an attack against a person rather than that person's position (ad hominem), Kim et al. (2017) expected that they would stimulate negative thoughts among audience members. And they argued that audience members would view the insults in these messages as constituting an intentional and unjustifiable attack (see p. 936) which, in turn, would result in audience members feeling anger toward the source of the persuasive message. So, in sum, they expected that those exposed to insults, weak arguments, and threats would resist the persuasive message appeal or change in the direction opposite of that advocated.

Their results proved unfavorable to the idea that argument strength and threat produce CMEs. No effect of these message variations emerged. Put differently, the amount of attitude change generated in the low-argument quality and high-argument quality conditions differed very little; the amount of attitude change found in the no threat and threat conditions differed very little. Indeed, the authors claimed that resistance occurred in the low-argument quality, and threat conditions fail to fit the observed pattern of results, as we would conclude that resistance took place if less change arose in these conditions than in their high-argument quality and no threat counterparts. Moreover, their failure to produce the usual argument quality effect raises questions as to the validity of their argument quality induction.

In contrast, the authors concluded, "Weak yet consistent evidence of persuasive boomerang emerged for personal insult" (p. 940). Those in the insult condition changed in a direction opposite to that advocated in the persuasive message. Moreover, they changed more in that direction than did those in the no insult and, marginally, control conditions. The authors term the evidence "weak" because of the modest magnitude of these differences.

To see the most striking feature of the Abelson and Miller (1967) and the Kim et al. (2017) experiments requires that we focus on the extremes to which they had to go to produce even small CMEs. Their messages lack realism when contrasted with what persuasion professionals would do when trying to convince an audience, although they may not lack realism so much for those who do not fit into the category of persuasion professionals. Persuasion professionals would not refer to an audience that they actually wanted to persuade as inconsiderate, rude, or as composed of obnoxious idiots, although they might insult the enemies of those they want to persuade.

Pertinent to that point, we find it instructive to reexamine an incident that occurred during the 2016 U.S. presidential campaign. Speaking at a fundraiser in New York, Hillary Clinton referred to half of Donald Trump's supporters as a "basket of deplorables." She went on to characterize them as racist, sexist, homophobic, xenophobic, and Islamophobic. In juxtaposition, she characterized the other half of his supporters as desperate for change. The former characterizations certainly merit the label "insult." Nevertheless, given the audience she addressed that day (composed of members of her base) and given that she had likely abandoned hope of convincing hard-core Trump supporters to vote for her, the insult may have served to promote an important persuasive goal. She might have reinforced and energized her base.

AUDIENCE-CENTERED VERSUS SOURCE-CENTERED VIEWS OF CMEs

Our definition of a CME focuses on the perspective of the audience members. After exposure to a persuasive message, they form some idea of what position that message advocates and why. Subsequently, they may not change their attitudes, or they may change them to some extent either toward or away from the position they perceive the message advocated. Modifying attitudes such that they move away from the position the audience perceives the message advocates defines a CME.

We can contrast that position with those who focus on the intentions of the source of the persuasive message. Sources have an idea of what attitude they would like the audience to adopt after exposure to their message. Audience members' attitudinal responses may or may not correspond to that idea. When their attitudes change by moving away from the position that the source intended them to adopt, then advocates of this position claim that a boomerang, or CME, has occurred. As Hart and Nisbet (2011) put it, "A boomerang effect occurs when a message is strategically constructed with a specific intent but produces a result that is the opposite of that intent" (p. 704).

Our preference for the audience-centered definition of a CME stems from the possibility that sources may intend to advocate a particular position, say opposition to capital punishment, but the audience members may think that the message advocates the opposite position, say support for capital punishment. In a case such as this one, we would not refer to the message effect as counterproductive; instead, we would say that the source of the persuasive message needed to *clarify* the message, *disambiguate* it, or both before we could judge whether or not it produced a CME.

Generally, a message lacks clarity when one cannot attribute meaning to it. Specifically, a persuasive message can lack clarity when audience members cannot judge what, if anything, it advocates. Allow us a personal example of a message lacking clarity. Once one of us (Frank) participated in a faculty meeting. A discussion item appeared on the agendum, and a faculty member (not Frank) spoke long (maybe 3 minutes) and passionately (as indicated by his loud voice and red face) on the matter. The rest of the faculty looked uncomfortable and perplexed. After a pregnant silence, a senior faculty member asked, "Well, Egbert (obviously not his real name), does that mean that you favor it or oppose it?" He went on for another 3 minutes, but even after this addition, no one knew what he favored (or opposed). And no one asked again for clarification. Frank still has no idea what he had in mind.

Generally, we characterize a message as ambiguous when we can generate multiple interpretations of it. A persuasive message can have ambiguity when audience members cannot ascertain which of a number of positions it advocates. Put another way, audience members can think of several different positions that the message might advocate.

Message organization provides one avenue by which ambiguity could enter into a persuasive message. Specifically, message sources may produce more or less explicit persuasive messages. When designing a persuasive message, sources can make several features of the message more or less explicit. One relevant dimension of explicitness involves stating the conclusion of the persuasive message, what you want the audience to endorse, more or less explicitly.

Many scholars have designed experiments to assess the relative effectiveness of making the persuasive message conclusion explicit versus leaving it implicit. Approximately half of the experimental participants might receive exposure to a persuasive message with the conclusion stated explicitly (explicit condition), such as, "Therefore, I recommend that we adopt comprehensive examinations as a graduation requirement at this university." The other participants receive exposure to the exact same persuasive message, except it does not include this sentence. Both O'Keefe (1997) and Cruz (1998) performed thorough reviews of these experiments, concluding that explicit conclusions confer a slight persuasive advantage.

After pointing out that the data require him to reject common explanations for this result, such as the intelligence of the audience and the initial attitudinal position of the audience, O'Keefe (1997) made an interesting and insightful observation. Referring back to the ideas of assimilation and contrast from social judgment theory (see Table 7.2), he suggested that when message sources make conclusions explicit, the audience perceives the position advocated more accurately than they do when message sources leave the conclusion implicit. Consequently, those exposed to persuasive messages with implicit conclusions tend to assimilate or contrast the message more than those exposed to persuasive messages with explicit conclusions. To the extent that O'Keefe's suggestion provides an accurate description of the audience's behavior, it follows that those exposed to persuasive messages with implicit conclusions may perceive the position advocated in the persuasive message as differing substantially from what the source of the message intended.

Subsequently, O'Keefe (1998) pointed out that features of persuasive messages other than the conclusion may also vary in explicitness. Specifically, he noted three of them: (1) articulation of the premises of the argument (**argument completeness**), (2) explicitness of **citing sources**, and (3) the provision or failure to provide specific **quantitative information**.

The first of these dimensions of explicitness refers to the extent to which the persuasive argument includes all of the premises that warrant the conclusion. In the second chapter, we referred to missing premises as enthymemes. So reframing the point, a persuasive argument has greater explicitness when it includes all premises, or lacks enthymemes. O'Keefe reported a persuasive advantage for persuasive messages with greater argument completeness (more explicitness). He also reported that people view the sources of persuasive messages as more credible when they include complete arguments (more explicitness).

The second dimension refers to the disclosure of sources. A persuasive argument might provide evidence for a premise by citing an expert opinion or a scientific study.

The message may or may not name that expert; it may or may not provide a reference for the study. When the message includes the name of the expert or a reference to the study, or both, we may speak of it as more explicit than when it does not. O'Keefe reported a persuasive advantage for persuasive messages which cited their sources (more explicitness). Again, he reports that people view the sources of persuasive messages as more credible when they cite their sources or the studies to which they refer (more explicitness).

The third of these dimensions refers to the specificity with which the message cites evidence. To borrow an O'Keefe (1998) example, a persuasive message that reports that "75% of the population supports a policy" has greater specificity (explicitness) than one that reports that "a majority of the population supports a policy." He did not find sufficient information to allow him to conclude that this dimension of explicitness had or did not have a persuasive advantage or that it affected source credibility.

In sum, explicitness affords influencing agents a persuasive advantage. Specifically, if the persuasive message includes explicit conclusions, complete arguments, and citations, then the audience tends to find it more compelling and the source of the message more credible. The converse of this proposition has important implications for us as well; to the extent that our messages lack these characteristics, audiences will view them as less persuasive and their sources as less credible. This result may emerge from the audience not understanding the position advocated in the persuasive message when the source of the message fails to make the conclusion, completeness of the arguments, and citations explicit.

A second method of clarifying and reducing ambiguity requires attending to the sidedness of the persuasive message. In a program of persuasion research designed to motivate the American soldier during WWII, Hovland et al. (1949) distinguished between one-sided persuasive messages and two-sided persuasive messages. In a one-sided persuasive message, influencing agents present only those arguments that lead to the conclusion that they want you to adopt. In a two-sided persuasive message, influencing agents present both arguments that lead to the conclusion that they want you to adopt and arguments that lead to a conclusion that they do *not* want you to adopt.

Subsequently, Allen (1991; Allen et al., 1990) pointed out that studies of message sidedness may employ one (or both) of two types of two-sided messages. *Nonrefutational two-sided* messages merely present both sides of a controversy; they present arguments both for the advocated conclusion and for a different conclusion. Refutational two-sided messages do the same, but they also go on to provide arguments that refute those arguments that lead to the conclusion that they do *not* want you to adopt. Thus the message sidedness research presents three options: (1) the one-sided message, (2) the two-sided nonrefutational message, and (3) the two-sided refutational message.

Let us consider two examples. Suppose that the topic involves the question of whether to eliminate the Electoral College as a means of electing the president of the United States. Some advocate the status quo, retaining the Electoral College system. Others advocate eliminating the Electoral College and adopting a direct vote system in which the candidate with a plurality (most votes) wins. Let us suppose you prefer a direct vote system in which the candidate with the most votes wins. A one-sided persuasive message would expose the audience only to those arguments that favor the direct vote/plurality position. A two-sided nonrefutational argument would expose the audience both to arguments that favor the direct vote/plurality position *and* to arguments that favor the Electoral College position. A two-sided refutational argument would expose the audience to arguments that favor the direct vote/plurality position, arguments that favor the Electoral College position, and then arguments refuting those Electoral College arguments.

Or suppose that you have the task of developing an advertisement for the product Sweet-Tooth Cola, which, in the competitive cola market, vies for dominance with *Sugar-High Cola*. You could develop a one-sided advertisement in which you laud the virtues of *Sweet-Tooth Cola*, such as refreshing and tasty. Alternatively, you could list the virtues of *Sweet-Tooth Cola* and the virtues of *Sugar-High Cola*, fewer calories and environmentally friendly (pure water, the company promotes recycling, etc.), to produce a two-sided nonrefutational message. And the third alternative, the two-sided refutational message would include the material presented in the two-sided nonrefutational message plus reasons why the attributes of caloric content and environmental friendliness do not matter, why *Sugar-High Cola* does not actually have these attributes, or that *Sweet-Tooth Cola* has these attributes as well (or perhaps more so). In sum, it would include refutations of the pro-*Sugar-High Cola* arguments.

Allen (1991; see also, Allen, 1993; Eisend, 2006; O'Keefe, 1993) summarized the results of numerous experiments conducted for the purpose of examining the relative persuasive effectiveness of these three forms of message organization. He reported that two-sided refutational messages have a more powerful persuasive impact than one-sided messages, which, in turn, produce persuasive outcomes superior to those of two-sided nonrefutational messages. Although some disagreement with these results has emerged (e.g., Eisend, 2006; O'Keefe, 1993), we can have quite a bit of confidence that the two-sided nonrefutational message has little suasory effect.

Notice that the two-sided nonrefutational message either lacks clarity or has a substantial amount of ambiguity associated with what it advocates and why it does so. Those reading the message examining the merits and flaws of the Electoral College might find the pro-Electoral College arguments (or any anti-direct vote/plurality arguments) contained in the two-sided nonrefutational message more compelling than the pro-direct vote/plurality arguments, in which case they would likely modify their attitude in the direction of more favorability toward the Electoral College. Or they may find the pro-direct vote/plurality arguments (or anti-Electoral College) arguments more persuasive than the pro-Electoral College (or anti-direct vote/plurality) arguments, in which case they would likely modify their attitude in the direction of greater favorability toward the direct vote/plurality position. Or they may find both sets of arguments equally compelling (or not compelling), in which case they would likely not change their attitude on the subject. A two-sided refutational message or a one-sided message would remove much of this unclarity and ambiguity.

Both the explicitness of the persuasive message and its sidedness could produce the illusion of an audience-centered CME (review Figure 7.5). A case of such a misperceived "message" arose in the 1970s with the airing on CBS of the situation comedy *All in the Family*. *All in the Family*, an American adaptation of a British situation comedy, proved a very successful program, running from 1971 to 1979 and topping the Nielsen Ratings for 5 consecutive years. It also spawned a number of spin-off situation comedies. The story line involved a working-class family living in Queens, New York. The cast revolved around the father, Archie Bunker (Carroll O'Connor), his wife Edith (Jean Stapleton), daughter Gloria (Sally Struthers), and son-in-law Michael (Rob Reiner). Most episodes featured conflict between Archie, the lovable bigot, and Michael, the liberal college student. From producer Norman Lear's point of view, the show satirized Archie's bigoted views, with Michael getting the best of Archie in their arguments.

Psychologists Neil Vidmar and Milton Rokeach (1974) had doubts about Lear's claim. Thus they surveyed a sample of American high school students and a sample of Canadian adults, asking them a number of questions about *All in the Family*. The responses reinforced Vidmar and Rokeach's skepticism. First, these respondents evaluated the show positively. Approximately half of them indicated that they watched the show every week or almost every week. And more than 80% of the respondents in both samples reported that they found it either enjoyable or very enjoyable. Furthermore, more than 50% said that they found it either extremely funny or very funny.

But when asked who they admired more, Archie or Michael, more than 60% chose Archie. And slightly more than 40% thought that Archie won at the end of the show. More concerning, when asked if they found anything wrong with Archie's use of racial epithets (common on the show), 35% of the students and 43% of the adults reported that they found nothing wrong about the practice. The students also responded to an item asking them to which of the major characters in the show would they have the most similarity in 20 years: 23% reported "Archie."

In addition, Vidmar and Rokeach asked a series of questions to assess the degree of prejudice among their respondents. These items proved of importance in making sense of their data. They found no evidence of differences between those low and high in prejudice of their enjoyment of the show or the extent to which they found it funny. In contrast, the highly prejudiced respondents indicated that they liked Archie more than Mike, thought that Archie made more sense than Mike, thought that Archie won more of the arguments than did Mike, and found the ethnic slurs more acceptable than did the low-prejudice respondents. In addition, high-prejudice students reported a greater likelihood of resembling Archie in the future than did low-prejudice students. Finally, they found that among the student sample, but not the adult sample, the more prejudiced students watched the program more frequently than did the less prejudiced students.

In sum, the conclusions that the respondents drew from watching the show depended on the prejudicial attitudes that they brought with them to the living room sofa. For those high in prejudice, they saw the "message" as advocating their point of view, one congruent with Archie's bigotry. For those low in prejudice, they saw the "message" as advocating a different point of view—namely, one congruent with Michael's liberalism.

To anticipate an objection, a critic might assert that a persuasive message, such as a PSA, an advertisement for a product, or a political speech, differs substantially and in important ways from the script of a television show or from a film. In response, scholars who study the mass media would emphasize numerous examples of influential television programs, radio programs, and films, such as the famed Mercury Theater radio production of *War of the Worlds*; the impact of sex and violence in television and film; the *Why We Fight* films shown to American soldiers during WWII; and entertainment-education programs, such as the radio show Apwe Plezi in St. Lucia (for additional examples, see Lowery & DeFleur, 1995; Singhal & Rogers, 1999). We grant that media such as film, radio, and television can influence people, and we also agree with critics who argue for these media messages differing in important ways from PSAs, advertisements, and speeches. Furthermore, we suggest that those films and other media products, created with the intent to persuade an audience, present products that often lack explicitness and often appear as two-sided nonrefutational messages. Those who perform experiments using such materials bear the burden of showing that their audience members perceive them as advocating what they intend to advocate, something that those associated with creating and producing *All in the Family* did not do. Unless and until they meet that standard, whether a media production results in a CME remains unclear.

SOME SUGGESTIONS FOR AVOIDING SNATCHING DEFEAT FROM THE JAWS OF VICTORY

Suppose that we have the task of persuading someone or an audience of someones. In the interest of having our target audience understand the position we want them to adopt, we create either a one-sided persuasive message or a two-sided refutational persuasive message with the conclusion that we wish our target to adopt stated explicitly. What else might we focus on so as to avoid producing a CME (having them agree with us less after message exposure than prior to message exposure)?

One focal factor involves the quality of the arguments that comprise the persuasive message. We would seek to create strong arguments by checking the logical structure of the message for fallacies, eliminating them if they exist, and doing our research so that we provide strong and plentiful evidence to support the premises of the arguments. Park et al. (2007) reported a boomerang effect for weak arguments, although Kim et al. (2017) and other experiments have not replicated this finding. So although a consistent

CME for weak arguments has not emerged, we would want to err on the side of caution by attending to this message factor.

A second factor would focus our attention on the extent to which the audience sees us as credible. Although no consistent evidence of a CME emerges for low-credibility sources, nevertheless, we would want to present ourselves in a manner that enhances audience perceptions of our expertise, trustworthiness, goodwill, and other favorable attributes as a means of avoiding a CME.

Third, although Hovland et al. (1957) did not produce evidence of a boomerang effect or CME, we would want to attend to the discrepancy between the position we want to advocate and the audience's attitude. We know that the greater the discrepancy between the position advocated and the audience's attitude, the more likely the message will fall into the audience's LOR. To persuade them, we might take an incremental approach, attempting to move audience members in the intended direction by small amounts with either a series of messages or perhaps with a cleverly constructed single message.

The famed Antony Funeral Speech in Act 3, Scene 2 of Shakespeare's *Julius Caesar* provides an example of the latter. Brutus and his co-conspirators have murdered Caesar. Brutus first speaks to the crowd and provides a defense of his actions. He argues that he did so to prevent Caesar from becoming a tyrant ("not that I loved Caesar less, but that I loved Rome more"). After having convinced the audience to approve of their action, he then provides an opportunity for Antony to address the crowd under the stipulation that he will not blame him and his co-conspirators. He also allows that Antony can speak well of Caesar, and then Brutus (inexplicably) leaves. Antony's subsequent persuasive message begins by attempting to render the crowd's attitude toward Caesar (very negative after Brutus's speech) less negative, then somewhat positive, and, finally, very positive. By the end of the speech, the crowd also has a very negative attitude toward Brutus and his co-conspirators.

Fourth, although little evidence suggests that reactance results in a CME, we could still avoid including statements such as, "You have no choice but to agree with me," in the persuasive message. As Brehm (1966) suggested. "When referring to inducing reactance by claiming that the audience has no choice but to agree with the communicator, ... the unusualness of this approach attests to the fact that it may be bad practice for someone studied in the arts of persuasion" (p. 108).

And fifth, we would want to avoid insulting our audience. Kim et al. (2017) claimed to produce modest evidence of a CME when the speaker insults audience members. Furthermore, Abelson and Miller's (1967) findings trend in that direction.

These suggestions illustrate an important point about CMEs: they occur rarely. Moreover, one must employ extremely poor persuasive message design tactics for them to emerge.

Conclusion

Abelson and Miller (1967) wrote, "In controlled experimental studies of attitude change, some degree of change in the direction advocated by the communicator is almost always observed, even under seemingly unfavorable conditions such as the use of communicators of very low credibility ... It is extremely unusual for negative influence—the so-called 'boomerang effect'—to occur, in which the mean attitude change score differs significantly from zero in the direction away from the advocated position" (p. 321). We echo their conclusion, as we find CMEs rare indeed. Insulting your audience may produce a relatively small consistent CME across experiments, but the absence of an extensive set of experimental evidence renders even that conclusion premature. Otherwise, one does not encounter CMEs consistently in studies meeting the criteria outlined in this chapter.

Suppose that you want to convince an audience with diverse views to adopt your position on an issue important to you. As an example, let us say that you want to convince people to recycle more than they do presently, the audience ranging from avid recyclers to those who oppose doing so on ideological grounds. One strategy would involve constructing a strong persuasive message advocating that members of your audience engage in recycling. You could develop several strong arguments entailing the explicit conclusion that your audience members recycle. You could add to your message anti-recycling arguments with refutations of them (two-sided refutational message). You could make each premise of each argument explicit (no enthymemes), include ample evidence to support each premise, and cite explicitly the sources of each piece of evidence.

But if we thought that our messages frequently produced powerful CMEs, we have another strategy available to us. We could construct the opposite of the kind of message we sketched in the preceding paragraph. We could expose them to a persuasive message arguing against recycling. We might insult them for recycling (e.g., "only people with nothing better to do recycle"), provide them with weak arguments opposed to recycling (e.g., "recycling will fail to help the environment because we have too few people to work at recycling centers"), try to induce reactance by telling them that they have no choice but to adopt an anti-recycling point of view, and use other counterproductive message design strategies in the hope of producing a CME. In sum, by advocating poorly for what we do *not* want them to embrace, we could try to move them to adopt our position.

Which strategy would you choose? Given the research available to us at this time, how consistently could we generate a CME if we desired to do so? Our answer tends toward the "very unlikely" side of a continuum ranging from "very unlikely" to "very likely." And given the research available to us at this time, and assuming that we could produce a CME with this strategy, how much could we get people to change their attitudes? Our answer: "A modest amount at best" on a continuum ranging from "none" to "a large amount."

How Can We Encourage Resistance to Persuasion?

Hopes were high. It was possible that many of the students on campus had never been leafleted before in their entire lives, and had developed no immunities at all against leafletting.

—Jane Smiley, *Moo*

IN THIS CHAPTER, WE SHALL approach the issue of persuasion from the opposite direction of every other chapter in this book. When addressing the other questions, we ask about ways to change the audience's attitudes, beliefs, and behavior. In this chapter, we focus on situations in which scholars have grappled with the opposite problem. In one early and important text in the scientific study of persuasion, Hovland et al. asked, "What types of communications create opinions that are enduring and resistant to change once they have been altered?" (1953, p. 241).

This question may seem odd to you. But if the applied goal of persuasion involves using messages to encourage better choices, in a variety of situations, resisting persuasion would produce more desirable outcomes. For example, most children in sixth grade have a negative attitude toward recreationally using heroin. Public health officials and most of the rest of us very much want children to retain that negative attitude and remain free of addiction to such a dangerous drug. People working in potentially unsafe environments usually have positive attitudes toward new safety regulations. But over time, they may see or hear their coworkers discussing how they ignore those regulations without incident. The employer wants that worker to retain a positive orientation toward safe behavior. Someone with a negative attitude toward conspiracy theories may watch a series of videos online and conclude that government aid programs that might help him instead hide a sinister plot to steal his fingernails. In many important situations, people would be better off resisting persuasion.

In addition, understanding how people resist persuasion helps us better understand persuasion in general. If we know why people successfully resist persuasion, we can discover better ways of persuading. An engineer designing a car looks both at ways to improve the power of the car while simultaneously trying to reduce air resistance to the car's forward motion. So too must persuasion researchers understand how to produce more thrust to our messages while at the same time trying to understand what weakens their impact. In particular, understanding resistance helps us understand the "hard-core" people who exhibit particularly strong resistance to change. You cannot use science to understand a phenomenon until you understand how to make it occur and how to make it fail to occur.

To help us answer this question, we first examine evidence of the existence of resistance so that we know it when we see it. Then we look at methods that temporarily increase resistance. Finally, we assess how to make an attitude more permanently resistant to persuasion. This last part will involve grappling with the issue of the relative contributions of cognitive structures and motivations in conferring resistance.

HOW DO WE KNOW IF AN ATTITUDE RESISTS CHANGE?

We can think about this question in a variety of ways. You can measure an audience's attitudes on a topic, expose them to a counterattitudinal message on the topic, and measure their attitudes again. Those whose attitudes remain the same have demonstrated resistance. You would probably also add a measure of comprehension of the message to make sure they understood the message. We resist most persuasive messages simply by ignoring them, but the kind of resistance we explore in this chapter requires people to at least understand the message. An attitude change experiment offers one simple method of assessing resistance.

For example, one early study looked at the extent to which a persuasive message can cause people to resist changes in their beliefs, even after a major public event contradicted these beliefs. Social psychologist Irving Janis and his colleagues (1951) took advantage of a major news event. In May of 1949, they measured 110 high school students' beliefs that the Soviet Union would develop a large number of nuclear weapons in the next 5 years. Then in early June, they exposed half of those high school students to a 20-minute audio recording of a persuasive message, indicating that the Soviet

Union would probably not develop a large number of nuclear weapons in the next 5 years. A control group heard a message about social changes in Italy. In late June, they measured their beliefs again and found that the experimental group had shifted their beliefs to positions more consistent with the message. Control group beliefs did not change. Then in September, President Truman announced that Russia had tested its first nuclear weapon. This event represented a major repudiation of the arguments in the experimental persuasive message that Russia had not yet developed sufficiently in their atomic science to produce nuclear weapons. The researchers took advantage of the event and measured the students' attitudes again. Although both groups shifted their beliefs such that they believed the Soviet Union now had a greater likelihood of developing many nuclear weapons sooner, the group members who heard the experimental message in June showed less change. Their beliefs resisted change to some extent, unlike the control group that showed a larger change. You can see the differential attitude change in Figure 8.1. In the pre-message survey, the groups showed similar attitudes. After the message, nearly everyone in the experimental message group agreed with the message, but the control group showed little change. Then after the news about the Russian nuclear test, you can see that the experimental message group showed less decline. This study illustrates what may be the gold standard in measuring resistance, the extent to which new arguments or information can change people's attitudes or beliefs.

Another option for measuring resistance requires examining what people do during and after message exposure. Some argue that resistance occurs when people actively try to think of reasons to reject the message claims, i.e., **counterarguing** against the message. You can measure counterarguing in a variety of ways. You can ask people what they thought during message exposure and then look at what kinds of thoughts they have. One simple method of examining their thoughts counts how many negative thoughts they had relative to positive thoughts (Petty & Cacioppo, 1979). But others offer more complex methods of parsing exactly what kind of resistance the audience used by categorizing the various types of negative thoughts (Jacks & Cameron, 2003).

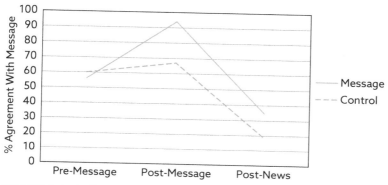

FIGURE 8.1   Difference in resistance in the Janis experiment.

These options require you to conduct a persuasion study. An interpretive difficulty exists, however, with methods that measure attitude change as an indication of resistance. What if people do not change their attitudes, not because their attitudes resisted persuasion but because your persuasive message used arguments that included information irrelevant to their needs and values? You might think that the audience had particularly resistant attitudes, but actually, you just wrote an inept message.

If you do not want to go to the trouble of conducting an entire persuasion study, you can also use a self-report survey measure that includes questions asking people how strongly they hold their attitudes regarding a particular object. This approach assumes that, generally, people know if their attitudes could easily resist persuasive messages or if they think they could easily change their minds. We put together such a measure once by expanding on an existing one and found that it worked to our satisfaction, although it still requires additional validation evidence (Carpenter & Boster, 2013b).

Alternatively, you can also look at how people respond to the attitude questions in and of themselves. People with extreme attitudes tend to have attitudes more resistant to persuasion (Sherif et al., 1965), possibly because they perceive even moderate positions as very discrepant from their own. Also, people who respond very quickly to the attitude questions tend to have highly resistant attitudes on that topic, possibly because highly accessible attitudes have a more accessible set of information and arguments to defend them as well (Bassili, 1996).

Unfortunately, persuasion researchers have not fully settled which of these methods of identifying highly resistant attitudes best captures the phenomenon. The *method of assessing attitude change* leaves open the possibility that rather than the audience possessing resistant attitudes, the persuasive message may have simply lacked persuasive force (i.e., a weak argument). Researchers usually supplement that method with a control group that did not receive some resistance-inducing treatment so that they can see what persuasive strength the message ordinarily possesses.

Examining people's *self-reported thoughts* offers myriad ways of examining the content of those thoughts, but no consensus exists as to which, if any, of these measures best captures resistance. Even if you simply count how many thoughts appear negative and how many appear positive, researchers can use the ratio of negative to positive, the ratio of negative to all thoughts (including those that do not clearly fall into either), the difference between the number of negative and positive, or even just the number of negative thoughts. But that method only captures resistance that involves substantial thinking. We probably resist many messages without much thinking at all by quickly dismissing them as "biased" or "stupid" without thinking carefully about why we produced that assessment.

Attitude extremity as a measure of resistance denies the possibility of someone feeling very committed to a neutral position. Many of us resist persuasive arguments from people who share their political ideologies when those people express a more extreme position (e.g., moderate liberals who feel wary of those advocating government-run health care or moderate conservatives who feel wary of privatizing all public schools).

Usually, extremity tends to correlate positively and moderately with resistance, but moderately correlated does not provide a sufficient measure.

Attitude accessibility probably seems like the indicator of resistance that has the least direct connection to what we want to measure. Why would how quickly you respond to an attitude question indicate how hard of a time someone would have trying to persuade you to change that position? Persuasion researchers do not agree on why attitude accessibility indicates a resistant attitude. Explaining how attitude accessibility works remains a busy area of research for persuasion researchers. Yet attitude accessibility has fewer problems as an indicator of resistance than some of the others. Measuring attitude accessibility well, on the other hand, does require specialized equipment so that researchers can precisely capture the latency between the subject's exposure to the attitude question and their response.

In general, you will see resistance researchers using any of these methods in contemporary research, even though the extent to which they all measure the same thing remains an open question (Krosnick et al., 1993). Assuming for a moment though that we know attitude resistance when we see it, we need to next explore ways to make attitudes more resistant. Researchers have identified ways both of increasing attitude resistance temporarily and more permanently.

HOW CAN WE TEMPORARILY INCREASE RESISTANCE?

Surprisingly, telling people that they will soon hear someone try to persuade them offers a sufficient spur to increase resistance (decrease persuasion). Persuasion researchers use the term forewarning to describe warning the audience of a coming persuasive message. Even a few seconds might make the difference. For example, social psychologists Stanley Milgram and John Sabini (1983) wanted to know if people would give up their seats on a New York subway if asked. In one condition of their experiment, the experimenters approached someone sitting on the subway and asked, "Excuse me. May I have your seat?" (p. 189), finding that 68.3% of those so approached either got up or moved over to make room. But in another condition of the experiment, the requester and a research confederate had a brief discussion. The experimenter said to the confederate, "Do you think it would be alright if I asked someone for a seat?" The confederate replied, "I don't know" (pp. 188–189). Then the experimenter paused for 10 seconds and asked someone within hearing of their conversation for their seat using the same request as before. With this forewarning that someone might be about to ask for their seat, only 36.5% gave up their seats. People gave up their seats 3.5 times more often when they did not receive forewarning of the request.

But Milgram and Sabini's (1983) interesting method does not represent how most persuasion researchers study the topic. One early study by social psychologists Jonathan Freedman and David Sears (1965) ran more like a typical persuasion study.

High school students served as subjects in this study. The message argued that the government should not allow teenagers to drive, a counterattitudinal message for this audience. For those of you able to drive as a teenager, you can see why the audience would not easily move their position closer to the speaker's. The researchers measured all the subjects' attitudes several weeks in advance. Then on the day of the experiment, 10 minutes before message exposure, the researchers told one-third of the subjects that the speaker had high expertise and that he wanted to ban teenage driving. Another one-third received the same warning 2 minutes in advance. The final one-third heard about the topic only seconds before the speaker began his speech. So the 10-minute group received a longer forewarning, the 2-minute group a shorter forewarning, and the last group received no forewarning.

As you probably guessed, the group that had 10 minutes to sit and think about teen driving showed the smallest amount of attitude change. The members of the 2-minute group shifted their attitudes a bit more toward the speaker's anti-teen-driving stance, and the members of the no-warning group shifted their attitudes still more. On average, everyone shifted their attitudes at least somewhat toward the speaker's position. But the longer the audience had to think about the topic beforehand, the less they shifted their attitudes.

This same basic pattern has replicated many times. A meta-analysis by social psychologists Wendy Wood and Jeffrey Quinn (2003) examined the average effect across the 17 available studies on the topic. They found that the audiences that received a forewarning about the speaker's intended claim in these studies changed their attitudes less than the audiences that did not receive a forewarning. A small but substantial difference in persuasiveness warranted attention. The meta-analysis looked at the various ways that researchers warned the audience. In some studies, the researchers merely told the audience that someone wanted to persuade them, some only told the audience the topic of the speech but not the speaker's position, and some, like the Freedman and Sears (1965) study about teen drivers, told the audience the speaker's position on the topic. The researchers found that the effect on resistance did not vary among these various types of forewarnings. So even if you do not know what the speaker plans on saying, if you just tell the audience members that the speaker will try to persuade them, the available research suggests you may temporarily increase the audience's resistance.

On the other hand, the researchers did find a pattern across studies such that if you forewarned the audience and then distracted them during the time between the warning and the persuasive message, the forewarning tended not to affect persuasion. So the available research suggests that people need to have the ability to think about the topic for the forewarning to induce resistance.

Forewarning appears to offer people the ability to resist a persuasive message. But if you turn over the ability coin, you always find motivation. Other researchers have attempted to temporarily increase people's motivation to resist persuasion. As we saw in the previous chapter, insulting your audience offers one method of motivating your audience to resist your persuasive message (Abelson & Miller, 1967). Such insult effects can also occur when people read pushy healthy behavior messages. A study by Quick and Stephenson (2008) encouraged people either to use sunscreen or to exercise more. Half of the messages included pushy language, such as, "You must stop the denial. There is a problem and you must be a part of the solution" (p. 475). Relative to subjects who read a message without pushy language, the subjects who read a pushy language message reported more anger, more negative thoughts, and lower intentions of adopting the healthy behavior advocated in the message. In both of these studies, any kind of attempt to bully the audience into accepting the message produced an immediate increase in resistance. But for situations in which we want people to resist persuasion in the long term, these short-term remedies may not work. So we will next turn to efforts at producing long-term resistance.

HOW CAN WE INCREASE RESISTANCE LONG TERM?

One of the ongoing controversies in the resistance literature concerns why some attitudes resist change. One group argues that people resist persuasion on certain issues because those attitudes have a particular cognitive structure such that when they encounter a persuasive message, those people tend to recall information and arguments that enable them to feel that the message does not make a good enough case for them to change their minds (Roskos-Ewoldsen, 1997). On the other hand, there exists a long tradition rooted in cognitive dissonance theory that argues that people resist persuasive messages because those messages threaten some aspect of their self-concept, such as their social group or their positive self-image (Aronson, 1968b; Carpenter, 2019; Rokeach, 1973). We shall explore what these divergent perspectives on the relative importance of ability and motivation to resist suggest for increasing people's resistance to persuasion for particular topics.

Improving People's Ability to Resist Persuasion

The ability to resist persuasion stems from people developing cognitive structures that allow them to resist persuasion on particular topics more easily. One of the variations on this theme focused on increasing people's knowledge about a topic as a means of encouraging later resistance to persuasion. Social psychologist Wendy Wood (1982) argued that if you know a lot about a topic, your attitude may resist change more vigorously. The more you know about an issue, the lower the chances that a persuasive message would offer anything new to you. You likely have heard all the arguments before. You will also have a greater store of information to use to generate counterarguments to defend your attitude. Consider a guy named Brandon who has a favorite Women's National Basketball Association player. Brandon knows a lot about her, so if you wanted to convince Brandon that a different player played better, you would have an uphill battle because Brandon could quote statistics and other information to defend his choice.

But can you increase someone's knowledge and thereby increase their attitude's resistance to new attacks? One early study from social psychologists Paul Lewan and Ezra Stotland (1961) sought to test the effect of previous knowledge on the persuasiveness of a subsequent message. They went to a high school and gave half of the students a fact sheet containing information about a very small European country called Andorra or about the region of Italy called Etruria. The researchers then measured all of the subjects' attitudes about Andorra and found trivial differences in their attitudes. Next, the students listened to a speech that attacked the people of Andorra in a bigoted way by calling them a "backward, ignorant, unprincipled, provincial, undemocratic people" and stated that "if you were to ask a well-informed person what is the one thing for which Andorra is noted, the answer would probably be 'the absence of morality'" (pp. 451–452). After the speech, the students again completed attitude measures. The researchers found that the students who had learned some facts about the Andorran people's government and currency resisted the change in their attitudes more than the control group who learned about a part of Italy. This finding suggests that having some knowledge about a topic provides some resistance to persuasion. We might also note that as far as we can tell from a brief survey of their Wikipedia page, Andorra looks like a lovely country of mountains and valleys with a rich cultural heritage.

Their study demonstrated the possibility of neutral information providing more resistant attitudes. But what about receiving additional persuasive information? One advertising study by Curtis Haugtvedt and his colleagues (1994) may support this strategy. They provided their subjects with comic books that contained various types of advertisements for a pen. They had a variety of experimental variations but two interest us here. In one version, subjects saw three ads for a new pen brand, and each ad contained different strong arguments for the pen. Another group of subjects saw three ads for the pen, but instead of varying the arguments, the three ads merely varied in superficial aspects, such as the name of the endorser and the font. They found that, as you might expect, people who saw the variety of information knew more about the pen on follow-up tests. You can see the results for their attitudes graphed in Figure 8.2. Right after they read the comic book containing those ads, measures of their attitudes on the post-test showed little

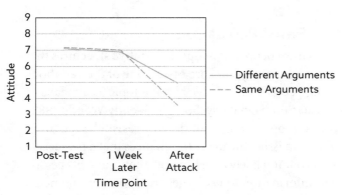

FIGURE 8.2 Experimental results in the Haugtvedt experiment.

difference based on whether they had varied or repetitive ads. A week later, their attitudes still showed little difference. But after they expressed their attitudes in the 1-week follow-up, the researchers gave them new information that attacked the quality of the pen. After the attack message, the subjects reported less attitude change against the pen if they had seen the varied information ads than those who saw the ads that merely varied surface features. Although the researchers did not conduct any statistical analysis to assess if the change in knowledge was the likely cause, this study does suggest that giving people more information may increase resistance to persuasion.

So far, we have looked at studies that showed a link between knowledge and resistance. But social psychologists Michael Biek and colleagues (1996) suggested another possibility. They proposed that people might think like Olympic judges. The Olympics hires such people based on their high degree of knowledge about a particular sport, such as gymnastics. That knowledge might enable them to render objective evaluations of a gymnast's floor routine. Or it might enable them to rationalize expertly a highly biased evaluation against the performance of a gymnast from a rival country. So, too, they suggested knowledge can affect our responses to messages. Like the biased judge, we might use our knowledge to resist all persuasive messages against our current attitude. Or we might use our knowledge critically but objectively such that we do change our attitudes when presented with credible information.

Biek and colleagues conducted a study to assess their hypothesis. They used the topic of HIV prevention. Remember, in the 1990s, infection by the HIV virus was far deadlier than now. They predicted that people with high knowledge would react objectively to information about the likelihood of becoming infected with HIV if they did not worry about HIV. On the other hand, knowledgeable people who did worry about HIV infection would react in a biased way such that their reaction to the information would depend heavily on their preexisting attitudes such that they would react favorably to information confirming their attitudes and unfavorably to information disconfirming their attitudes. They used a two-phase study. In the first phase, the researchers measured the subjects' knowledge, attitudes, and amount of negative emotional reaction to HIV (worry). They found knowledge and emotional reaction essentially uncorrelated such that one variable did not seem related to the other. Then 3 weeks later, the researchers had the subjects read a series of scenarios concerning different types of sexual behavior and the person in the scenario's likelihood of contracting the virus. Half received information indicating a high risk and the other half a low risk.

The results showed that both measures of thought favorability and agreement with the risk estimates showed the expected pattern of resistance. In particular, people with low knowledge did not tend to react to the message based on what they already believed. Their previous attitudes did not affect the favorability of their thoughts or their agreement with the message. The people with high knowledge but low emotional reaction to HIV showed a similar pattern. Neither their thought favorability nor their agreement with the message showed a substantial relationship to their preexisting attitudes. They may have had high knowledge about the topic, but they did not appear to use that knowledge to resist the message when they lacked the emotional drive. But the group members who had a lot of knowledge and a strong emotional reaction to HIV infection showed substantial relationships between their preexisting attitudes and both their thought favorability and agreement with the message. They had both the ability (preexisting knowledge) and motivation (emotional involvement), so their knowledge translated into resistant attitudes. This study raises the possibility that mere knowledge may not always be enough to produce resistant attitudes. At least sometimes that knowledge must couple with some kind of motivation to resist persuasion. We shall discuss motivations shortly. But first, we discuss another proposed method of increasing attitude resistance: message elaboration.

We discussed Richard Petty and John Cacioppo's (1986) elaboration likelihood model in our chapter on argument strength. The portion of their model relevant here concerns the effects of thinking carefully about a persuasive message. They argued that cognitive elaboration (i.e., careful thought about message arguments in which the audience evaluates the information and compares it to previously known information), would produce attitudes that would subsequently resist persuasion. They produced some studies showing attitudes formed under conditions of more careful thinking resisted attacks that came immediately after formation in the same experimental session (e.g., Haugtvedt & Petty, 1992). But more recent research showed that attitude elaboration may produce attitudes that resist persuasion 2 days later.

A group of Spanish scholars led by Miguel Cárdaba (2013) investigated methods of reducing prejudice against immigrants from South America. Their Spanish subjects either read a message containing seven strong arguments from highly credible sources that favored South American immigrants, or they read a control message about a proposed university policy. The investigators also measured the subjects' NC (see Chapter 3), a personality trait that tends to predict how much an audience will think about a message (Cacioppo et al., 1996). People who score higher on the NC measure tend to think substantially more about any given message than those with low scores. They found that immediately after the message, both high and low NC people had more positive attitudes toward South American immigrants if they heard the pro-immigration message rather than the control. But when researchers measured their attitudes again 2 days later, only those higher in NC and who had heard the pro-immigrant message retained their positive attitudes. Although the study does not show that the more highly elaborated messages resisted attack in the lab, the study does show that whatever forces managed to change the attitudes of the low NC subjects, it did not as strongly affect those high in NC and who presumably thought more about the pro-immigration message. We have not found any studies showing that more careful thinking about a message by itself produces resistant attitudes over a longer period of time.

These studies on knowledge and amount of thinking about the issues suggest that although these variables play a role in predicting the increased resistance to persuasion, motivation to resist persuasion likely also plays a role. We quoted Carl Hovland and his colleagues (1953) when writing an early version of the question addressed in this chapter. Regarding this issue, they also wrote, "If one remembers none of the arguments from the communication, one's opinion about the issue may revert to its initial level. Or if one is no longer motivated to accept what was said, the opinion change will not persist" (p. 244). They concluded that both factors likely exert influence on resistance.

Motivations to Resist Persuasion

Next, we will discuss some methods of increasing the audience's motivation to resist future attempts to change their attitudes. Investigators ground some of these methods in various types of consistency theories. To begin, consider New Year's resolutions. Suppose Chet and Marcel both make New Year's resolutions to give up smoking. Their behavioral intentions to quit smoking will have to deal with a variety of attacks. For example, they may see some advertising in gas stations. They may even have friends and coworkers who smoke and who will offer them cigarettes. Of course, they will also likely experience physical cravings. Their behavioral intention will need strong fortification to resist all of that. On January 1, Chet posted on all of his various social media accounts that he intended to quit smoking. Marcel told no one. Who do you think will have the more resistant behavioral intention?

Social psychologist Charles Kiesler (1971) would predict that Chet has a better chance of permanently avoiding cigarettes than Marcel. Kiesler developed a model of commitment to help predict when **commitments** to an attitude, belief, or behavior would create resistance to changing that attitude, belief, or behavior. He explained that when people behave in ways consistent with their attitudes, it causes them to feel more committed to those attitudes. The attitude becomes more and more associated with the self-concept so that a particularly strong commitment binds the attitude closely to the self-concept. Consequently, changing the attitude would make people feel they failed to live up to their core beliefs. Kiesler argued that a variety of factors help determine how strongly the commitment increases resistance. Like Chet making his New Year's resolution, the more public a committing behavior, the stronger the resistance. Other methods of increasing commitment include performing the behavior more often, engaging in a behavior that cannot be reversed (e.g., if you decide you hate an artist and burn one of his paintings, you cannot unburn it), and knowing that you freely chose the behavior.

To test some of his predictions, Kiesler and Sakumura (1966) conducted an experiment. They measured their subjects' attitudes toward the topic of voting-age changes. Then the experimenter told the subjects that they needed them to record a message about voting ages. The message the experimenter asked them to read into the tape recorder supported whichever stance the subject already supported on the topic. They merely elaborated on their existing opinions. But half of the subjects received $1 to make the recording and the other half received $5 (about $8 and $40 in today's money). Then the researcher told both groups that they would next participate in a separate experiment. In this alleged second experiment, all subjects read a persuasive message that opposed their own stance on voting age. Then their subjects reported their attitudes again.

The results of Kiesler and Sakumura's study illustrate the prediction that behavior for which the subject feels more responsible (i.e., receiving a smaller amount of money rather than a larger amount of money for advocating their own beliefs) produces more commitment. Those who received $1 changed their attitudes after the new persuasive message less than those who received $5, showing greater resistance to persuasion. Greater commitment to their original attitude occurred when they received lower pay for attitude-consistent behavior (recording the message). Kiesler's commitment theory predicts that when you attribute your behavior more to the situation than your own free choice, the behavior does not strengthen your commitment as much as if you attributed the behavior to your own choice. People who received more money probably felt like they put effort into the recording about voting age because they received the money for their effort, whereas the people who received less money may have felt like they put effort into the recording because they believed strongly in the policy. If you feel that you did something because you wanted to, you feel more committed than if you feel you acted that way to gain a large cash reward.

This study might feel familiar to you. Kiesler and Sakumura chose that study design because they wanted to show how an important element from cognitive dissonance theory could explain commitment too. In the original Festinger and Carlsmith (1959) study, subjects performed a boring task, and then the researchers paid them either $1 or $20 to lie about how much they enjoyed the task. Then the researchers measured how much the subjects believed they enjoyed the task. Those who received only $1 to lie reported enjoying the boring task more than those who received $20. Festinger and Carlsmith's study showed that cognitive dissonance can explain how when we believe we freely chose attitude-discrepant behavior, we shift our attitudes toward the behavior. Knowing we did something we usually would not (lie to strangers) causes us to shift our attitudes to avoid feeling bad about the behavior. Kiesler and Sakumura showed that when the freely chosen behavior does not violate our attitudes, our attitudes instead develop stronger resistance to persuasion. Kiesler argued that commitment represented a different kind of process than cognitive dissonance. But one of the early proponents of cognitive dissonance, Elliot Aronson (1968a), argued that commitment effects represented the other side of the same cognitive dissonance coin. Regardless, publicly pledging to recycle motivated subjects in another study to recycle more over a 4-week period (Wang & Katzev, 1990). When people freely choose to commit to something, it appears that their attitudes resist change.

But what does commitment really mean? Some have argued that when we decided to commit to something, it means we have tied our self-concept to that object or idea (Aronson, 1968b; Carpenter, 2019; Rokeach, 1973). Consider your attitude toward bicycling. If a doctor told you that new research showed that bicycling produced negative health effects, some of you might shift your attitudes to a slightly more negative position toward bicycling. But some of you identify as bicyclists. When people ask you to describe yourself, you first say that you regularly and vigorously engage in bicycling. A doctor telling you bicycling had negative health effects may have produced anger and negative thoughts. You may have even counterargued this imaginary doctor by calling to mind cases where other doctors presented false recommendations. Thus you would likely resist any change in your attitude. The same process likely helps people resist attitude change on hot-button political topics like gun control and abortion.

For example, if you have a smartphone, what would it take to convince you to switch brands? You might think about phone features, such as the quality of the camera or the speed with which it can connect to the Internet. If someone told you that you could switch phone brands and get a phone with more advanced features for the same price, would you do it? Some of you probably would, but some of you probably would not. A team of consumer science researchers led by Lam et al. (2010) investigated phone-brand switching in Spain when the iPhone was first released for sale in that country.

Some months before the scheduled release of the iPhone, Lam and colleagues measured the current phone brand of over 679 people living in Spain. They measured the extent to which their subjects perceived they had a phone with quality features at a good price—the utilitarian features of a phone. But they also measured the extent to which their subjects **identified** with their phone brand. They wanted to know how much their subjects thought of their phone brand as part of their identity. Then months later the iPhone was released in Spain. Shortly after the release, they measured these issues again in the same sample and then several times more every 2 months. They found that the utilitarian features of their subjects' phones relative to the iPhone and the extent to which they identified with their phone brands predicted the extent to which people switched to the iPhone. So the practical aspects and the identity aspects both had an effect such that people switched more if they perceived the iPhone offered a better, more inexpensive product and switched less if they expressed a strong identity connection to their old phone brand. But, more importantly, over time, the identity issues exerted a stronger effect on phone switching than the utilitarian issues. During the release of the iPhone, they likely encountered many advertisements, as well as people in their social circle extolling the virtues of the iPhone. But people who personally identified with their old brand resisted those persuasive efforts. As Lam and colleagues noted, "The findings suggest that building a strong brand identity can immunize brands from market disruptions" (2010, p. 142).

Unfortunately, too few studies have investigated how to connect people's attitudes, beliefs, and behaviors to their self-concepts. One study by social psychologists Thomas Ostrom and Timothy Brock (1969) encouraged people to think about the connections between an issue and their values by circling words in a transcript of a speech about the concept and drawing an arrow to the value that it represented. The researchers carefully chose values that previous studies on similar subjects showed had high or low importance to the subjects. Those who drew connections to high-importance values resisted a subsequent persuasive message on the topic more than those asked to connect the issue to low-importance values. Your values represent particularly central parts of your self-concept so such methods would logically increase resistance. Unfortunately, only a few studies have followed up on this method, and the idea of increasing resistance by deliberately tying important self-concepts to attitudes remains an under-researched topic.

Much of the research focusing on the connection between people's self-concept and persuasion has attempted to find ways to overcome the resistance produced by that connection. Yet the process of improving people's motivation to resist persuasion by tying issues to their self-concepts has received relatively less attention. One area of research on resistance to persuasion has managed to merge traditions focusing on the ability to resist persuasion with motivations to resist. We turn to inoculation research next.

INOCULATION THEORY: CAN WE VACCINATE AGAINST PERSUASION?

Remember the study on high school students becoming resistant to the idea of the Soviet Union developing a large number of nuclear weapons if they had heard a persuasive message first? Well, some of the researchers in that study actually collected data on a variety of message types as part of that project. Specifically, Arthur Lumsdaine and Irving Janis (1953) looked at variations in the content of the messages the high school students heard. One variation concerned the presence or absence of arguments presenting the other side of the issue, what persuasion researchers call a one- or two-sided message. Recall from Chapter 7 that in a one-sided message, the speaker presents only the arguments in favor of the speaker's position. In a two-sided message, the speaker also mentions arguments that others have produced that oppose the speaker's position.

In this study, some subjects received only a one-sided message asserting the low likelihood of the Soviet Union quickly developing nuclear weapons. The two-sided message contained the same message as the one-sided but also wove some of the opposing arguments into the message so that in some cases, the speaker's arguments refuted the opposition arguments (refutational). In other cases, the speaker merely mentioned the opposing arguments without directly contradicting them (nonrefutational). Then after a week had gone by, the researchers exposed the same subjects to a message that argued that the Soviet Union would likely develop many nuclear weapons in a short time frame, opposing the previous message the subjects had heard. Next, the researchers measured the subjects' attitudes to determine how well their attitudes would resist the new persuasive attempt. Half of the original group did not hear a new message (control groups). The researchers merely measured their attitudes to determine if the one- or two-sided message produced different outcomes.

The subjects who did not receive a new message had beliefs that showed equal favorability to the position advocated by the speaker. One- and two-sided messages did not differentially persuade in this study. But the other half of the subjects received a message attacking the previous speaker's position. Only those who had originally heard a one-sided message substantially changed their beliefs. Those who had heard a two-sided message in the previous session changed their beliefs very little. The researchers concluded that people who hear at least some of the opposition arguments will have more resistant beliefs than those who do not hear the opposition. Indeed, the change scores showed that those who heard the two-sided message had beliefs almost the same as the control subjects who did not even hear an opposing message.

When describing the results of the experiment, the researchers explained that the subjects in the two-sided-message condition had already considered arguments against their positions when they heard those arguments in the two-sided message, whereas the subjects in the one-sided message had not really considered arguments against their own position. The researchers explained this phenomenon by writing, "In effect, he has been given an advance basis for ignoring or discounting the opposing communication and thus 'inoculated', he will tend to retain the positive conclusion" (p. 318).

This early study was part of the prominent "Yale School" of persuasion program. William McGuire worked in that program as a graduate student around that same time. Although inoculating against persuasive messages may have started as a one-sentence metaphor in the Lumsdaine and Janis (1953) paper, in McGuire's hands, it flourished into a theory. After conducting a number of experiments on inoculation, McGuire (1964) summarized the process in a seminal paper on resistance. He argued that just as inoculations can improve the immune system of the body to protect the body from diseases, certain types of messages can **inoculate** people's attitudes and beliefs against persuasion.

In the medical sciences, some inoculations (also known as vaccines) operate by a medical professional injecting a weakened or dead form of a virus into healthy people. Those people's immune systems then attack and defeat the weakened or dead virus. Then if the people who have received an inoculation get some of the live virus in their bodies from another person, the body will have defenses that can fight it off.

McGuire believed that people's attitudes and beliefs can develop similar resistance. Instead of resisting a disease, people can resist attitude change. Inoculation theory specifies the series of steps necessary to do so. You may see some of the elements we discussed previously coming together. First, people must believe that their attitudes may face a **threat** from people trying to persuade them. Oftentimes, those attempting to inoculate an audience will tell them that people will want to change their attitudes (similar to a forewarning). Then the researchers describe some of the arguments the subjects might hear that challenge their existing attitudes. For example, if they wanted to inoculate your anti-smoking attitudes, they might tell you that others will offer you cigarettes and claim that just one cigarette will not hurt you. Then the investigators refute those arguments. They might say that even one cigarette can produce chemical changes that make you more likely to develop an addiction. Thus someone who wants to remain a nonsmoker will first receive the threat that someone might try to convince them to smoke. Then they receive the arguments in favor of smoking and hear why those arguments contain flaws. This series of steps completes the inoculation. Then after some small number of weeks, perhaps two, the subjects return to the laboratory and receive exposure to a message that attempts to change their position. If the inoculated subjects change their attitudes substantially less than a control group who received no inoculation, then the inoculation succeeded in providing resistance to persuasion.

Numerous studies have shown the effectiveness of this system for producing stronger attitudes. A review of the existing studies on inoculation conducted in 2010 by communication scientists John Banas and Stephen Raines showed that inoculation generally produced more resistance to later persuasion attempts than a control group that received no message. They also found that inoculation produces more resistance than a control message that merely supports the subjects' original attitudes or beliefs without including the other steps in the inoculation process.

Inoculation theorists have used inoculation processes to create resistant attitudes in a wide variety of areas, including image protection for corporations advocating social issues (Burgoon et al., 1995), avoiding unhealthy behavior (Parker et al., 2012), resisting conspiracy theories online (Banas & Miller, 2013), and resisting false news stories with a game (Roozenbeek & Linden, 2019). Communication scholars Josh Compton and Brian Kaylor (2013) even found elements of inoculation theory in an early 18th-century pamphlet promoting the smallpox inoculation. But beyond a simple diversity of topics, inoculation theorists have made a variety of advances in the scope of the theory and its implementation in recent decades as part of major resurgence in inoculation theory research among communication scholars.

Some interesting studies took inoculation theory in surprising directions. A study by communication scholar Kimberly Parker and colleagues (2012) sought to test how inoculation might affect attitudes in addition to the targeted attitude. They obtained a group of college student subjects who favored wearing condoms during sex and opposed binge drinking. They used a standard inoculation induction in which the subjects received a warning that people might try to change their minds about condoms and then presented them with arguments against wearing condoms, along with refutations of those arguments. Two weeks later, Parker et al. exposed them to arguments against wearing condoms and again measured their attitudes. As usual, the inoculated subjects showed more resistance to changing their attitudes than members of a control group who did not receive the inoculation treatment. But the unusual part came next. After the attack message and measures concerning condoms, the researchers then showed the subjects a message arguing in favor of binge drinking and measured the subjects' attitudes toward binge drinking. The subjects who had received an inoculation about condoms also resisted pro-binge-drinking arguments better than the control group.

Just as inoculation can protect people's attitudes against both the arguments in the inoculation message and novel arguments, these investigators argued that inoculation can protect people's attitudes against attacks on attitudes that have a connection to those focal attitudes. Previously, we discussed how attitudes might connect with one another. Changing one attitude can sometimes produce changes in another (generalization effects). Similarly, making one attitude more resistant to persuasion may also make related attitudes resistant to persuasion. Currently, we do not know exactly how this process works. Perhaps inoculation strengthens more abstract attitudes such as attitudes against risky behavior in general. Or perhaps the subjects need to have a direct connection between the attitudes. Notably, people often associate risky sexual behavior with binge drinking. Research in this area may produce interesting fruit for theories of both inoculation and attitude structure.

Another development in inoculation theory suggests that the boundaries of inoculation may extend beyond resistance to persuasion. Communication scholar Bobi Ivanov and colleagues (2017) decided to examine the extent to which inoculation inductions can both increase resistance to persuasion and persuade. They conducted a standard inoculation theory study in which the messages concerned the desirability of various tourist destinations. In the first phase, they assessed the subjects' attitudes toward the tourist spots. Then in the second phase, the subjects received a control message about unrelated subjects—a message that discussed the merits of a particular destination or an inoculation message about a destination that included forewarning messages against the destination followed by refutations of arguments against visiting that destination. Subjects then all reported their attitudes again. Two weeks later, all subjects received a message that tried to persuade them that the destination had many negative features and thus that they should avoid it.

Several interesting findings emerged. First, the inoculation message produced attitude *modification* such that people who reported negative or neutral attitudes toward those destinations reported more positive attitudes after the inoculation treatment relative to those in the control condition, whose attitudes did not change. Not only that, but after the attack message in the final phase, those whose attitudes had shifted to a more positive attitude toward the destination also showed resistance to attack. Those who already had positive attitudes also showed the usual resistance to persuasion. This study raises the possibility that inoculation treatments not only make attitudes more resistant but also such treatments might first modify attitudes *and* then make them more resistant. Enthusiasm for these findings must be tempered because in some cases, the merely positive message also showed similar, although often somewhat weaker, effects. Nevertheless, this study opens an exciting new frontier in inoculation research.

Inoculation research blends several aspects of increasing resistance. First, the introduction and refutation of arguments against the initial position offer subjects the ability to better defend their existing positions. The forewarning aspects offer the motivation to defend themselves. Generally, the research suggests that both components produce the strongest resistance effects (Banas & Raines, 2010). The technique and research in this area suggest that resistance arises most effectively when people receive both knowledge and motives to resist persuasion.

Conclusion

Scholars conceptualize resistance to persuasion in a variety of ways. As you probably noticed, we focused on studies that demonstrated increased resistance as simply showing less attitude change relative to a control group. Conceptualizations involving attitude accessibility remain promising, but most resistance researchers tend to focus on resistance to particular persuasive messages. We examined a variety of aspects of persuasion and concluded with a focus on the most popular area: inoculation research. Generally, one can answer this chapter's question by saying that resistance can be induced by motivating people to resist and then giving them the cognitive tools to do so.

We will offer one more issue to consider about these studies. Most of this research focuses on these inductions as present or absent rather than to a degree of intensity. How strongly should a forewarning threaten people's existing attitudes? Would a message induce more resistance by including outright insults to the audience, perhaps by telling them they will likely face brainwashing unless they consider the refutations we subsequently offer? How much refutation produces the most resistance? Should we force them to hear 30 minutes of arguments and refutations, or can one find an optimal Goldilocks point such that the audience members receive the forearming they need to protect their attitudes without getting completely bored? In general, the social sciences tend to think about inductions as present or absent, so this issue applies to many areas, but the high level of research activity in this area may make it ripe for exploration along these lines.

Credits

To What Extent Does Action Follow From Attitudes?

Defining Action (Behavior)

Attitude-Behavior Consistency Pressures

Evidence Pertaining to the Strength of the Attitude-Action Relationship
   Subsequent Attitude-Action Research

Explaining the Attitude-Action Relationship
   The TRA
   The MODE Model

Beware of false prophets, which come to you in sheep's clothing,
but inwardly they are ravening wolves. Ye shall know them by
their fruits.

—**Matthew: 7:15–16**

ALTHOUGH CONTROVERSY SURROUNDS THE MATTER, most New Testament Biblical scholars date the book of Matthew to late in the 1st century CE. As the quotation from Matthew 7:15–16 indicates, we have long known that attitude-action inconsistencies occur. Sometimes, as the quotation suggests, these inconsistencies result from an attempt to gain an advantage, but not always. As an example of the former, a televangelist may prey on poor, uneducated people by promising heavenly rewards while soliciting funds from them. But in a much more mundane manner, each of us might exhibit inconsistencies as well. We might, for instance, have a very positive attitude toward wearing sunscreen, believing that we should put it on 20 minutes before going into the sun, using at least a 15 SPF, and covering all exposed parts of our bodies. Nevertheless, when in a hurry to leave the house, we may fail to act consistently with our attitudes by failing to apply it.

One of the persistent and enduring questions that persuasion scholars continue to address revolves around this issue. As persuasion scholars state the issue, to what extent, if any, do attitudes predict action? Notice that we frame the question quantitatively: *to what extent*? We suspect that people behave consistently with their attitudes some of the time, indeed most of the time, but not all of the time. Thus the question reduces to *how much*?

We can generate several plausible answers to that question. Consider the following nine possibilities.

1. No relationship or only a trivial relationship. Knowing someone's attitude does not help us predict what they will do, and knowing how someone behaves does not help us predict their attitudes. Although this hypothesis appears implausible on the face of it, we must examine it empirically. Only if we find it false can we dismiss it and move on to more complex possibilities.

2. We might uncover an association between attitudes and action, either the more favorable the attitude the more likely consistent action ensues (positive) or the opposite (negative). Nevertheless, this association might not indicate a causal connection between the two because both attitudes and action share a common cause. Scholars characterize such associations as spurious (false).

3. Attitudes could cause behavior directly.

4. Attitudes could cause behavior indirectly. They could cause something which, in turn, then exerts a direct effect on behavior.

5. Attitudes could cause action either directly or indirectly, but the effects may differ depending on other circumstances. For example, a stronger effect may emerge for older adults than children. Scholars refer to such effects as *moderated*.

6. Behavior could cause attitudes directly.

7. Behavior could cause attitudes indirectly.

8. Behavior could cause attitudes either directly or indirectly, but the effects may depend on other circumstances.

9. Some combination of one through eight.

In this chapter, we shall examine these possible answers to the question of the relationship between attitude and action.

DEFINING ACTION (BEHAVIOR)

In the first chapter, we defined the term "attitude" as a basic evaluative orientation toward some object. In contrast, defining the term behavior reveals it as somewhat ambiguous. The term might refer to frequency of action (e.g., the proportion of time someone votes Republican, wears a bicycle helmet, or purchases a soft drink). Alternatively, it might refer to latency of action (e.g., how promptly one responds to a request for assistance, how quickly in a campaign someone endorses a candidate, or how quickly one moves to purchase the newest electronic device). As an additional alternative, it might refer to potency of action (intensity, duration, or both)—for example, how much money one contributes to a political campaign (or how long one continues to sport one's political candidate's sign in one's yard), how hard (or long) one engages in physical exercise, or the extremity (or duration) of one's drug use.

It benefits our thinking about the relationship between attitudes and action to keep these distinctions in mind. The frequency with which one exercises and the duration of our exercise sessions may differ dramatically. How soon one endorses a political candidate and the intensity of that support might also differ dramatically. The relationship between attitudes and action may vary for these different dimensions of action.

ATTITUDE-BEHAVIOR CONSISTENCY PRESSURES

Generally, we do not treat kindly those who behave inconsistently with their professed attitudes. We might label a politician who professes to favor women's rights but who then votes against an equal rights amendment to the U.S. Constitution a flip-flopper (or worse). We may refer to a Christian minister caught in an extramarital affair as a hypocrite. People who profess principles but who then violate them when they conflict with self-interest might receive labels such as "phony," "fraud," or "fake." Notably, none of these labels have positive connotations.

Consequently, you might expect people to act in ways to avoid attitude-action inconsistencies. One of the most influential persuasion theories examines this very issue in detail. Psychologist Leon Festinger's theory of cognitive dissonance (Festinger, 1957) asserts that inconsistencies of this sort produce psychological discomfort, which he terms dissonance.

For Festinger, any piece of knowledge a person has constitutes a cognition (Cooper, 2007). And according to Festinger, a dissonant relationship between two cognitions, say X and Y, arises when X implies not Y and the reverse. So let us say that you know that you dislike the idea of tax increases, perhaps because your ideology favors a reduced role for government in the affairs of its citizens. Nevertheless, you find yourself in a voting booth checking a box favoring the increase of a millage designed to raise money for your city's public schools. Under these conditions, Festinger would say that you experience dissonance.

The amount of dissonance that we experience varies as the discrepancy between our attitudes and our actions expands. In the previous example, our hypothetical voter would experience more dissonance as a strong and vocal proponent of decreasing taxes than if he had only mild opposition to tax increases, and he largely kept his opinions to himself.

Because experiencing dissonance produces psychological discomfort, Festinger argued that when we experience it, we have a drive to reduce it. And Festinger suggested several ways in which we might do so. For example, we might compartmentalize (i.e., ignore it). This strategy has some utility for relatively mild experiences of dissonance but will likely fail for severely dissonant action. We could think of consonant elements, bits of knowledge consistent with our action. So after voting, our hypothetical voter's thoughts may turn to his last visit to the local middle school, and he might recall its dilapidated condition. Thus he may now consider his vote as promoting a necessary public service, not as a tax increase. Alternatively, or additionally, we could seek social support for our belief. For example, after voting, our hypothetical voter could seek out others whom he suspects voted in favor of the millage and turn the conversation to the necessity of this particular millage. Finally, we could change our attitude. To continue the example, after voting, our hypothetical voter could begin to evaluate tax increases more favorably. Most of us find this method extreme. We would prefer one of the three previous options and only if we cannot employ at least one of them would we turn to it.

In a classic experiment, Festinger and his colleague Merrill Carlsmith (1959) demonstrated the extreme lengths to which people will go to reduce their dissonance. In this experiment, naïve subjects engaged in one of the most boring tasks imaginable. With a board full of pegs in front of them, the investigators instructed the subjects to turn each of the many pegs one-half turn to the right, then a quarter turn to the left, and so on—repeatedly.

After the subjects performed this task for some time, the experimenter took them aside and explained (falsely) that the experiment dealt with the effect of instructions on performance. The experimenter continued by saying that some people, like them, entered the experiment without receiving instructions. Others, however, received instructions from a fellow student serving as a confederate to the effect that they found the experiment fun and interesting. The experimenter went on to note that the next subject assigned to receive the instructions sat in a waiting room. Finally, the experimenter, in a rather embarrassed fashion, mentioned that the student confederate had not come to the lab that day. He then asked the naïve subjects if they would help out by telling the next subject (actually a confederate) how interesting, fun, and intriguing he found the experiment. For their help, the experimenter promised the subjects either $1 or $20. All agreed to do so. Note that Festinger and Carlsmith conducted this experiment in the late 1950s and that $1 then equals approximately $9 today, and $20 then equals approximately $180 dollars today. In addition, the experimental procedure assigned some of the subjects to a control condition. Control subjects only performed the task.

When meeting with the confederate, supposedly the next subject, the naïve subjects responded dutifully with enthusiasm about the task, describing it in terms such as "interesting," "fun," and "challenging." The confederate, however, made them work at it, challenging their assertions with comments such as, "Really, it sounds pretty boring to me," or "I had a friend who participated in this experiment, and he found it tedious." Thus they forced the naïve subjects to defend their positions, further enhancing the discrepancy between what they had done (they had participated in a boring experiment) and what they told the confederate (they had participated in an interesting experiment).

Last, before terminating the session, the experimenter asked the naïve subjects some questions. They included items such as how enjoyable the naïve subjects found the experiment, the scientific importance of the experiment, and whether they would participate in similar experiments in the future. The results indicated that for each of these questions, those paid $1 reported more favorable attitudes toward the experiment than did those paid $20.

But why? Festinger had predicted the outcome, arguing that getting only $1 produces a lot of dissonance. The vast majority of people have negative attitudes about lying, and getting very little for telling a lie to an innocent person creates a big discrepancy between attitude and action. Those receiving $1 cannot change their actions, so they change their attitudes toward the experiment. That change reduces or eliminates the inconsistency (i.e., they might now reason "I found it an interesting experiment and I told the confederate just that"). In contrast, getting $20 for telling the same lie produces less, perhaps no, dissonance. The $20 subjects might reason, "Sure I lied, but I made a made a lot of money on the deal. I am willing to tell a lie like this one for that much money." (Ironically, none of the subjects received payment; the experimenter lied again.)

Notice that in this experiment, Festinger and Carlsmith blocked alternative methods of dissonance reduction. The salience of the lie makes it impossible to ignore it. The setting provides little or no opportunity to add consonant elements, nor does it furnish similar others who might provide social support by characterizing the experiment as interesting. The subject cannot undo the action. The only method of dissonance reduction available requires changing one's attitude toward the experiment.

Several other important features of the experiment contribute to the experimental outcome. First, the naïve subjects must believe that they chose freely to perform the dissonance-producing act. The experimenter did not force them to lie to the confederate; he induced them to do so, but they made the choice. Second, the naïve subjects must commit to the dissonance-producing act. Commitment involved exhibiting a high degree of dedication, a willingness to persevere in the face of opposition, and a willingness to provide resources toward the cause to which one commits. The confederate's challenge to the naïve subject's claim of an interesting experiment pressured the naïve subjects to argue for their position. In this way, it fostered commitment. Third, the dissonance-producing act must lead to **aversive consequences**. Telling a lie about the nature of the experiment to a pleasant stranger meets this criterion. And the naïve subjects must see their act as one for which they take **personal responsibility**. In the Festinger and Carlsmith experiment, the setting included no one else for the naïve subject to blame.

The Festinger and Carlsmith experiment demonstrates a close causal link between attitude and action, with the causality running from behavior to attitude. Put differently, it produces a context in which behavior causes attitudes. In contrast, others posit a causal relationship between attitudes and action but one that goes in the opposite direction (i.e., they hypothesize that attitudes cause action; e.g., Fishbein & Ajzen, 1975).

EVIDENCE PERTAINING TO THE STRENGTH OF THE ATTITUDE-ACTION RELATIONSHIP

With cognitive dissonance and other forces motivating people toward a state of attitude-action consistency, what reason(s) exists to doubt the presence of a strong relationship between attitudes and action? A report by sociologist Richard LaPiere in 1934 planted the first seeds of doubt.

The LaPiere Study. LaPiere traveled the United States from 1930 to 1932 with a young Chinese couple. He estimated that they drove more than 10,000 miles. During that time, they requested services from restaurants, motels, and other businesses. Sometimes the Chinese couple solicited the services, whereas other times both LaPiere *and* the couple did so. When he returned to his academic post, he mailed a survey to a sample of these and other establishments and asked, "Will you accept members of the Chinese race as guests in your establishment?" He found that in only 1 of 251 instances did the proprietors *actually* refuse service, but in the overwhelming number of cases (92%), proprietors *reported* that they would refuse service to a Chinese couple. Clearly, the questionnaire evidence and the observational evidence did not agree. Thus some scholars have cited this paper as demonstrating that attitudes and action do not correspond.

Others have criticized the study. For example, LaPiere's presence may have affected the outcome. After all, the questionnaire did not ask about an Chinese couple accompanied by a white male. Others have pointed out that the question, "Will you accept members of the Chinese race as guests in your establishment?" likely does not measure attitudes toward those from China. Put differently, the responses to the question may not reflect the proprietor's attitudes. They might instead have had the aim of discouraging future requests, or they might have assumed that the person sending the questionnaire would not stay at their establishment if they admitted accepting Chinese customers. Notably, the United States found itself in the midst of the Great Depression at this time. Proprietors would have coveted the business of most potential customers, regardless of their own prejudices. Might an attitude toward personal financial well-being, overpowering the prejudices of the time, have driven their action? Yet others have noted that LaPiere could have spoken to a very different set of people than those who provided the services. After all, only 12.8% of those who provided services returned the questionnaire.

In any case, the result appears peculiar. Usually, people protest their biases, which may then gain expression in their actions. But in this case, the reverse occurred; the sample voiced their biases, which then did not exhibit behavioral expression. And if these proprietors who exhibited no bigotry toward the Chinese couple truly lacked prejudice as their actions indicate, then why did "Oriental" Americans, mainly Japanese, find themselves stripped of their property and incarcerated approximately a decade later? One way to begin approaching these questions requires us to ask what scholars have found in subsequent studies of the attitude-action relationship.

Subsequent Attitude-Action Research

Thirty-five years after the publication of LaPiere's study, psychologist Allan Wicker (1969) found enough additional studies of the attitude-action relationship to warrant a detailed review of the evidence. Specifically, he examined more than 30 research papers that investigated topics ranging from attitudes toward one's job and behavioral manifestations of job performance, attitudes toward minority groups and the nature of subsequent interactions with members of these groups, attitudes toward cheating and cheating behavior, and attitudes toward breastfeeding one's children and participation in the practice. He did not disagree substantially with LaPiere, characterizing the relationship between attitudes and action as, at best, weak.

In contrast, only 5 years later, sociologist Allen Liska's (1974) review provided a more optimistic analysis, arguing for a stronger attitude-action relationship and noting that several features of the studies he reviewed served to dampen the magnitude of the attitude-action relationship. Twenty-one years later, psychologist Steve Kraus (1995) performed a meta-analysis of 88 attitude-behavior studies. He reported a moderate effect that varied depending on certain conditions of the study. And in more recent reviews, psychologist Dolores Albarracin and her colleagues (Albarracin et al., 2001; Glasman & Albarracin, 2006) reported evidence of yet larger effects, as well as evidence that more accessible attitudes lead to closer attitude-action correspondence.

In our view, however, the most compelling evidence for a strong relationship between attitudes and action comes from two papers by communication scholar Min-Sun Kim and psychologist Jack Hunter (Kim & Hunter, 1993a, 1993b). Kim and Hunter restricted their review to studies examining behavior over which the subjects had **volitional control**. So, for example, their analysis included voting behavior studies because we can choose those candidates for whom we wish to vote. But they did not include studies of addictive behaviors, as one may have little, if any, control over such actions.

Their review encompassed 138 separate tests of the attitude-action relationship. Nearly 91,000 people participated in these studies. Moreover, Kim and Hunter took exceptional care in attending to, and correcting for, methodological limitations known to make observed effects smaller than warranted. They found evidence of a very strong attitude-action relationship. In addition, they reported a second and very important finding: the attitude-action relationship gets stronger as the match between the attitude measure and the behavior measure increased. This last point requires elaboration.

Suppose that an investigator wanted to predict whether each member of a sample of women would get a mammogram as a means of screening for breast cancer. The women's attitudes toward mammograms would predict the act more accurately than would their more general attitudes toward early detection of diseases. And their attitudes toward early detection of diseases would predict the act more accurately than would their even more general concern with health. Putting the matter another way, matching the specificity of the attitude and action measures maximizes one's ability to predict action from attitude.

EXPLAINING THE ATTITUDE-ACTION RELATIONSHIP

A number of "models" purport to explain why attitudes and action correspond. We shall first consider the best known of these models, Fishbein and Ajzen's (1975) theory of reasoned action (TRA). Like the Kim and Hunter meta-analysis, this model restricts its treatment of the attitude-action relationship to instances of volitional behavior: those acts over which we can exert control. Thus the TRA does not apply to action requiring special skills or abilities, opportunities, or cooperation of others.

The TRA

The TRA has four primary components relevant to the relationship between attitudes and action: attitude toward the behavior, subjective norm, behavioral intentions, and behavior. First, we shall examine each of these components.

Attitude toward the behavior, like attitudes generally, refers to a basic evaluative orientation toward an object. Fishbein and Ajzen thought of these evaluations as the sum of the products of our relevant beliefs and our evaluations of them. An example will help clarify this important conceptual point.

Suppose that you want to know about people's attitudes toward the very specific proposal of engaging in 30 minutes of aerobic exercise five times a week. Beliefs relevant to your attitude might include (albeit not limited to) (1) your belief that such an exercise program promotes heart health, (2) your belief that it increases lung capacity, (3) your belief that it makes you feel better, and (4) your belief that it will lengthen your life. I could ask you questions about each of these beliefs. Following up on each of these items, I could ask you how desirable you find each of these outcomes. Perhaps the first item would look like the following:

Thirty minutes of aerobic exercise 5 days a week promotes heart health.
___ 5 ___ agree strongly
___ 4 ___ agree
___ 3 ___ neither agree nor disagree
___ 2 ___ disagree
___ 1 ___ disagree strongly

How desirable is it that you do things to promote your heart's health?
___ 5 ___ highly desirable
___ 4 ___ desirable
___ 3 ___ neither desirable nor undesirable
___ 2 ___ undesirable
___ 1 ___ highly undesirable

Now suppose that Pat said that he agreed that 30 minutes of aerobic exercise 5 days a week promotes heart health and that he evaluates promoting heart health as very desirable. His first evaluative belief score would then equal $(4) \times (5) = 20$. We could perform the same operation for each of the other three items and then add them up. That number would represent Pat's attitude toward this issue. Notice that maximally, Pat could score 5 on both parts of the item, so the maximum score obtainable for a single item would equal 25, and if Pat scored 25 on each of the four items, his maximum score would equal 100. His minimum score on each item would equal $(1) \times (1) = 1$, and if he responded that way across all four items, his minimal score would equal 4. The higher his score, the more positive his attitude toward engaging in this form and duration of exercise.

According to Fishbein and Ajzen, the attitude object in this example (30 minutes of aerobic exercise 5 days a week) must correspond closely to the very specific act under investigation (30 minutes of aerobic exercise 5 days a week). Thus as in the Kim and Hunter meta-analysis, Fishbein and Ajzen posited that the attitude and behavior must match: one must assess both of them at the same level of specificity.

Whereas attitudes reside within each individual person, the subjective norm concept adds a more social dimension to the TRA. Generally, norms refer to what others do, expect us to do, or both. And others' actions and their expectations do affect our behavior. For example, we may face the temptation of tossing a flyer we find on our car windshield on the ground, but we refrain from doing so because of anti-littering norms. We do so because we believe that most others frown on such activity and that they do not engage in such acts. We may drink more than we want to at the bar on Saturday night because we believe that our peers drink to excess and because we think they might think less of us if we did not. We might refrain from cheating on an exam, even if we know we would not get caught, because we know that others would disapprove.

Fishbein and Ajzen's concept of a subjective norm incorporates some of these ideas. For them, the subjective norm has two components: (1) what we believe important others would want us to do, or normative beliefs, and (2) the strength of our motivation to comply with what these others would have us do. Once again, an example can clarify matters.

We might ask Pat to list three people about whom opinions regarding exercise matter to him. Suppose that Pat lists his significant other, his mother, and his primary care physician. Now we can ask him what these people would want him to do and then ask him the strength of his motivation to comply with their wishes. So we might ask him to respond to the following items:

Your primary care physician would want you to engage in 30 minutes of aerobic exercise five times a week.

_____ 5 _____ agree strongly
_____ 4 _____ agree
_____ 3 _____ neither agree nor disagree
_____ 2 _____ disagree
_____ 1 _____ disagree strongly

It is important for me to do what my primary care physician wants me to do when it comes to exercising.

_____ 5 _____ agree strongly
_____ 4 _____ agree
_____ 3 _____ neither agree nor disagree
_____ 2 _____ disagree
_____ 1 _____ disagree strongly

Once again, we could calculate the product of Pat's responses. Say that he thinks that his primary care physician would agree strongly with the first statement and that he neither agrees nor disagrees with the second statement. We calculate his subjective norm score on this item as $(5) \times (3) = 15$. And once again, we could make the same calculation for this response to his significant other and his mother, sum them, and obtain an indication of his subjective norm on the issue of engaging in 30 minutes of aerobic exercise 5 days a week. His score would fall into the range from 3 to 75. The higher the score, the stronger the normative pressure on Pat to begin exercising aerobically 30 minutes a day, 5 days a week.

Since Fishbein and Ajzen developed their idea of subjective norms, the focus of conceptual thinking has shifted. Presently, scholars focus on **descriptive** and **injunctive** norms. The phrase "descriptive norm" refers to our perception of what other people do. If most people avoid littering, then we speak of an anti-littering norm, and the larger the majority, the stronger the norm. The phrase "injunctive norm" refers to our perception of what others approve/disapprove or what they "ought to"/"ought not to" do. If we believe that the majority of others approve of cleaning up after their dogs when they take them for a walk and disapprove when they do not do so, then we speak of this activity as normative. Once again, the larger the majority who approve/ disapprove, the stronger the norm.

Under many circumstances, we would expect these two kinds of norms to align. For example, if people disapprove of littering, then we would expect them to avoid doing it. But exceptions do arise. In a classic article, sociologist Alvin Gouldner wrote about the **norm of reciprocity** (Gouldner, 1960). As he pointed out, this norm makes at least two demands of us: first, that we should help those who have helped us, and second, that we should avoid hurting those who have helped us. Notice that Gouldner framed the norm of reciprocity as an injunctive norm ("should"). It may also serve as a description of what most people do. Nevertheless, most of us can think of numerous occasions in which recipients of our help did not reciprocate it. If we face up to the matter honestly, no doubt we can generate examples of our own failures to reciprocate favors from others. Some even argue that among friends, a descriptive norm of reciprocity does not exist (e.g., see Boster et al., 1995; Clark & Mills, 1979).

Miller's (1999) work on the **norm of self-interest** provides a second example. He argued that we can expect most people to act in their best interests most of the time. Miller framed the norm of self-interest as a descriptive norm. Nevertheless, many have advocated strongly for doing the opposite, arguing that higher ideals "should" (injunctive norm) motivate us. For example, our religious leaders often nudge us in this direction.

Descriptive and injunctive norms may work at cross-purposes, but they may also work together to create very strong normative influence. An experiment by Schultz and colleagues (2007) illustrated this point well. Schultz et al. applied normative influence to the problem of conserving energy. They sent a descriptive norm message to the inhabitants of a particular neighborhood by simply providing them with power usage data. Specifically, they informed them of how much power they had used in a particular billing period, and they told them how much power people in their neighborhood used *on average*. And it worked! Sort of. Those who used more power than the average did decrease their power use toward the average (or the norm), a clear example of the influence of descriptive norms. But those who used less energy than the average increased their usage. The descriptive norm affected them as well but not in the manner in which Schultz et al. wanted. To take advantage of the strong normative influence for those using more than an average amount of power while harnessing the power of the descriptive norm for those using less than an average amount of power, they added a subtle injunctive norm cue. Those who used less power than average received their power usage statistics, the community average usage, and *a sticker with a smiley face*. The sticker provided a subtle cue that others judged their actions laudable. As a result, the power usage data for those using below-average amounts of power continued to stay low. Clearly, a savvy use of the combination of a descriptive norm and an injunctive norm led to substantial influence and to what many of us would consider a positive social outcome.

Behavior intentions refer to our plans for action. This concept carries some ambiguity. At times, we speak of behavioral intentions as what we think we will do. At other times, we speak of behavioral intentions as what we would like to do—likely the use of the phrase that gave rise to the adage that "the road to hell is paved with good intentions." Engaging in exercise illustrates this difference. If asked how much exercise we intend to do tomorrow, we might think about the question with an overabundance of optimism and respond, "I will take a twenty-mile bicycle ride; lift weights for my shoulders, arms, and chest for forty-five minutes; and then stretch thoroughly." Alternatively, we might think about the question with a sobering dose of realism and respond, "Thinking about my schedule tomorrow, I realize that I can only get in a thirty-minute walk." In the context of the TRA, behavioral intentions refer to the latter, more carefully thought out plans for action.

We discussed behavior, the final key TRA concept, in Chapter 1 and again at the beginning of this chapter. As a quick refresher, behavior refers to overt action. We might focus on several features of it such as its frequency, intensity, or duration. The TRA includes all of these dimensions of action in its conception of behavior.

Figure 9.1 provides a depiction of the TRA. The figure includes the four focal concepts. Notice that some of the concepts link to each other by a one-way arrow. The links represent causal relationships, with the arrow pointing from the cause to the effect. The lack of arrows connecting concepts also proves instructive, as it indicates a lack of a *direct* causal effect. We shall examine these links, and nonlinks, for each pair of concepts.

First, we shall consider the lack of a link between attitude toward the behavior and subjective norm. The lack of a link between these two concepts may strike you as odd. You might think that those others who form our subjective norms have some effect on our attitudes. Alternatively, you might think that our attitudes affect those persons with whom we affiliate so that they ultimately affect our subjective norms. You might think both. Data collected from experiments in which measures of both attitude toward the behavior and subjective norm generally report a positive correlation between the two. This correlation varies across studies, but investigators usually report a moderate-sized coefficient.

Nevertheless, we know that the presence of a correlation between two concepts does not always imply a causal relationship between them. One possibility, and one endorsed by Fishbein and Ajzen, involves a common cause(s) driving both attitude toward the behavior and subjective norm so that we speak of the attitude-norm relationship as spurious. As an

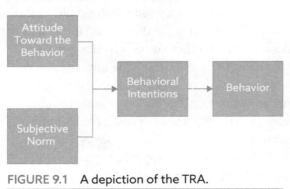

FIGURE 9.1   A depiction of the TRA.

example, a persuasive message might serve as a common cause of both attitude toward the behavior and subjective norm. Specifically, we might construct a persuasive argument designed to produce a more positive attitude toward financial planning, and it might do so. In addition, at the same time, it might bring to mind a small set of people you know who have expectations about the way in which you plan (or fail to plan) for your financial future. They might include your parents, a friend who does financial planning, your spouse, and your in-laws. The message changed your attitude toward financial planning in a positive direction. The people brought to mind by the message would also urge you to engage carefully and frequently in financial planning. Consequently, your attitude and subjective norm would now correlate positively with each other, not because one caused the other but rather because a common cause drove both of them.

Second, as Figure 9.1 shows, the TRA posits that attitude toward the behavior has a direct causal effect on your behavioral intention. Specifically, Fishbein and Ajzen asserted that the more positive your attitude toward the behavior, the more likely you will plan to enact that behavior. The TRA conceives of behavioral intentions as carefully crafted plans, and our attitudes play a central, and causal, role in the planning process.

Third, the figure implies that the subjective norm also has a direct effect on behavioral intention. As with attitude toward the behavior, Fishbein and Ajzen claimed that the more positive your subjective norm, the more likely you will plan to enact the behavior. As with attitudes, what important others would have us do plays an important, and causal, role in forming our intentions.

Fourth, the figure includes no causal arrow from attitude toward the behavior to behavior. But it does include the previously mentioned causal arrow from attitude toward the behavior and behavior intention, and we also notice a causal arrow from behavioral intention to behavior. So we can trace the causal arrows from attitude toward the behavior to behavioral intentions to behavior. We refer to such a structure as an *indirect* effect and say that attitude toward the behavior exerts an indirect effect on behavior. Alternatively, we may put the matter slightly differently. Instead, we may say that behavioral intentions mediate (comes between) the relationship between attitude and behavior. In either case, Fishbein and Ajzen argued, attitudes affect behavioral intentions, which, in turn affect behavior.

Fifth, as with attitude toward the behavior, we can see that the subjective norm has an indirect effect on behavior—the effect mediated again by behavioral intention. So subjective norms also affect behavioral intentions, which, in turn, affect behavior.

Finally, the TRA claims that behavioral intentions exert a direct causal effect on behavior. According to the TRA, the stronger our plans to act in a particular manner, the more likely we do so. But recent research findings have produced new and important findings about the behavioral intention—behavior relationship.

The **mere measurement effect** refers to the difference in behavior produced by either asking or not asking our research subjects to report their behavioral intentions (Levav & Fitzsimons, 2006). Specifically, behavior emerges more frequently when we first ask our subjects to report their behavioral intentions than when we do not do so. Thus the mere act of asking the question increases people's performance of the focal act. As a specific example, we may be able to induce a target person to engage in more exercise merely by asking her about her plan to exercise in the near future. In sum, we could think about asking a behavioral intention question as a means of influencing people to act in a particular manner.

But why? Levav and Fitzsimons speculated that thinking about and stating our intentions make the thought of acting more accessible, and more accessible thoughts facilitate action. Alternatively, it may render the action more easily imaginable so that we know better how to go about performing the focal act. Possibly, the mere measurement effect involves both of these processes.

We must keep in mind that the TRA provides a framework for understanding, among other things, the relationship between attitudes and action. The value of a theoretical framework lies in the empirical tests of it. Ample data have reflected favorably on the TRA's claim that behavioral intentions mediate the attitude-action relationship. For example, both Kim and Hunter's and Albarracin et al.'s meta-analyses have reported outcomes consistent with the TRA. They have found strong relationships, on average, between attitude toward the behavior and behavior intentions, strong behavioral intentions–behavior relationships, and relationships between attitude toward the behavior and behavior of the predicted magnitude.

Nevertheless, we must keep in mind that the TRA and the Kim and Hunter and Albarracin et al. meta-analyses focus on voluntary behavior. What might we say about **nonvolitional** or less volitional behavior? Addressing this issue, Ajzen (1991) proposed the theory of planned behavior (TPB). The TPB differs from the TRA primarily by its addition of one variable, **perceived behavior control** (PBC). PBC refers to the extent to which we believe that we have the ability to control our actions to bring about or to avoid the focal behavior. For example, let us consider engaging in 30 minutes or more of aerobic exercise at least five times per week as the focal behavior. To have high PBC would require reporting that doing this behavior lies within our control; to have low PBC would mean that we lack the ability to meet these behavioral criteria.

Figure 9.2 provides a graphic depiction of the TPB. The addition of PBC adds three possible new links, as it remains ambiguous as to how PBC contributes to predicting

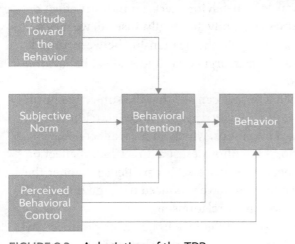

FIGURE 9.2   A depiction of the TPB.

behavioral intentions and behavior. A link between PBC and behavioral intentions provides one possibility. Perhaps those who believe that they possess the ability to control the focal behavior form stronger behavioral intentions than those who perceived that they lack the ability to do so. This possibility implies that PBC exerts an indirect effect on behavior. Alternatively, PBC may affect behavior directly so that those with high PBC exhibit no difference in their intentions from those low in PBC, but they do engage in the focal action more frequently than those low with PBC. A third possibility, represented as an arrow from PBC to the link between behavioral intention and behavior, views PBC as changing the relationship between behavioral intentions and behavior. Specifically, the effect of behavioral intentions on behavior increases in strength as PBC increases. Hence for those high in PBC, their behavioral intentions exert a powerful effect on their behavior, but the behavioral intentions of those low in PBC have a lower likelihood of leading to enacting the behavior.

Boster and colleagues (2014) suggested an alternative to the TPB. They argued that for those with high PBC, the TRA explains how attitudes help us predict action. But for those low in PBC, they suggested that the causal sequence presented in the TRA reverses—a model they term the Reverse TRA. Figure 9.3 depicts this model. In their view, low PBC leads us to reflect on how we usually act and to conclude that because we appear able to do little to change it, we must intend to continue behaving in this manner in the future. To promote cognitive harmony between our intentions and our attitudes, we change our attitudes, if necessary, and make them consistent with our intentions. For the same reason, we also adjust our set of important others so that our subjective norm becomes consistent with our intentions.

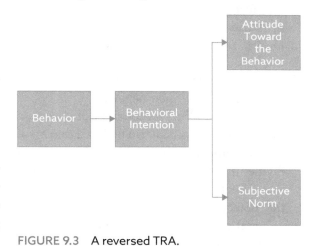

FIGURE 9.3 A reversed TRA.

The MODE Model

Social psychologist Russel Fazio (1990) offered an alternative to the TRA: the MODE model. This model specifies that the processes described by the TRA sometimes operate as predicted and sometimes not. A laundry metaphor will help it. Imagine you do not keep your clothing hung neatly in a closet, folded neatly in a chest of drawers, or both (some of you will imagine this state of affairs more easily than others). Instead, your clothing lies piled around your bedroom. Suppose that you want to choose a T-shirt for a date. If you really wanted a particular shirt, you might dig around for it. In some circumstances, you might have enough motivation to dig through the pile because you think that particular shirt might impress your date. On the other hand, perhaps you do not care to impress your date all that much, so you just grab the shirt on top of the most convenient pile. Alternatively, you may have sufficient motivation, but your date has just pulled up, and you need to dress quickly. Thus, again, you just grab the most available shirt. But what if you did not need to dig because you wear that shirt so often that it naturally ends up at the top of the pile? Perhaps halfway through this metaphor, you began to wonder what this scenario has to do with attitudes.

Think of your attitudes as those piles of clothing. Your attitudes, beliefs, memories, and whatever you currently perceive fill your mind. Some of your attitudes do not get much use, so they end up buried deeper like an ugly sweater you received from a well-meaning, but sartorially challenged, relative. If you want to use those attitudes for making a decision, you will have to put in a little mental effort to dig them out. In contrast, you find other attitudes near the top so that you can use them effortlessly. Perhaps you might even use those attitudes to make decisions without even thinking about it. Like a favorite T-shirt on top of the pile, you might automatically grab whatever you find on top and go with it. On the other hand, if you do not want to dig, you may just go with whatever you find lying around.

Fazio made this concept of attitude accessibility the centerpiece of his MODE model. The letters in MODE stand for motivation and opportunity as determinants. Like Fishbein and Ajzen, Fazio wanted to understand when attitudes would predict behavior, but he believed that under some circumstances, people's attitudes would not accurately predict their behavior.

You can think of his model as a dual-process model, similar to the ones we described in previous chapters. Fazio believed that automatic processes tended to drive most of our behavior such that we operate on a kind of autopilot. This automatic processing divides into two possibilities. When we encounter an attitude object, various cognitive elements pop up, including memories associated with that object, beliefs about that object, and possibly attitudes about that object. If an attitude pops up easily and automatically, Fazio argued that we use that attitude to assess rapidly the situation. That attitude tends to guide whether we engage in a particular behavior. For example, when you order fast food at a restaurant at which you have eaten many times before, you might automatically remember what kind of food you like and order it with little thought. The likelihood of relying on that accessible attitude increases if a line of people behind you pressures you to order quickly. Such scenarios exemplify a highly accessible attitude; the attitude comes to mind quickly.

On the other hand, you might have an attitude about what you like at a fast-food restaurant but you have not ordered any food there in a long time. Again, you feel rushed. So you glance around and see that management has chosen the fish sandwich for the special discounted meal of the day. Your positive attitude toward paying less pops up, and you order the fish sandwich. Such a situation represents what the MODE model predicts happens when you do *not* have an accessible attitude. You rely on whatever attitudes do pop up and whatever information you perceive in your environment to help guide you. In this situation, you might even rely on local norms such that you order the fish sandwich because all of your friends ahead of you in line ordered it.

The fast-food example illustrates that either you cannot think carefully and deliberately about what you want, or you lack the motivation to do so. An automatic process then causes you to rely on whatever lies on top of the laundry pile of your mind. If you have an accessible attitude, then it guides your action. If not, you employ an attitude that allows you to make a quick choice.

Notably, attitudes become more accessible when they get called up more often. Put differently, frequently accessed attitudes become more accessible. Stronger attitudes also tend to have higher accessibility. That is, they come to mind more quickly and easily. Hence when you care strongly about an issue, you can easily access that attitude.

But not all food ordering situations carry this much urgency. Suppose that you went to a fancy restaurant where you could peruse the menu at your leisure. In addition, suppose that you wanted to make a good impression on your dining companion by choosing something that you would particularly enjoy rather than ordering something at which you would only nibble. This situation would likely spur the second of Fazio's two processes: the deliberative process. In this situation, you go to the trouble of digging up your attitudes toward the dishes available on the menu. You might think carefully about the kinds of sauces and vegetables you tend to like and dislike. With Fazio's deliberative process, you would make an effort to dig up those less accessible attitudes. Consequently, according to Fazio, your attitudes would likely guide your behavior. Should the attitudes have high accessibility, so much the better. Nevertheless, highly accessible or not, your attitudes will likely guide your behavior. Fazio argued that only in the deliberative process will the TRA predictions prove accurate. Yet in our fancy restaurant scenario, you will likely fall back on what attitudes you can access quickly in automatic processing if either you decide you do not care what you eat (lack of motivation) or you find your dining companion so beguiling that you cannot think clearly (lack of opportunity).

These two determinants of automatic versus deliberative processing deserve further development. Your motivation to decide carefully what to do has many sources. Fazio identifies a need to impress others as one possible motive such that you think carefully about the decision because you believe others will evaluate you based on your behavior. Fazio also argued that situations in which your choice has important consequences for your life also cause deliberative processing. You probably used deliberative processing when deciding which college or university to attend. Fazio believed that we lack motivation for most of our behavioral choices, so automatic processing likely guides most of our behavior. Your opportunity to engage in deliberative processing parallels the previous types of dual-process models such that distraction and time pressure can both prevent deliberative processing and thus cause you to use automatic processing to guide your behavior. If you lack either motivation or opportunity, automatic processing will occur. Only when both motivation and opportunity exist does deliberative processing emerge.

So Fazio and his MODE model answer the question about whether attitudes predict behavior with an "it depends," the fifth of our original list of options (i.e., moderation). For the MODE model, if you engage in deliberative processing, then yes, your attitudes strongly guide your behavior. If you lack motivation or opportunity for thinking carefully, then it depends. For easily accessible attitudes, then, again, yes, your attitudes strongly guide your behavior. But if that attitude does not come to mind easily (i.e., if that attitude exhibits low accessibility), then no, a weak attitude-action correlation emerges. Recently, others have expanded the MODE model to explain prejudiced behavior and reactions to mass media content (see Ewoldsen et al., 2015; Fazio & Olson, 2014, for reviews).

Conclusion

An ample amount of empirical evidence demonstrates that attitudes affect behavior. Consistently, studies report a positive and substantial correlation between the two. Thus we can dismiss the first possibility mentioned at the beginning of this chapter—namely, that of no association between attitude and action. Furthermore, we can clarify the second possibility: the data show a positive correlation so that attitudes and action tend to correspond to, not oppose, one another.

Theories such as the TRA and TPB predict that behavioral intentions mediate the relationship between attitudes and behavior. Attitudes toward the behavior exert a direct causal effect on behavioral intentions, which, in turn, exert a direct causal effect on behavior. Thus we properly characterize the attitude-action relationship as mediated or indirect. Once again, scholars have amassed an ample amount of empirical evidence consistent with this claim. Thus we may dismiss the third possibility and embrace the fourth.

But a more thorough understanding of the attitude-action relationship requires that we understand the contingencies associated with it. As the Kim and Hunter meta-analyses demonstrated, the match between the specificity of the attitude and action measures affects the magnitude of the relationship between the two. When they match, a larger effect emerges than when we fail to match. Moreover, as the MODE model and the studies testing it demonstrate, the strength of the attitude-action relationship varies as a result of other factors. When we deliberate (i.e., we have both strong motivation and opportunity to think about our actions), then we can expect a strong attitude-action association. In addition, for highly accessible attitudes, we can expect strong attitude-action associations. But when we lack motivation, opportunity, or both, *and* when our attitudes lack accessibility, then they no longer predict action well. Consequently, we can embrace the fifth possibility mentioned at the beginning of this chapter.

We also find that the ways in which we act can affect our attitudes. Festinger's cognitive dissonance theory, and the subsequent experiments testing it, inform us that a number of factors must exist to produce dissonance. These factors include choice, commitment, aversive consequences, and personal responsibility and serve as moderators of the effect of action on attitudes. Hence we can embrace the sixth or seventh, as well as the eighth possibility mentioned at the beginning of this chapter.

We can profit by stepping back from the technical details revolving around the attitude-action relationship presented in this chapter so as to obtain a broader view. When we do so, we observe an interesting dynamic. Generally, how we evaluate objects in our environment affects how we act toward them, and how we act toward them affects how we evaluate them. Consider an example.

One of Frank's friends, let us refer to him as P, served as a consultant for a corporation, let us refer to it as Q, which, among other things, manufactured asbestos. Today, those working in manufacturing processes as dangerous as this one would wear protective equipment at all times. They would do so as a means of avoiding asbestosis, a chronic lung condition brought about by inhaling asbestos fibers into the lungs. To our knowledge, no cure exists for this disease.

In his consulting role, P conducted interviews with and observed both workers who had asbestosis and their families. To P's surprise, he found that the workers had very positive attitudes toward Q. In contrast, their family members hated Q. You can image the very straightforward explanation for the family members' attitudes. They viewed Q as responsible for the illness, and eventual death, of a loved one—a husband, father, brother, cousin, or uncle. But why did the workers have positive attitudes toward Q?

M found that a typical worker, say Jim, had a positive attitude toward Q initially because Q paid well and because Jim had few other job options (especially in the area) that would allow him to provide for his family nearly as well. Jim felt happy, and perhaps a bit blessed or lucky, to have gotten such a good job. He had a positive attitude toward his employer, and his behavior reflected it. He came to work on time and had good things to say about the company when asked.

The effects of asbestosis cumulate so that Jim would not exhibit symptoms of asbestosis for some time. When he did begin to exhibit symptoms, his family began urging him to quit his job. They argued that Q knew the dangers of asbestos and that it did not inform Jim and his fellow workers about it, and it did not provide the necessary protective equipment. Often in loud and emotional appeals, they portrayed Q as a heartless corporation concerned only about profits and not at all about people. Because Jim had a positive attitude toward Q, he defended his employer. In addition, however, Jim's constant defense of Q, his behavior, also served to strengthen his positive attitude toward his employer.

This cycle of attitude leading to behavior that, in turn, strengthened the attitude prevented Jim from quitting until the severity of his asbestosis rendered him unable to work any longer. And, ultimately, he died of the disease.

Hardly an uplifting story, but we might imagine the same dynamic producing a much more prosocial outcome spiral. We can imagine someone like Mary Teresa Bojaxhiu (Mother Teresa) observing the suffering among the poor and sick in Calcutta, these observations giving rise to feelings of sympathy, and, ultimately, very positive attitudes toward the poor—attitudes that led her to minister to them. And we can imagine that the acts of ministering to the poor subsequently reinforced her positive attitudes toward them, which led her to expand her ministry, and so on.

Finally, we can also profit by remembering that under very specific conditions, attitudes fail to predict behavior well. When we lack motivation, opportunity, and accessible attitudes, we must look to other factors to predict our behavior. So, for example, we might have to look elsewhere to explain binge purchasing behavior. So, in the main, attitudes and action correspond with one another, but not always.

Do We Have All the Answers?

So there ain't nothing more to write about, and I am rotten glad of it, because if I'd "a" knowed what a trouble it was to make a book I wouldn't "a" tackled it.

        —Mark Twain, *The Adventures of Huckleberry Finn*

No.

    Frank

No way.

    Chris

    (The responses to the question posed in this chapter's title.)

S O WE COME TO THE end of our treatment of the issues we view as fundamental to the study of persuasion. We began by discussing several different processes of social influence, ending by defining the focal process of this book: persuasion. We defined persuasive communication as those social influence situations in which a source transmits a message to an audience through some channel with the purpose of changing an attitude. And we distinguished persuasive communication from the other forms of social influence: means control, obedience to authority, identification, and compliance gaining. Let us now consider what we concluded regarding the eight fundamental issues that form the substantive focus of this volume.

A SUMMARY

Argument Quality

We reached some conclusions about the role of argument quality in the persuasion process. We view a strong argument as one that effectively addresses the components of the Toulmin model. Strong arguments contain premises that entail a conclusion, with, if necessary, rebuttals that mark conditions under which the claim may not follow from the premises. We clarified what constitutes strong evidence: factual statements originating from a source other than the speaker, objects not created by the speaker, and opinions of persons other than the speaker, each relevant to and offered in support of the speaker's claims. We concluded that strong arguments with strong evidence (data and backing in Toulmin model terminology) contribute to our ability to convince our audience. We concluded that the credibility of the source mattered as well. Audiences find messages attributed to highly credible sources as more compelling than messages attributed to less credible sources. But we also found it difficult to disentangle the effect of the message source from the effect of the quality of the argument. When sources make strong arguments, the audience tends to view them as highly credible; when audiences attribute high credibility to sources, they tend to view their cited evidence as strong.

And we learned the importance of the audience understanding our arguments, for without doing so, our strong arguments will fail to yield persuasive successes. Often, our audience will have the ability to understand our arguments. The more important challenge may be motivating them to employ their ability. And this point leads us to perhaps the most formidable challenge to understanding the relationship between argument quality and changing attitudes. Our knowledge of how people think about persuasive messages remains inadequate and elusive.

Persuasibility

Despite our best efforts to advance high-quality arguments, however, some audience members will remain difficult to convince. A number of individual differences affect the difficulty of convincing others (persuasibility). Some of them involve demographic differences. The sex/gender of the audience members matters, with women showing slightly more susceptibility to persuasive messages than men. This modest difference appears to result from the priming of sex/gender stereotypes. Age also matters with the life-stages hypothesis and accompanying data indicating that those younger and older have more susceptibility to persuasive appeals than do those in the midyears.

Psychological differences emerged as well. Those highly dogmatic tend to accept the recommendations of persuasive messages from sources they respect but not the recommendations of the persuasive messages transmitted by those they do not respect. For those lower in dogmatism, this tendency decreases and then vanishes. Those high in need for cognition (NC) tend to yield to message recommendations less so than do those lower in NC. Research in this area also indicates that those high in NC require strong arguments to change their attitudes, whereas for those low in NC, argument strength exerts little effect on their attitudes. And those with moderate self-esteem tend to have greater susceptibility to persuasive messages than do those either low or high in self-esteem.

We found that other dimensions of individual differences matter too. The Rhodes and Woods (1992) review indicated that the higher one's IQ, the less likely one would yield to a persuasive appeal. Furthermore, a documented hereditary component affects at least some of our attitudes.

But as an article of faith, persuasion scholars believe that the right message from the right source transmitted through the right channel can persuade any one of us, regardless of sex/gender, age, intelligence, dogmatism, NC, self-esteem, and genetic predispositions. And what might constitute the right message? We distinguished generic, targeted, and tailored messages and shared the belief that tailored messages would have a suasory advantage over targeted messages, which would have a suasory advantage over generic messages.

Nevertheless, although different approaches to tailoring have emerged, such as personality, approach/avoidance orientation, attitude functions, attitude structure, and neuroscience, it remains unclear what attributes to tailor persuasive messages on so as to maximize their effectiveness. Furthermore, those that form the hard core and the avant-garde cause us to question our faith that under the right circumstances, we can persuade anyone. We even question if, with its greater reach, the effectiveness of targeting may exceed that of tailoring. Once again, our knowledge of these matters requires substantial expansion before we can provide more definitive answers.

Side Effects

Argument quality and individual differences in persuasibility pertain to changing people's attitudes. Perhaps of equal importance, however, we find that our persuasive message attempts have side effects. People might comprehend more or less of our persuasion attempt. If we have a strong message, we would prefer that they comprehend most or all of it, a state of affairs that we can promote by using the active voice, avoiding negation, right branching, and structuring the persuasion setting so as to minimize distraction. Nevertheless, the amount of the message that people comprehend only correlates with the success of our persuasion attempt when our persuasive targets process the message in a memory-based fashion. On the other hand, if we only have a weak argument to offer, we enhance our chances of persuading successfully when our audience does not remember very much of it. And we improve our chances even more when the audience experiences distractions. In contrast, when the audience processes in an online manner rather than a memory-based manner, message comprehension matters little. Instead, the valence of the audience's thoughts emerges as a stronger determinant of our persuasive effectiveness.

One important kind of thinking that arises during exposure to a persuasive message involves audience members counterarguing the message. They might generate reasons why they believe the reasoning erroneous or the evidence unconvincing. These kinds of thoughts, as well as source derogation, can blunt the effect of a persuasive message. Scholars have examined methods of thwarting people's ability to counterargue by distracting them and by making the persuasive case in a story or narrative, with both methods producing limited success.

We also find that our persuasive messages may affect related attitudes as well as the targeted attitude, a generalization effect, or related attitudes in lieu of the targeted attitude—a displacement effect. Much remains unknown about the way in which generalization and displacement effects emerge—an important challenge for subsequent scholars to address.

Research evidence also shows that our persuasive messages affect the audience's perception of important dimensions of our credibility, as well as our relationships with those to whom we target our suasory appeals. Strong arguments tend to enhance audience members' perceptions of the expertise dimension of our credibility, with weak arguments generating the opposite result. The issues for which we argue and the manner in which we present ourselves and our persuasive case may affect the audience's perceptions of our trustworthiness and goodwill, two other important dimensions of credibility. And the manner of presentation, particularly avoiding threatening our audience members' positive and negative faces, may also have important implications for our relationship and subsequent interactions with audience members.

Also, our persuasive messages may affect other material pertaining to the focal topic in the future. In some cases, our messages may motivate others to find out more about the topic. In others, it may lead them to pursue only attitude-consistent information about the topic or avoid attitude-inconsistent information.

In sum, our persuasive messages have a much wider sphere of influence than only their effects on audience attitudes. Because these areas of study tend to receive less attention from persuasion scholars than does the examination of the effect of the message on attitudes, much remains for us to know about them.

The Buzz

In addition, we find that the effects of our persuasive messages also might have more extensive effects on attitudes. The buzz refers to the extent to which, and the ways in which, people discuss with others the merits of arguments raised in persuasive discourse. So those who we persuade on some issue, or fail to persuade on that issue, may talk with others about it. In that way, our persuasive message might have greater reach by persuading others who did not hear (or read) it directly from us. Research results indicate that the buzz can shape attitudes and that the buzz can modify attitudes. We hope that our message creates a positive buzz so that those we persuaded to embrace our position convince others to do the same. But we also see research examples in which our persuasive messages create a negative buzz so that our message gives rise to a determined minority seeking to persuade others not to embrace our message recommendations. They may even seek to convince others to believe and do the opposite of what we would have them believe or do.

Our review of some classical and contemporary research indicated that opinion leaders (OLs) facilitate creating buzz. OLs have numerous connections to other people, both within the groups of people with whom they interact frequently and with selected others from other groups to which they do not belong. They tend to have exceptional persuasive skills, and they tend to have substantial expertise in some particular domain, such as politics, health, and music. So, for example, they may use their expertise and persuasive skills to persuade their extensive lists of contacts to eat healthier and exercise more. Their contacts, in turn, may try to do the same with their friends and acquaintances. Although, because of their lesser expertise and persuasive ability, they might have less success influencing others than do OLs, they likely have at least some successes so that the reach of the OLs' influence expands.

As we noted in one program of research, some have tried and succeeded at using OLs to aid in a communication campaign. If we can identify them, convince them to help us in our persuasive efforts, and perhaps give them some issue-specific training, they may control the buzz for us.

As we also noticed, OLs may not be the only persons who create buzz. Some have argued that it may take more than just an OL to convince us. Perhaps at times, we change our minds only after exposure to the same message from many people who form our social network. Or perhaps even one person, even someone other than an OL, may convince us with a message well tailored to persuade us.

Nevertheless, many important questions related to the buzz remain unanswered. We cannot predict accurately at this moment in history how much buzz a message will generate or the valence (how much negative, how much positive) of the buzz. We would also find it difficult to predict who generated most of the buzz, with whom they would speak, and to what effect.

Decay

Controlling the buzz would improve substantially the effectiveness of persuasive communication campaigns. But for how long would they do so? Stated differently, if we convinced teenagers to avoid tobacco products, illegal drugs, or alcohol, how long would they remain convinced? When we say that attitudes modified by a persuasive message or by a communication campaign revert to their original, pre-message level after a short period of time, we refer to the process as attitude decay. Of the experiments focusing on attitude decay, some produce evidence of decay and others do not. In the latter instance, we speak of attitude maintenance.

We discussed a number of reasons to expect attitudes to decay. The internal messages generated by more abstract attitudes, or values (the most abstract entity in an attitude hierarchy), can result in more concrete attitudes in that hierarchy decaying. Post-message information seeking, as well as additional external messages from people in our social networks who might want our attitudes to revert to their pre-message level, can also produce decay. And we find that our genetic inheritance might contribute to attitude decay as well. Finally, what appears as decay, or in some cases attitude maintenance, may result from random fluctuation in our responses to attitude items on questionnaires for topics on which we do not actually have attitudes (i.e., what we have termed nonattitudes).

Those attempting to modify attitudes would find attitude decay an undesirable state of affairs, so they would seek means of avoiding decay and promoting attitude maintenance instead. And we find many ideas as to how to go about promoting that goal. We see some evidence that message repetition thwarts attitude decay. Booster messages may have similar effects. Instead of one person constructing a persuasive message and delivering it to an audience, using group discussion to promote attitude modification may also promote attitude change maintenance. Finally, constructing sticky messages holds promise, both for modifying attitudes and reducing decay.

Decay involves initial attitude modification, followed by reverting to the original attitude. Interestingly, however, we find that sometimes the opposite effect occurs; our message may have no initial effect on attitudes, but at some later point, our audience does change and in the direction advocated in the message. This outcome might result when we disassociate the source and message over time. Put another way, a source low in trustworthiness may fail to convince an audience initially, even if she has strong arguments. But given the passage of a sufficient amount of time, the audience may forget that an untrustworthy person transmitted this message but remember the highly compelling argument. Such a process can result in this type of delayed attitude change to which we have referred as the sleeper effect.

There remain, however, numerous things that we would like to know about attitude decay, attitude maintenance, and the sleeper effect. We should like to know more about the conditions under which each of these three outcomes occur and why. We should like to know how to promote attitude maintenance. And we need to know much more about timing. We would especially like to know at what duration message effects decay.

Moreover, because we expect that not all message effects would decay at the same rate, we also need to know what factors (such as type of message, source) affect that duration. Notably, knowing such information could then inform us as to when we need to send booster messages or engage in some other intervention to prevent decay.

Counterproductive Message Effects (CME)

But influencing agents have a fear greater than attitude decay. They worry that their messages could have CMEs. Specifically, they fear that audience attitudes will move away from the message recommendation so that audiences agree less with the influencing agent after exposure to the message than before exposure to the message. Notably, we view the message recommendation as the attitude position that audience members think the message source wants them to adopt. Because the source may send ambiguous or unclear messages at times, this perception may differ from what the source intended. In particular, this difference between audience perception and source intent might arise when the source constructs a two-sided nonrefutational message.

For us to conclude that a CME occurred in a single experiment requires that it meet a number of criteria. First, people must have actual attitudes on the topic in question so that we study attitude modification rather than attitude shaping. Second, our audience must perceive the position advocated in the message as intended. Third, the investigator must measure change, requiring that subjects complete both a pretest and a posttest. Fourth, the experiment must include both an experimental group and a control group. Fifth, the results must produce evidence of substantial attitude modification in the direction opposite of the message recommendation for experimental group subjects and less negative modification (or positive modification or no modification) for control group subjects. Furthermore, for us to have confidence in the consistency of a CME, as opposed to an outlying change finding, we must find many experiments that produce a CME under specified conditions.

Social judgment theory (SJT) provides a theoretical framework that scholars have used to predict when CMEs might occur. Specifically, SJT hints that when exposed to a persuasive message that falls into our latitude of rejection, the set of attitudinal positions we deem unacceptable, a CME may emerge. Direct tests of this hypothesis have not, however, fared particularly well. Scholars have suggested other ideas, such as CMEs emerging under conditions of threat to behavioral freedom, weak arguments, low credibility, and insults to name a few. The last of these suggestions, instances in which the source of the persuasive message insults the audience, has provided some weak evidence of a CME.

Most who study persuasion want to examine the properties of messages that convince people or that block persuasive efforts. They do not strive to find properties of messages that fail to persuade or produce counterproductive effects. Thus we can characterize the area of CMEs as "understudied." The conditions under which CMEs might emerge, if any, remain unknown. The magnitude of CMEs, if they exist, remain unknown. The area requires additional study because of its importance. Certainly, influencing agents want to avoid CMEs.

Preventing Persuasion

In numerous situations, practitioners of persuasion may prefer that their audience retain their existing attitudes, and resist, when necessary, the persuasive appeals of others. Religious institutions want their congregation members to retain their convictions rather than modify them. Politicians want party members to continue to vote for, contribute time, and contribute money to the party rather than switch their allegiance to another party. Public health officials want pro-vaccination citizens to continue to have their children vaccinated rather than become opponents of vaccination. Notice that this issue differs from our treatment of attitude decay/maintenance in one important way. Discussion of the means of maintaining attitudes that our messages previously modified arose in a context with an absence of attack messages or counterarguments. Preventing persuasion, on the other hand, arises in the context of rendering our audience resistant to counterpersuasion attempts.

To study resistance requires that we can identify it when it occurs. Scholars have developed a number of methods of doing so. They include observing a lack of attitude change, measuring thought valences, measuring attitude extremity, and measuring attitude accessibility. Each method has some disadvantages and limitations; each has some advantages. None of the methods has shown itself as far superior to the others.

Regardless of method, audience members forewarned that someone would attempt to persuade them proved more resistant to the subsequent appeal than did those not forewarned. In addition, as discussed in the previous chapter, when the speaker insults the audience, that audience demonstrates more resistance to the appeal than when the speaker does not insult the audience. Nevertheless, these outcomes prove temporary so that scholars have searched for more permanent strategies of inducing resistance.

Some of these more permanent strategies include providing our audience with additional information. Some studies have shown adding information to produce resistance, perhaps because the additional information provides audience members with a stronger foundation to resist counterpersuasion. Promoting message elaboration has also provided some evidence of effectiveness in promoting resistance, as have both inducing commitment and facilitating the connection of the focal attitude with values fundamental to audience members' self-concepts.

The most frequently studied technique, and possibly the most effective as well, requires that we attempt to inoculate our audience. Inoculation occurs in three stages. Initially, audience members receive a warning that someone will try to change their attitude on a particular topic. Next, those conducting the experiment provide the audience with weak arguments that challenge the audience's attitudinal position and provide arguments that refute those weak arguments. Finally, the audience members receive a message attacking their position. Typically, we find that those receiving this inoculation induction resist those attack messages to a greater extent than do those who do not receive the inoculation treatment. Notice that scholars employ two components especially important to resistance in the inoculation induction. First, the forewarning provides motivation to resist and, second, the weak counterarguments and their refutations provide the knowledge required to resist.

Despite the excellent work in this area, some important issues remain unaddressed. Particularly, we could characterize the area as marked by dichotomous thinking: we either inoculate, for example, or we do not inoculate. Rarely might we see an experiment in which the investigators vary the strength of forewarning. Similarly, rarely might we see an experiment in which researchers vary the strength of the counterargument or the thoroughness of its refutation. Such extensions, among others, will serve as fruitful directions for future investigations.

Attitudes and Action

The relationship between attitudes and action might take a number of forms: no association between them, attitudes as direct causes of action, attitudes as indirect causes of action, behavior as a direct cause of action, behavior as an indirect cause of action, moderators might change the relationship, and so on. Our best evidence suggests that for volitional behavior, a strong association exists and that when the specificity of the attitude matches the specificity of the action, a very strong association exists.

Cognitive dissonance theory provides one reason to expect an association between attitudes and action but other theories/models do as well. For example, the theory of reasoned action (TRA) posits that attitudes and subjective norms both affect behavioral intentions, which, in turn, exert a direct causal effect on behavior. Therefore, this theory asserts that attitudes have an indirect cause and effect on behavior, with this effect mediated by behavioral intentions. Notably, those who developed the TRA restrict its applicability to cases involving voluntary action.

To explain the attitude-action relationship for cases of nonvoluntary action, scholars have suggested another idea: the theory of planned behavior (TPB). Perceived behavioral control (PBC) forms the pivotal construct for this idea. When we perceive that we lack behavioral control, as we might if we have an addiction, our behavioral intentions might weaken, behavior might correspond less with our attitudes, the strength of the behavioral intention-behavior relationship might weaken, or some combination of these three outcomes might emerge. Hence this theory asserts an indirect relationship between attitudes and action and that PBC might moderate the relationship as well.

Others have suggested an alternative for nonvoluntary action. This suggestion claims that the causal sequence characteristic of the TRA and TPB might reverse for nonvoluntary action. Thus this idea suggests that behavior drives attitudes and that behavioral intentions mediate the relationship between them.

Recently, the MODE model advances a different kind of explanation. The ideas of motivation and opportunity provide the keys to this explanation. According to the MODE model, when people have both motive and opportunity, they respond as the TRA predicts. But what if we lack either motive or opportunity or both? In that case, the MODE model predicts that if we have highly accessible attitudes, then our attitudes still drive our behavior. But if we lack accessible attitudes, then only a weak relationship between attitudes and action emerges. We could ask what does drive action in those cases in which we lack motive and opportunity, as well as highly accessible attitudes. Firm answers to that question remain elusive at the moment.

EVOLUTION AND UNCERTAINTY

Our reading and analysis inform us that these eight issues comprise the most basic and important issues in the study of persuasion, and our treatment of them in Chapters 2–9 summarizes what we think we know about them. Despite the importance of the issues and the length of time that scholars have pondered and studied these issues, definitive answers to them remain elusive. We suggest that you do not let this fact lead you to dismiss the study of persuasion or become dismayed at the lack of answers to some of your questions. Instead, we ask you to consider *embracing the uncertainty*. Regarding this point, Moore and Kaag (2020) wrote,

> "Philosophers have long warned that this desire for certainty can lead us astray. To think and learn about the world, we must be willing to be uncertain: to accept that we don't yet know everything ... In the year 2020 it seems even more so. Many of us rely on political or tribal loyalties, dismissing any argument that could make us less certain of our views. At its worst, the desire for certainty crushes all subtlety and complexity under its heel" (p. 32).

The study of persuasion has evolved substantially over the centuries, so much so that what we consider foundational issues differs from what we would have considered foundational issues 50 years ago. Moreover, what scholars in 2070 consider foundational will likely differ from what we consider foundational today. Change accelerated in the 20th century and continues to accelerate, but at a faster rate, in the 21st century. The answers tomorrow will improve on the answers we have today. Even at a single moment in time, communication scientists will disagree on at least some of the answers. Moore and Kaag (2020) addressed this point as well when they wrote, "It requires us to respect each other's views but insists on our right to question them. It admits our ignorance while remaining optimistic that we can learn more. It insists that there is a truth that we can and should pursue together – but that this pursuit is endless, with uncertainty our constant companion" (p. 32).

WHEN WE MIGHT PROFIT FROM REFRAINING FROM TRYING TO PERSUADE

We also hope that from the preceding nine chapters you have gathered that sometimes you will gain more from listening than trying to persuade. You encounter many people with opinions that differ substantially from your own. You may encounter them in face-to-face conversations or read them online. These differences in opinion may occur on topics about which you feel very passionately so that persuading this person seems urgent. But consider the following reasons why, instead, you may profit from listening; not just failing to speak, but asking questions and attempting to understand thoroughly this person's position instead of, or before, trying to change it.

First, consider the possibility that the beliefs upon which you have based your attitude do not map onto the facts of the situation as well as you might think. We live in an exceedingly complex world. There exists a fairly low likelihood that you possess perfectly accurate knowledge of all relevant facts for every possible opinion about which you might feel strongly. Rather than displaying your lack of knowledge, you may consider asking the person to explain why they believe as they do. Intellectual honesty requires us to admit the possibility of our own unawareness.

In addition, if you listen rather than trying to attack your interlocutor's position immediately, you sometimes find you actually had a **pseudoconflict**, a term introduced by Miller and Steinberg (1975) in their classic interpersonal text. A pseudoconflict occurs when people think they disagree, but they only believe that because they misperceive each other's positions. The disagreement feels very real and can escalate to an unpleasant conflict. As much as you want to jump right in and tell them why they should change, you should at least assess the possibility that you agree, lest you make a mountain out of a molehill.

Consider also that you can only attempt to persuade a particular person so many times before they find your company odious. As we discussed in Chapter 4, trying to persuade sometimes results in damaging your relationship with the person you want to persuade. So if you want to try to persuade someone, you may want to consider whether you might save your disagreement for a topic you consider more important. The phrase "winning the battle but losing the war" applies here. As we discussed in Chapter 4, people like those who seem similar to themselves. The more frequently you disagree with someone, the less similar you seem to that person and perhaps the less they will like you.

Finally, stopping to listen first might enable you to persuade them more effectively. You mind find out that they have difficulty reconciling your position with an important value they hold, thus making any persuasion temporary at best (as we discussed in our chapter on attitude decay). But you might also find that you can tailor your message to show how your position enables them to adhere to their values more closely than they currently do. As we discussed in our chapter on adapting messages, people can hold the same attitude for many different reasons, and thus there exist myriad persuasive messages that can shift someone's attitude to greater favorability or disfavorability. The message that persuaded you may not persuade the person with whom you find yourself disagreeing. People often seem eager to pull out what they consider a devastating argument because they found it persuasive, only to discover their opponent remains unimpressed. If you listen to someone explain the combination of beliefs and values that produced their current attitude, you will find yourself in a much better position to tailor your argument in a way that they might find persuasive.

A classic *xkcd* comic depicts someone sitting at a computer while someone out of frame exhorts the person at the computer to come to bed. He replies that he cannot because "someone is <u>WRONG</u> on the internet" (Munroe, 2008). We advise that sometimes you should just let it go and go to bed. You might not persuade the person on the other end of the computer, but at least you will please the person waiting for you to go to bed.

OUR APPROACH TO THE STUDY OF PERSUASION

Multiple disciplines informed our treatment of the eight fundamental issues that form the gist of this book. We drew from our home discipline of communication, but we also attended to the ample persuasion literature in psychology, sociology, political science, and other related disciplines. We consider a multidisciplinary approach a strength. Or, to put it negatively, we find it counterproductive to ignore pertinent research from other disciplines to preserve disciplinary hygiene.

We share an important commonality with these other disciplines. All of us approach the study of persuasion scientifically. We and they seek to describe persuasive behavior, explain and understand it, predict it, and, in some cases, find ways to control it. We search for generalities in our study of persuasion. Thus the texts to which we attend include journal articles, books, book chapters, and other monographs replete with details of experimental designs, sampling, survey items, measurement details, statistical analyses, and the like.

Within our discipline of communication resides a group of scholars who also focus frequently on the study of persuasion. They would define their field of study as *rhetoric*. You might think of rhetoric as Aristotle did, focusing on describing all available means of persuasion. Or we might think of it as Quintilian did, focusing on the art of speaking well. Or both.

Although we (Frank and Chris) have received some exposure to rhetorical research, we cannot and would not claim expertise in rhetorical scholarship. But perhaps we have enough exposure to provide a brief characterization of this important discipline. We would describe it as humanistic, as opposed to scientific, inquiry. Rhetoricians tend to focus on individual persuaders or persuasion occasions and not as much on generalizations about persuasion. They study important existing texts, such as Lincoln's Gettysburg Address, and analyze them in detail, searching for what might have rendered them effective or ineffective.

We have great respect for rhetorical scholarship and the insights it has added to the study of persuasion. But because writing about it requires a skill set for which neither of us received training, we must follow Wittgenstein's dictum that comprises the last line in his *Tractatus Logico-Philosophicus*, "Whereof one cannot speak, thereof one must be silent." Our lack of rhetorical knowledge provides one of the reasons why both of us answered "no" to the question that forms the title of this chapter.

PAST, PRESENT, AND FUTURE

Scholarship suffers seriously when we fail to attend sufficiently to the past. Not only can we learn from past successes, such as the Asch and Milgram experiments, but we profit from learning about theoretical, methodological, and analytic dead ends as well. Attention to past scholarship also prevents us from reinventing the wheel, which happens with more frequency than we might like to believe. Moreover, the reinventions frequently do not work out quite as well as the originals. For these reasons, we have spent considerable space presenting and discussing classic, or seminal, studies.

The present provides its own challenges. Trying to describe an academic area of study in which we find ourselves immersed can lead us to miss ideas, findings, and theories that over time will emerge as important. On the other side of this coin, we generally clutch our pet ideas closely, perhaps too closely, only to learn 20 years later the folly of our ways.

A *paradigm* consists of concepts, ways of thinking, theories, research methodological standards, and ideas taken for granted. In describing in Chapters 2–9 what we think we know about eight substantive issues, we employed these components of the paradigm in which we work presently. Yet when we try to step back and gain a more detached vantage point, we find that we may lack a dominant paradigm or that we may work under multiple paradigms, at the moment. In some ways, we may benefit from that state of affairs. Consider the methods we employ to study persuasion. The classic passive experimental public address paradigm, survey studies of media exposure and attitude change, communication campaigns and other interventions, Internet experiments, and other diverse approaches have all enriched our knowledge of persuasion in ways that no single method could have. Similar, neither theoretical nor applied research dominate the persuasive research agendum. Both have made, and continue to make, important contributions.

We lack consensus on a dominant theoretical perspective as well. Dual-process models once appeared dominant, particularly because they appeared to make sense of seemingly contradictory research results. But as we pointed out, scholars have demonstrated, and amply so, the weaknesses in the Heuristic-Systemic Model and Elaboration Likelihood Model. The unimodel emerges as a challenger to the dual-process models but oddly has received substantially less empirical attention than it warrants. Just as the ascension of the dual-process models to a place of dominance gave rise to important findings about the persuasion process, so too do we expect its successor to do so. What that successor might look like, however, remains beyond our ken at this moment.

One part of a paradigm involves what we have referred to as articles of faith. Because we take them for granted as truths, we often fail to examine them. And oftentimes, new paradigms expose their taken-for-granted status. We pointed out one of them, the notion that given the right set of circumstances, we can persuade anyone, and we challenged it. We likely embrace more ideas of this type but lack awareness of them. Exposing them can only serve to improve our understanding of the persuasion process.

In his last book, Leon Festinger (1983) noted our inability as a species to predict the future. He claimed that if ever another species supplanted us on this planet (as we did the Neanderthals) it would result from that species having a better ability to predict the future. In our desire to avoid futile pursuits, we shall not make an attempt in this direction. Instead, we shall content ourselves with some comments about progress in persuasion research.

New theoretical ideas that can synthesize and explain the empirical regularities that we have observed would represent immense progress. Ludwig Boltzman once asserted, "There is nothing so practical as a good theory." Theories direct us where to look and at what to look. They provide an important set of principles for organizing our thoughts and understanding the world. Of course, by directing our attention and thoughts, they may also miss important phenomena, at which point we must search for new organizing principles. That appears to describe our current position.

Beyond that, however, we need to fill in gaps in our knowledge. That activity forms the crux of normal science. And we have many gaps to fill. Plugging those gaps in knowledge requires an agendum. We believe that the eight fundamental issues that we have identified in this volume provide that agendum.

Glossary

Acute self-esteem Someone's temporary level of self-esteem usually caused by contextual cues regarding that person's self-worth. Also called state self-esteem.

Ad hominem A type of informal fallacy in which someone attacks a person rather than the argument that person advocates.

Affirming the consequent A type of informal fallacy in which someone observes an effect has occurred and then incorrectly assumes that because the presence of a particular cause has produced that effect in other cases that cause must have brought about the effect in this case.

Agreeableness One of the Big Five personality traits in which those exhibiting high levels of this trait tend to be particularly friendly and cooperative.

Approach motivational orientation A personality orientation in which people tend to feel driven to seek positive outcomes.

Approval The positive regard of others to the self.

Argument A message designed to persuade by using evidence

Argument completeness The extent to which a persuasive message contains all of the premises supporting the argument such that a complete argument includes all of the premises that form the argument.

Argument from ignorance A type of informal fallacy in which because something is not known or cannot be known, the speaker argues it is true.

Assimilate In the context of social judgment theory, someone perceives that a speaker advocates a position that is closer to that person's own position than the speaker attempts to present.

Attitude A basic evaluative orientation toward an object.

Attitude accessibility The speed with which someone recalls their attitude towards a given object.

Attitude bolstering A type of resistance to a persuasive message in which someone focuses on reasons for the superiority of their original position.

Attitude change Modifying, reinforcing, or shaping an attitude.

Attitude decay The process by which the attitudes of someone who experienced attitude change in response to a persuasive message returns to their original pre-message level after a period of time has elapsed.

Attitude extremity The extent to which someone's attitude deviates from neutrality.

Attitude functions In the context of functional attitude theory, the purposes for which someone has an attitude.

Attitude structure The way someone's attitudes are related to each other in cognitive networks such that an attitude towards a particular object will have stronger connections to attitudes towards similar objects than dissimilar objects.

Attitude toward the behavior A basic evaluative orientation toward a behavior.

Audience The person or persons that a speaker tries to persuade.

Audience adaptation When someone tries to compose their message to change the attitudes of a particular audience based on the characteristics of that audience.

Avant garde People whose attitudes on a topic differ from the popular view but they resist persuasion because they believe their attitudes will one day become popular.

Aversive consequences In the context of cognitive dissonance theory, when someone's behavior produces negative outcomes for others.

Avoid motivational orientation A personality orientation in which people tend to feel driven to escape negative outcomes.

Backing In the context of Toulmin's model of argumentation, backing refers to the support for the warrant that provides a reason to accept the soundness of the warrant.

Begging the question (circular reasoning) A type of information fallacy in which someone assumes the truth of the conclusion as part of their argument for the conclusion.

Behavior The actions someone performs that vary by duration, frequency, intensity, and latency.

Behavioral intention The plans for action someone has.

Belief A judgment of the correctness of a proposition.

Belonging (sense of) The extent to which someone feels included in a group by the members of the group.

Booster message In the context of behavior change interventions, when the targeted group receives an additional, shorter version of the initial intervention after some time has passed in order to extend the impact of the initial intervention.

Buzz The extent to which, and the ways in which, people discuss with others the merits of arguments raised in persuasive discourse.

Change (an attitude) Modifying, reinforcing, or shaping an attitude.

Channel The medium through which the source transmits the message.

Choice (choose freely) In the context of cognitive dissonance theory, choice refers to the extent to which people believe they had the freedom to behave differently than they did.

Chronic self-esteem The general level of self-esteem someone has which exists largely independent of context. Also called trait self-esteem.

Citing sources (explicitness of) The extent to which a message includes the name of the expert making a claim and/or a reference for the information.

Claim In the context of Toulmin's model of argumentation, backing refers to the belief that the speaker would like the audience to accept.

Cognition In the context of cognitive dissonance theory, a cognition refers to any piece of knowledge a person possesses.

Cognitive elaboration In the context of dual-process theories, cognitive elaboration refers to the extent to which someone thinks carefully and deeply about the merits of a persuasive message.

Commitment In the context of cognitive dissonance theory, commitment refers to engaging in behavior while showing a high degree of dedication to that behavior.

Communication campaigns Large-scale efforts of finite but relatively long duration that seek to persuade large numbers of people to change their attitudes, beliefs, and behaviors

Compartmentalize In the context of cognitive dissonance theory, compartmentalizing refers to ignoring aroused cognitive dissonance.

Compatibility In the context of diffusions of innovations, compatibility refers to the extent to which an innovation is consistent with the values, needs, and experiences of the target audience.

Complexity (of an innovation) In the context of diffusions of innovations, complexity refers to the extent to which an innovation presents many difficulties in implementation.

Conclusion The particular belief or attitude the speaker wants the audience to adopt. These vary in the degree to which the speaker makes them explicit.

Concreteness (message property) In the context of message stickiness, concreteness refers to the extent to which a message refers to detailed and specific situations.

Confirmation bias The tendency for people to look for information that confirms what they already believe

Connectors Those who know many people and know a diversity of people.

Conscientiousness One of the Big Five personality traits in which those exhibiting high levels of this trait tend to be particularly efficient and organized.

Consonant elements In the context of cognitive dissonance theory, consonant elements are pieces of someone's knowledge that show consistency with that person's previous actions.

Contrast In the context of social judgment theory, someone perceives that a speaker advocates a position that is more different from that person's own position than the speaker attempts to present.

Control In a persuasion experiment, the researcher randomly assigns some participants to receive no message at all or a version of the experimental message without some key element. This condition provides a comparison point to assess the effectiveness of the experimental message.

Counterarguing The thoughts of an audience member when that person thinks of reasons that disagree with the speaker's claims.

Counterproductive message effect (CME) When an audience shifts their attitudes away from, rather than toward, the position advocated in a persuasive message. Also called a "boomerang effect."

Credibility The perception by the audience that a speaker is willing and able to tell the truth.

Credibility (message property) In the context of message stickiness, credibility refers to the perception by the audience of the trustworthiness of the information in the message.

Cultural-level information The information about a person that can be inferred from merely knowing someone's background and visible characteristics.

Data In the context of Toulmin's model of argumentation, data represents the information that the speaker assumes the audience will likely believe and which the speaker wants to use to argue in favor of the claim.

Deduction Arguments in which conclusions follow necessarily from premises.

Descriptive norms Perceptions of what other people do.

Diffusion The spread of persuasive messages promoting an idea throughout a defined population of people.

Disapproval The negative regard of others towards the self

Displacement effect When a persuasive message fails to change the focal attitude but does change related attitudes in the desired direction.

Dissonance Psychological discomfort caused by one's inconsistency.

Dogmatism A psychological trait characterized by high levels of closed-mindedness.

Duration (of behavior) How long someone engages in a particular action.

Ego-defensive function In the context of functional attitude theory, the ego-defensive function refers to an attitude function such that the attitude helps people preserve their sense of themselves, or their self-concepts.

Ego-involvement When someone's stance on an issue is deeply connected to their values and sense of self-worth.

Ego-strength An older term for self-esteem, a persons' negative or positive evaluation or orientation toward themselves

Emotion (message property) In the context of message stickiness, emotion refers to giving people a reason to care about the outcome endorsed in the message recommendation.

Enthymeme An argument in which one of the premises is not stated.

Evidence "Factual statement originating from a source other than the speaker, objects not created by the speaker, and opinions of persons other than the speaker that are offered in support of the speaker's claims." (McCroskey, 1969).

Expertise A type of credibility that refers to the extent to which the speaker possesses the relevant knowledge to produce arguments backed by facts for the audience on that topic.

Explicit persuasive message When all of the aspects of the message are clearly stated, such as the conclusion and the sources of information.

External messages In hierarchical attitude theory, external messages refers to influences on someone's attitude that come from outside the person, such as advertisements and statements from others.

Extraversion One of the Big Five personality traits in which those exhibiting high levels of this trait tend to be particularly outgoing and energetic.

Forewarning effect An audience who learns that someone will soon try to persuade them tends to resist persuasion more than an audience who did not receive that information.

Free behaviors In the context of reactance theory, free behaviors refers to behaviors that people believe they could potentially choose to perform or not to perform.

Frequency (of behavior) The proportion of time that someone performs a behavior.

Gain-framed message Messages emphasizing the benefits from adopting the persuasive message recommendations. Thought to enhance persuasiveness when the audience has an approach motivational orientation.

Generalization effect A situation in which a persuasive message modifies not only the focal attitude but also a related attitude.

Generic messages In the context of audience adaptation, generic messages refers to messages adapted to the cultural level of information about the audience, reflecting very minimal adaptation.

Goodwill A type of credibility that refers to the extent to which the audience believes the speaker has their best interests at heart

Hardcore In the context of spiral of silence theory, hardcore refers to people who hold unpopular positions and show a general indifference to social pressure.

Hard-core People who exhibit particularly strong resistance to attitude change.

Hierarchical model A model of attitude structure and change that posits that attitude networks show evidence consistent with a structure with more abstract attitudes and values at the top exerting conformity pressure on increasingly concrete attitudes in the lower areas.

Identification When people attempt to model their behavior on an individual or group with whom the person wants to resemble as much as possible.

Identified When people think of some object or group as part of their own self-concept.

Ideology A consistent set of views on a constellation of related attitudes.

Imagined supporter explanation (of a CME) An explanation of why insults may cause a CME such that someone who receives an insult calls to mind someone respectable who holds the opposite opinion as the insulter. The target of the insult then adopts the attitude of this respectable person.

Immediacy The extent to which someone can communicate with nearby others.

Impressionable years explanation The hypotheses that the likelihood of persuasion declines as people get older such that their attitudes change easily until they reach early adulthood, at which point the likelihood of attitude change declines rapidly.

Increasing-persistence explanation The hypothesis that the likelihood of changing someone's attitudes declines slowly as they age.

Inductive argument An argument in which the conclusion follows from the premises with more or less certainty or higher or lower probability.

Ineffective persuasion attempt When the audience's attitudes remain unchanged after someone tries to persuade them.

Informal fallacy A type of poor reasoning in which the fault lies in the premises.

Information overload When having access to large amounts of information makes decisions harder rather than easier because people have difficulty sorting through all the information available.

Information seeking When people attempt to find more information about a topic after exposure to a persuasive message.

Information sufficiency When people believe they have enough information to form a useful attitude, they stop seeking more information.

Injunctive norms The perception of what others approve/disapprove or what people "ought to"/"ought not to" do.

Inoculation In the context of inoculation theory, inoculation refers to the process of causing people's attitudes to resist persuasion better by first exposing them to a weak persuasive message and then offering them arguments to help refute that message.

Intelligence The capacity to learn and to apply that knowledge

Intensity (of behavior) How difficult or time consuming the behavior related to an attitude one performs is.

Internal messages In hierarchical attitude theory, internal messages refers to the consistent pressure exerted on attitudes and values at the higher parts of the hierarchy on attitudes in the lower part.

Interpersonal level information The most specific level of knowing someone such that you know information specific to that person.

Intra-audience effects The effect of others in our immediate physical environment on our judgments, affect, and behavior.

Knowledge function When attitudes serve to help us make sense of our experiences, we say that they serve a knowledge function.

Latency (of behavior) The speed of an action, e.g., how quickly one buys a product after being exposed to an advertisement promoting it.

Legitimate power Influencing agents have legitimate power to the extent that others believe that the influencing agents have a legitimate right to tell them what to do.

Life-long openness explanation An explanation for the relationship between age and persuasibility. It asserts that there are no differences in persuasibility across the life course.

Life-stages explanation An explanation for the relationship between age and persuasibility. It asserts that younger and older people are more easily persuaded than those in their middle years.

LOA Latitude of acceptance. The LOA is a region on the attitude continuum consisting of those positions that one finds reasonable or tolerable. One's own attitude would be found in this region.

LON Latitude of noncommitment. The LON is a region on the attitude continuum consisting of those positions that one neither endorses nor finds unacceptable.

LOR Latitude of rejection. The LOR is a region on the attitude continuum consisting of those message positions that one finds unacceptable, unreasonable, and perhaps intolerable.

Loss-framed messages Persuasive messages emphasizing the costs of failing to adopt message recommendations.

Match (attitude-behavior) The extent to which a measure of attitude and a measure of behavior are equally specific. Equally specific (e.g., attitude toward getting a tetanus shot and the behavior of getting or not getting a tetanus shot) measures are said to match.

Mavens Experts in a specific knowledge domain.

Meaningful existence The way(s) in which a people justify their lives to themselves and others.

Means control Others have means control over us to the extent that they control what rewards us, what we find punishing, or both.

Memory-based processing The process of shaping, reinforcing, or modifying an attitude based upon what you can recall.

Mere measurement effect The difference in behavior produced by asking or not asking people to report their behavioral intention.

Message A set of symbolic stimuli designed to change attitudes.

Message environment The number and mix of messages on a particular topic to which one is exposed.

Message fatigue One experiences message fatigue when one tires of being exposed to similar messages.

Modify (an attitude) To make an attitude something other than it was initially, such as when a persuasive message might modify someone with a favorable attitude toward capital punishment to adopt an unfavorable attitude toward capital punishment.

Modus ponens (mode that affirms) A valid argument structure with premises of the form: (1) If A, then B and (2) A, and (3) the conclusion: Therefore B.

Need for cognition An intrinsic motive that leads to a tendency to engage in and enjoy thinking.

Negative affect Unpleasant feelings including emotions such as guilt, shame, and anger.

Negative face One's personal rights, including such things as freedom of action.

Neuroticism Those high in neuroticism are characterized by sensitivity and nervousness.

Nonattitude Attitudes that show no consistency when reported over time.

Non-volitional behavior Actions that people cannot perform with complete freedom, e.g., avoiding an addiction.

Norm of reciprocity The prescription that we should help others who have helped us, and that we should avoid harming others who have helped us.

Norm of self-interest The idea that we can expect most people to act in their best interests most of the time.

Number The quantity of sources who attempt to influence a member of a social network. A pivotal concept in Latane's Social Impact Theory.

Observability A property of an innovation. A highly observable innovation is one in which others can see the results of adopting the innovation.

One-sided persuasive message A form that a persuasive message might take in which sources present only arguments advocating their point of view.

On-line processing One way in which people think about a persuasive message. When processing on-line, they form their attitude while reading or listening to the message.

Openness to experience One of the Big Five personality traits. Persons high in openness to experience are marked by inventiveness and curiosity.

Opinion The verbal expression of a belief.

Ostracism A process in which someone is excluded from a group and its activities.

Outcome involvement A property of a persuasive topic in which the manner in which the issue is settled has important personal consequences for the audience.

Overshoot An outcome of a persuasion experiment in which audience members change in the direction of the position advocated in the persuasive message to the extent that they adopt a position even more extreme than that advocated.

Partial persistence An outcome associated with the duration of persuasive message effects. Partial persistence occurs when, after an initial change in attitude as a result of exposure to a persuasive message, the attitude moves back somewhat toward its pre-message exposure position. Nevertheless, it remains closer to the initially changed attitude than it does toward the original attitude.

Perceived behavioral control A sense that one has the ability to control an aspect of their behavior, self-efficacy.

Persistence explanation An explanation of the effect of age on persuasibility. It asserts that persuasibility remains uniform across the life course.

Personal responsibility In dissonance theory, personal responsibility is proposed as a condition necessary to bring about cognitive dissonance. It refers to being unable to blame anyone else for the performance of an act that harms another.

Persuaders In the context of diffusion, a persuader is a member of a social network who is exceptionally skilled at convincing others. Persuaders engage in argument frequently, are audience adapted, and are reluctant to concede contested points.

Persuasibility The extent to which one is easily persuaded.

Persuasive communication Persuasive communication occurs when a source transmits a message to an audience through a channel with the purpose of changing an attitude.

Positive face The desire to be appreciated and respected by others.

Potency A property of action (behavior) which focuses on the intensity, duration, or both of the act.

Pragmatic (evaluation of an argument) A method of argument criticism in which one examines additional lines of argument that leads to a different conclusion than the argument being criticized.

Premise A part of the structure of an argument, premises are statements that provide reasons for agreeing with the conclusion of the argument.

Priming The act of creating experiences that increase the likelihood of a particular idea coming to mind.

Punishment Physical or psychological stimuli that we judge as aversive. They serve as disincentives.

Qualifier The degree of force which the data confer on the claim, e.g, "definitely" or "probably."

Quantitative information (providing or not providing) A feature of a persuasive message that makes it more (when quantitative information is provided) or less (when it is not) explicit.

Reactance Classically, an unpleasant psychological state said to arise when free behaviors are eliminated or threatened with elimination. In contemporary work, reactance is thought of as occurring when a persuasive message generates negative thoughts and counterarguments on the part of the audience.

Rebuttal In the Toulmin Model, a rebuttal points out exceptions to the warrant.

Refutational two-sided message A type of persuasive message in which sources present an opponent's arguments, refute them (i.e., provides arguments counter to them), and presents arguments in favor of their own position.

Refute (refutation) A refutation refers to providing arguments that counter the position advocated in a persuasive message.

Reinforce To reinforce an attitude is to make it stronger.

Relative advantage A property of an innovation, relative advantage refers to the extent that it improves what it replaced.

Resistance Those whose attitudes remain the same after exposure to a persuasive message as they were before exposure to that message have exhibited resistance.

Rewards Physical objects or psychological states that people desire to obtain; incentives.

Selective exposure A tendency to seek or avoid information. Usually people seek information consistent with their attitudes and avoid information inconsistent with them.

Sleeper effect An empirical phenomenon in which audience attitudes do not change immediately after exposure to a persuasive message, but emerge later on delayed post-tests.

Shape To shape someone's attitude is to create an attitude on an issue for which they had no previous attitude.

Social equity explanation (of a CME) An explanation of how insults might produce a counterproductive message effect. Exposing oneself to a persuasive message is considered an investment or reward. A speaker would be expected to reciprocate by being polite. An insult is a violation of that agreement, and leads to reciprocating the insult by changing one's attitude so as to make it more objectionable to the source of the insulting persuasive message.

Social impact A theory developed by Bibb Latane and his colleagues that asserts that influence (social impact) results from three forces: the strength of the source of the influence, the immediacy of the influence, and the number of influencing agents.

Social support In the context of cognitive dissonance theory, "social support" refers to others who agree with our beliefs or who embrace our attitudes.

Social validation The process of drawing confidence in one of your attitudes from your memory of all of the people who agree with you.

Socialization The process of learning to act in ways expected by the groups of which one is a member.

Sociological level information Knowledge of some of the groups to which a persuasive target belongs.

Source Someone who transmits a persuasive message.

Source derogation A process in which a speaker's arguments are devalued because the audience focuses criticism on the speaker's motives or personal characteristics.

Spiral of silence A tendency for people who perceive that their position on an issue is in the minority to feel isolated, and thus to refrain from expressing their opinion. Such a process results in those who perceive that their position is held by the majority of others to dominate the message environment.

Stories/narratives (message property) A form a persuasive message might take. In an extreme case, the script of a film or television program may be constructed so as to convince the audience to adopt a certain attitude or action. In a less extreme case, the script may be a short depiction of a series of events, such as telling the story of a young person who developed skin cancer as a result of overexposure to the sun, as a means of promoting sunscreen use.

Strength (of a persuasive message) The strength of a persuasive message is assessed by how closely it moves the audience's attitude toward the attitude advocated by the speaker.

Subjective norm What we believe significant others, such as parents and friends, want us to do coupled with our motivation to conform to their wishes.

Successful persuasion attempt A completely successful persuasive attempt would result in the audience adopting the speaker's position. Moving the audience to adopt a position closer to the speaker's than they originally had would still be classified as successful, albeit less so.

Syntax (of an argument) In the context of argumentation, syntax refers to the structure of an argument, i.e., the number and type(s) of premises and the form of the conclusion.

Tailored messages Very personalized persuasive messages. At its most extreme a tailored message would be designed specially to persuade one person.

Targeted messages Messages designed to persuade someone based upon the (usually) demographic groups (e.g., teenagers, Latinas, males) of which they are a member.

Threat In the context of cognitive dissonance theory, persuasive message may challenge, and hence threaten, one's existing attitudes.

Total attitude decay When one's attitude changes in response to a persuasive message, but then, after a period of time, returns to its original position (decays).

Total persistence (maintenance) When one's attitude changes in response to a persuasive message, and then changes no longer.

Toulmin's model A schema designed by Stephen Toulmin to analyze reasoning. It included the components of data, warrant, claim, qualifier, backing, and rebuttal.

Transportation Transportation occurs when those listening to a persuasive narrative become so engaged in the story that they focus on it only, to the exclusion of other thoughts, such as critical thoughts.

Trialability Refers to the extent to which an adopter of an innovation or innovative idea can try it on a limited basis initially.

Trustworthiness A property of audience perceptions of the source of a persuasive message. The highly trustworthy source is someone who the audience expects will tell them the truth if the source knows the truth.

Two-sided persuasive message A type of persuasive message that presents arguments both for the side it advocates and for the opposing side. Two-sided refutational messages also include refutations of the arguments for the opposing side.

Two-step flow An explanation of how media affect people's attitude, beliefs, and behavior. Media are said to affect opinion leaders (first step) who, in turn, affect others who are not opinion leaders (second step).

Unexpectedness (message property) A property of a persuasive message that involves surprising the audience as a means of gaining their attention.

Utilitarian function (of attitudes) Attitudes that promote features of the environment found to be rewarding, and discourage those found as punitive. Synonyms include the "adjustive function" and the "instrumental function."

Valid argument A structure of related statements in which the conclusion follows necessarily, given rules of logic, from premises.

Value Exceptionally general or abstract attitudes, such as benevolence, power, or conformity.

Value-expressive function (of attitudes) Attitudes that exist to promote self-expression that might, in turn, result in receiving approval from important others or important reference groups.

Value-relevant involvement A property of an issue that helps them sustain their sense of identity, or a psychological state that results from focusing on attitudes that are linked closely to our values. See also, ego-involvement.

Volitional behavior Actions that people can choose to do freely, such as for whom to vote, as contrasted with action people cannot control, such as addiction.

Warrant The general rule that connects the data to the claim in the Toulmin Model.

References

Abelson, R. P., & Miller, J. C. (1967). Negative persuasion via personal insult. *Journal of Experimental Social Psychology*, 3(4), 321–333. https://doi.org/10.1016/0022-1031(67)90001-7

Ahn, A., & Min, D. (2018). Exploring the effect of time horizon perspective on persuasion: Focusing on both biological and embodied age. *Sustainability*, 10(12), 1–15. https://doi.org/10.3390/su10124375

Ajzen, I. (1991). The theory of planned behavior. *Organizational Behavior and Human Decision Processes*, 50(2), 179–211. https://doi.org/10.1016/0749-5978(91)90020-t

Albarracin, D., Johnson, B.T., Fishbein, M., & Muellerleile, P.A. (2001). Theories of reasoned action and planned behavior as models of condom use: A meta-analysis. *Psychological Bulletin*, 127(1), 142–161. https://doi.org/10.1037/0033-2909.127.1.142

Alkış, N., & Temizel, T. T. (2015). The impact of individual differences on influence strategies. *Personality and Individual Differences*, 87, 147–152. https://doi.org/10.1016/j.paid.2015.07.037

Allen, M. (1991). Meta-analysis comparing the persuasiveness of one-sided and two-sided messages. *Western Journal of Speech Communication*, 55(4), 390–404. https://doi.org/10.1080/00909889509365420

Allen, M. (1993). Determining the persuasiveness of message sidedness: A prudent note about utilizing research summaries. *Western Journal of Communication*, 57(1), 98–103. https://doi.org/10.1080/10570319309374433

Allen, M., Hale, J., Mongeau, P., Berkowitz-Stafford, S., Stafford, S., Shanahan, W., Agee, P., Dillon, K., Jackson, R., & Ray, C. (1990). Testing a model of message sidedness: Three replications. *Communication Monographs*, 57(4), 275–291. https://doi.org/org/10.1080/03637759009376203

Altheide, D. L., & Johnson, J. M. (1977). Counting souls: A study of counseling at evangelical crusades. *Pacific Sociological Review*, 20(3), 323–348. https://doi.org/10.2307/1388912

Alvaro, E. M., & Crano, W. D. (2017). Reflections on Gabriel Mugny's contributions to attitude-centric theory and research on minority influence. *International Review of Social Psychology*, 30(1), 161–171. https://doi.org/10.5334/irsp.25

Alwin, D. F., Cohen, R. L., & Newcomb, T. M. (1991). *Political attitudes over the lifespan: The Bennington women after fifty years*. University of Wisconsin Press.

Anderson, N. (1971). Integration theory and attitude change. *Psychological Review*, 78(3), 171–206. https://doi.org/10.1037/h0030834

Andrews, K. R., Carpenter, C. J., Shaw, A. S., & Boster, F. J. (2008). The legitimization of paltry favors effect: A review and meta-analysis. *Communication Reports,* 21(2), 59–69. https://doi.org/10.1080/08934210802305028

Appleby, J., & Ball, T. (1999). *Jefferson: Political writings*. Cambridge University Press. https://doi.org/10.1017/CBO9781139164351

Areni, C. S., & Lutz, R. J. (1988). The role of argument quality in the elaboration likelihood model. *Advances in Consumer Research*, 15, 197–203.

Aristotle. (335 BCE/1991). *On rhetoric*. (G. A. Kennedy, Trans.). Oxford University Press.

Aronson, E. (1968a). Discussion: Commitments about commitment. In R. P. Abelson, E. Aronson, W. J. McGuire, T. M. Newcomb, M. J. Rosenberg, & P. H. Tannenbaum (Eds.), *Theories of cognitive consistency: A sourcebook* (pp. 464–466). Rand McNally.

Aronson, E. (1968b). Dissonance theory: Progress and problems. In R. P. Abelson, E. Aronson, W. J. McGuire, T. M. Newcomb, M. J. Rosenberg, & P. H. Tannenbaum (Eds.), *Theories of cognitive consistency: A sourcebook* (pp. 5–27). Rand McNally.

Asch, S. E. (1948). The doctrine of suggestion, prestige, and imitation in social psychology. *Psychological Review, 55*(5), 250–276. https://doi.org/10.1037/h0057270

Asch, S. E. (1956). Studies of independence and conformity: A minority of one against a unanimous majority. *Psychological Monographs, 70*(9), 1–70. https://doi.org/10.1037/h0093718.

Banas, J. A., & Miller, G. (2013). Inducing resistance to conspiracy theory propaganda: Testing inoculation and metainoculation strategies. *Human Communication Research, 39*(2), 184–207. https://doi.org/10.1111/hcre.12000

Banas, J. A., & Rains, S. A. (2010). A meta-analysis of research on inoculation theory. *Communication Monographs, 77*(3), 281–311. https://doi.org/10.1080/03637751003758193

Bandura, A., Ross, D., & Ross, S. A. (1963). Imitation of film-mediated aggressive models. *Journal of Abnormal and Social Psychology, 66*(1), 3–11. https://doi.org/10.1037/h0048687

Barker, E. (1995). *The politics of Aristotle*. Oxford University Press.

Barry, J. M. (2018). *The great influenza: The story of the deadliest pandemic in history*. Penguin Books.

Bassili, J. N. (1996). Meta-judgmental versus operative indexes of psychological attributes: The case of measures of attitude strength. *Journal of Personality and Social Psychology, 71*(4), 637–653. https://doi.org/10.1037/0022-3514.71.4.637

Baumeister, R. F. (2005). *The cultural animal: Human nature, meaning, and social life*. Oxford University Press.

Baumgardner, M. H., Leippe, M. R., Ronis, D. L., & Greenwald, A. G. (1983). In search of reliable persuasion effects: II. Associate interference and persistence of persuasion in a message-dense environment. *Journal of Personality and Social Psychology, 45*(3), 524–537. https://doi.org/10.1037/0022-3514.45.3.524

Biek, M., Wood, W., & Chaiken, S. (1996). Working knowledge, cognitive processing, and attitudes: On the determinants of bias. *Personality and Social Psychology Bulletin, 22*(6), 547–556. https://doi.org/10.1177/0146167296226001

Bitner, M. J., & Obermiller, C. (1985). The elaboration likelihood model: Limitations and extensions in marketing. *Advances in Consumer Research, 12*, 420–425.

Bond, B. J., & Drogos, K. L. (2014). Sex on the shore: Wishful identification and parasocial relationships as mediators in the relationship between *Jersey Shore* exposure and emerging adults' sexual attitudes and behaviors. *Media Psychology, 17*(1), 102–126. https://doi.org/10.1080/15213269.2013.872039

Boster, F. J., Carpenter, C. J., & Kotowski, M. R. (2015). Validation studies of the maven scale. *Social Influence, 10*, 85–96. https://doi.org/10.1080/15534510.2014.939224

Boster, F. J., Fryrear, J. E., Mongeau, P. A., & Hunter, J. E. (1982). An unequal speaking linear discrepancy model: Implications for polarity shift. In M. Burgoon (Ed.), *Communication yearbook 6* (pp. 395–418). SAGE Publications. https://doi.org/10.1080/23808985.1982.11678505

Boster, F. J., Hunter, J. E., & Hale, J. L. (1991). An information-processing model of jury decision making. *Communication Research, 18*, 524–547. https://doi.org/10.1177/009365091018004004

Boster, F. J., Kotowski, M. R., Andrews, K. R., & Serota, K. (2011). Identifying influence: Development and validation of the connectivity, persuasiveness, and maven scales. *Journal of Communication, 61*, 178–196. https://doi.org/10.1111/j.1460-2466.2010.01531.x

Boster, F. J., Liu, R. W., Cheng, Y., Kim, W., & Shaikh, S. J. (2018). The suasory force of sticky messages: An application to the application of sunscreen. *Communication Studies, 69*(1), 4–22. https://doi.org/10.1080/10510974.2017.1414067

Boster, F. J., Mayer, M. E., Hunter, J. E., & Hale, J. L. (1980). Expanding the persuasive arguments explanation of the polarity shift: A linear discrepancy model. In D. Nimmo (Ed.), *Communication yearbook 4* (pp. 165–176). Transaction Books. https://doi.org/10.1080/23808985.1980. 11923801

Boster, F. J., Rodríguez, J. I., Cruz, M. G., & Marshall, L. (1995). The relative effectiveness of a direct request message and a pregiving message on friends and strangers. *Communication Research, 22*(4), 475–484. https://doi.org/10.1177/009365095022004005

Boster, F. J., Shaw, A. Z., Carpenter, C. J., & Lindsey, L. L. M. (2014). Simulation of a dynamic theory of reasoned action. *Simulation & Gaming, 45*(6), 699–731. https://doi.org/10.1177/1046878114562930

Bostrom, R. N. (1964). Dogmatism, rigidity, and rating behavior. *Speech Teacher, 13*(4), 283–287. https://doi.org/10.1080/03634526409377388

Braddock, K., & Dillard, J. P. (2016). Meta-analytic evidence for the persuasive effect of narratives on beliefs, attitudes, intentions, and behaviors. *Communication Monographs, 83*(4), 446–467. https://doi.org/10.1080/03637751.2015.1128555

Brehm, J. W. (1966). *A theory of psychological reactance.* Academic Press.

Brehm, S. S., & Brehm, J. W. (1981). *Psychological reactance: A theory of freedom and control.* Academic Press.

Buller, D. B. (1986). Distraction during persuasive communication: A meta-analytic review. *Communication Monographs, 53*(2), 91–114. https://doi.org/10.1080/03637758609376130

Burger, J. M. (2009). Replicating Milgram: Would people still obey today? *American Psychologist, 64*(1), 1–11. https://doi.org/10.1037/a0010932

Burgoon, M., Pfau, M., & Birk, T. S. (1995). An inoculation theory explanation for the effects of corporate issue/advocacy advertising campaigns. *Communication Research, 22*(4), 485–505. https://doi.org/10.1177/009365095022004006

Byrne, D. E. (1971). *The attraction paradigm.* Academic Press.

Cacioppo, J. T., & Petty, R. E. (1982). The need for cognition. *Journal of Personality and Social Psychology, 42*(1), 116–131. https://doi.org/10.1037//0022-3514.42.1.116

Cacioppo, J. T., Petty, R. E., Feinstein, J. A., & Jarvis, W.B.G. (1996). Dispositional differences in cognitive motivation: The life and times of individuals varying in need for cognition. *Psychological Bulletin, 119*(2), 197–253. https://doi.org/10.1037//0033-2909.119.2.197

Cacioppo, J. T., Petty, R. E., & Kao, C. F. (1984). The efficient assessment of need for cognition. *Journal of Personality Assessment, 48*(3), 306–307. https://doi.org/10.1207/s15327752jpa4803_13

Cárdaba, M.A.M., Briñol, P., Horcajo, J., & Petty, R. E. (2013). The need for cognition on the stability of prejudiced attitudes towards South American immigrants. *Psicothema, 25*(1), 73–78. https://doi.org/10.7334/psicothema2012.107

Carpenter, C. J. (2012). A meta-analysis of the functional matching effect based on functional attitude theory. *Southern Journal of Communication, 77*(5), 438–451. https://doi.org/10.1080/10570314.2012.662307.

Carpenter, C. J. (2013). A meta-analysis of the effectiveness of the "but you are free" compliance-gaining technique. *Communication Studies, 64*(1), 6–17. https://doi.org/10.1080/10510974.2012.727941

Carpenter, C. J. (2015). A meta-analysis of the ELM's argument quality X processing type predictions. *Human Communication Research, 41*(4), 501–534. https://doi.org/10.1111/hcre.12054

Carpenter, C. J. (2019). Cognitive dissonance, ego-involvement, and motivated reasoning. *Annals of the International Communication Association, 43*, 1–23. https://doi.org/10.1080/23808985.2018.1564881

Carpenter, C. J., & Boster, F. J. (2013a). Modeling the effects of processing effort and ability in response to persuasive message arguments. *Communication Quarterly, 61*(4), 413–430. https://doi.org/10.1080/01463373.2013.799509

Carpenter, C. J., & Boster, F. J. (2013b). The relationship between message recall and persuasion: More complex than it seems. *Journal of Communication, 63*(4), 661–681. https://doi.org/10.1111/jcom.12042

Carpenter, C. J., Boster, F. J., Kotowski, M. R., & Day, J. (2015). Evidence for the validity of a social connectedness scale: Connectors amass bridging social capital online and offline. *Communication Quarterly, 63*, 119–134. https://doi.org/10.1980/01463373.2015.1012217

Carpenter, C. J., Kotowski, M. R., Boster, F. J., Andrews, K. R., Serota, K., & Shaw, A. S. (2009). Do superdiffusers argue differently? An analysis of argumentation style as a function of diffusion ability. *Argumentation and Advocacy, 45*, 151–170. https://doi.org/10.1080/00028533.2009.11821704

Cha, M., Haddadi, H., Benevenuto, F., & Gummadi, P. K. (2010). Measuring user influence in Twitter: The million follower fallacy. *ICWSM, 10*, 10–17.

Chaiken, S. (1980). Heuristic versus systematic information processing and the use of source versus message cues in persuasion. *Journal of Personality and Social Psychology, 39*(5), 752–766. https://doi.org/10.1037/0022-3514.39.5.752

Chaiken, S., & Ledgerwood, A. (2012). A theory of heuristic and systematic information processing. In P. A. M. Van Lange, A. W. Kruglanski, & E. T. Higgins (Eds.), *Handbook of theories of social psychology* (Vol. 1, pp. 246–266). SAGE Publications.

Chaiken, S., Liberman, A., & Eagly, A. H. (1989). Heuristic and systematic information processing within and beyond the persuasion context. In J. S. Uleman, & J. A. Bargh (Eds.), *Unintended thought* (pp. 212–252). Guilford Press.

Cho, H., & Boster, F. J. (2005). Development and validation of value-, outcome-, and impression-relevant involvement scales. *Communication Research, 32*(2), 235–264. https://doi.org/10.1177/0093650204273764

Chua, H. F., Liberzon, I., Welsh, R. C., & Strecher, V. J. (2009). Neural correlates of message tailoring and self-relatedness in smoking cessation programming. *Biological Psychiatry, 65*(2), 165–168. https://doi.org/10.1016/j.biopsych.2008.08.030

Cialdini, R. B. (2008). *Influence: Science and practice* (5th ed.). Allyn & Bacon. https://doi.org/10.1037//0022-3514.34.3.366

Cialdini, R. B., Borden, R. J., Thorne, A., Walker, M. R., Freeman, S., & Sloan, L. R. (1976). Basking in reflected glory: Three (football) field studies. *Journal of Personality and Social Psychology, 34*(3), 366–375. https://doi.org/10.1037//0022-3514.34.3.366

Cialdini, R. B., & Schroeder, D. A. (1976). Increasing compliance by legitimizing paltry contributions: When even a penny helps. *Journal of Personality and Social Psychology, 34*(4), 599–604. https://doi.org/10.1037/0022-3514.34.4.599

Cialdini, R. B., Vincent, J. E., Lews, S. K., Catalan, J., Wheeler, D., & Darby, B. L. (1975). Reciprocal concessions procedure for inducing compliance: The door-in-the-face technique. *Journal of Personality and Social Psychology, 31*(2), 206–215. https://doi.org/10.1037/h0076284

Cionea, I. A., Piercy, C. W., & Carpenter, C. J. (2017). A profile of arguing behaviors on Facebook. *Computers in Human Behavior, 76*, 438–449. https://doi.org/10.1016/j.chb.2017.08.009

Clark, M. S., & Mills, J. (1979). Interpersonal attraction in exchange and communal relationships. *Journal of Personality and Social Psychology, 37*(1), 12–24. https://doi.org/10.1037//0022-3514.37.1.12

Clary, E. G., & Snyder, M. (1992). Persuasive communications strategies for recruiting volunteers. In D. R. Young, R. M. Hollister, & V. A. Hodgkinson (Eds.), *Governing, leading, and managing nonprofit organizations: New insights from research and practice* (pp. 121–137). Jossey-Bass.

Cohen, J. (2001). Defining identification: A theoretical look at the identification of audiences with media characters. *Mass Communication & Society, 4*(3), 245–264. https://doi.org/10.1207/s15327825mcs0403_01

Combs, D.J.Y., & Keller, P. S. (2010). Politicians and trustworthiness: Acting contrary to self-interest enhances trustworthiness. *Basic and Applied Social Psychology, 32*(4), 328–339. https://doi.org/10.1080/01973533.2010.519246

Compton, J., & Kaylor, B. (2013). Inoculating for small pox inoculation objections in Reverend Cooper's *Letter to a friend in the country. Journal of Communication and Religion, 36*(1), 92–107.

Converse, P. E. (1964). The nature of belief systems in mass publics. In D. E. Apter (Ed.), *Ideology and discontent* (pp. 206–261). Free Press of Glencoe.

Converse, P. E. (1974). Nonattitudes and American public opinion: The status of nonattitudes. *American Political Science Review, 68*(2), 650–660. https://doi.org/10.2307/1959510

Cook, T. D., & Flay, B. R. (1978). The persistence of experimentally induced attitude change. *Advances in Experimental Social Psychology, 2*, 1–57. https://doi.org/10.1016/s0065-2601(08)60004-0

Cooper, J. (2007). *Cognitive dissonance: Fifty years of a classic theory*. SAGE Publications.

Cronkhite, G., & Goetz, E. (1971). Dogmatism, persuasibility, and attitude instability. *Journal of Communication, 21*(4), 342–352. https://doi.org/10.1111/j.1460-2466.1971.tb02933.x

Crown, D. P., & Strickland, B. R. (1961). The conditioning of verbal behavior as a function of the need for social approval. *Journal of Abnormal and Social Psychology, 63*(2), 395–401. https://doi.org/10.1037/h0046330

Cruz, M. G. (1998). Explicit and implicit conclusions in persuasive messages. In M. Allen & R. W. Preiss (Eds.), *Persuasion: Advances through meta-analysis* (pp. 217–230). Hampton.

Dalege, J., Boorsboom, D., van Harreveld, F., van den Berg, H., Conner, M., & van den Maas, H.L.J. (2016). Toward a formalized account of attitudes: The causal attitude network (CAN) model. *Psychological Review, 123*(1), 2–22. https://doi.org/10.1037/a0039802.

Danes, J. E., Hunter, J. E., & Woelfel, J. (1978). Mass communication and belief change: A test of three mathematical models. *Human Communication Research, 4*(3), 243–252. https://doi.org/10.1111/j.1468-2958.1978.tb00613.x

David, C., Cappella, J. N., & Fishbein, M. (2006). The social diffusion of influence among adolescents: Group interaction in a chat room environment about antidrug advertisements. *Communication Theory, 16*(1), 118–140. https://doi.org/10.1111/j.1468-2885.2006.00008.x

Derzon, J. H., & Lipsey, M. W. (2002). A meta-analysis of the effectiveness of mass-communication for changing substance-use knowledge, attitudes, and behavior. In W. D. Crano, M. Burgoon, & S. Oskamp (Eds.), *Mass media and drug prevention: Classic and contemporary theories and research* (pp. 231–258). Lawrence Erlbaum Associates.

Dhanesh, G. S., & Duthler, G. (2019). Relationship management through social media influencers: Effects of followers' awareness of paid endorsement. *Public Relations Review, 45*(3). https://doi.org/10.1016/j.pubrev.2019.03.002

Dillard, J. P., Fitzpatrick, M. A. (1985). Compliance-gaining in marital interaction. *Personality and Social Psychology Bulletin, 11*(4), 419–433. https://doi.org/10.1177/0146167285114008

Dillard, J. P., & Knobloch, L. K. (2011). Interpersonal influence. In M. L. Knapp & J. A. Daly (Eds.), *The SAGE handbook of interpersonal communication* (4th ed., pp. 389–422). SAGE Publications.

Dillard, J. P., & Shen, L. (2005). On the nature of reactance and its role in persuasive health communication. *Communication Monographs, 72*(2), 144–168. https://doi.org/10.1080/03637750500111815

Eagly, A. H. (1974). Comprehensibility of persuasive arguments as a determinant of opinion change. *Journal of Personality and Social Psychology, 29*(6), 758–773. https://doi.org/10.1037/h0036202

Eagly, A. H. (1978). Sex differences in influenceability. *Psychological Bulletin, 85*(1), 86–116. https://doi.org/10.1037//0033-2909.85.1.86

Eagly, A. H., & Carli, L. L. (1981). Sex of researchers and sex-typed communications as determinants of sex differences in influenceability: A meta-analysis of social influence studies. *Psychological Bulletin, 90*(1), 1–20. https://doi.org/10.1037//0033-2909.90.1.1

Eaton, A. A., Visser, P. S., & Burns, V. (2017). How gender-role salience influences attitude strength and persuasive message processing. *Psychology of Women Quarterly, 41*(2), 223–239. https://doi.org/10.1177/0361684317696257

Eaton, A. A., Visser, P. S., Krosnick, J. A., & Anand, S. (2009). Social power and attitude strength over the life course. *Personality and Social Psychology Bulletin, 35*(12), 1646–1660. https://doi.org/10.1177/0146167209349114

Eisend, M. (2006). Two-sided advertising: A meta-analysis. *International Journal of Research in Marketing, 23*(2), 187–198. https://doi.org/10.1016/j.ijresmar.2005.11.001

Emerson, J. P. (1970). Behavior in private places: Sustaining definitions of reality in gynecological examinations. In H. P. Dreitzel (Ed.), *Recent sociology: Vol. 74*(2). *Patterns of communicative behavior* (pp. 74–97). Collier-Macmillan Ltd.

Ewoldsen, D. R., Rhodes, N., & Fazio, R. H. (2015). The MODE model and its implications for studying the media. *Media Psychology, 18*(3), 312–337. https://doi.org/10.1080/15213269.2014.937440

Fazio, R. H. (1990). Multiple processes by which attitudes guide behavior: The MODE model as an integrative framework. *Advances in Experimental Social Psychology, 23*, 75–109. https://doi.org/10.1016/s0065-2601(08)60318-4

Fazio, R. H., & Olson, M. A. (2014). The MODE model: Attitude-behavior processes as a function of motivation and opportunity. In J. W. Sherman, B. Gawronski, & Y. Trope (Eds.), *Dual process theories of the social mind* (pp. 155–171). Guildford.

Festinger, L. (1957). *A theory of cognitive dissonance.* Stanford University Press.

Festinger, L. (1964). Behavior support for opinion change. *Public Opinion Quarterly, 28*(3), 404–417. https://doi.org/10.1086/267263

Festinger, L. (1983). *The human legacy.* Columbia University Press.

Festinger, L., & Carlsmith, J. M. (1959). Cognitive consequences of forced compliance. *Journal of Abnormal and Social Psychology, 58*(2), 203–210. https://doi.org/10.1037/h0041593

Festinger, L., & Maccoby, N. (1964). On resistance to persuasive communications. *Journal of Abnormal and Social Psychology, 68*(4), 359–366. https://doi.org/10.1037/h0049073

Fishbein, M., & Ajzen, I. (1975). *Belief, attitude, intention, and behavior: An introduction to theory and research.* Addison-Wesley.

Flores, S. A., & Hartlaub, M. G. (1998). Reducing rape-myth acceptance in male college students: A meta-analysis of intervention studies. *Journal of College Student Development, 39*(5), 438–448.

Freeder, S., Lenz, G. S., & Turney, S. (2018). The importance of knowing "what goes with what": Reinterpreting the evidence on policy attitude stability. *Journal of Politics, 81*(1), 274–290. https://doi.org/10.1086/700005

Freedman, J. L., & Sears, D. O. (1965). Warning, distraction, and resistance to influence. *Journal of Personality and Social Psychology*, *1*(3), 262–266. https://doi.org/10.1037/h0021872

French, J.R.P. (1956). A formal theory of social power. *Psychological Review*, *63*(3), 181–194. https://doi.org/10.1037/h0046123

Frey, K. P., & Eagly, A. H. (1993). Vividness can undermine the persuasiveness of messages. *Journal of Personality and Social Psychology*, *65*(1), 32–44. https://doi.org/10.1037/0022-3514.65.1.32

Funk, C. L. (2011). Connecting the social and biological bases of public opinion. In G. C. Edwards, L. R. Jacobs, & R. Y. Shapiro (Eds.), *The Oxford handbook of American public opinion and the media* (pp. 418–436). Oxford University Press.

Gardikiotis, A. (2011). Minority influence. *Social and Personality Compass*, *5*, 679–693. https://doi.org/10.1111/j.1751-9004.2011.00377.x

Gerber, A. S., Gimpel, J. G., Green, D. P., & Shaw, D. R. (2011). How large and long-lasting are the persuasive effects of televised campaign ads? Results from a randomized field experiment. *American Political Science Review*, *105*(1), 135–150. https://doi.org/10.1017/s000305541000047x

Guéguen, N., Silone, F., & David, M. (2015). The effect of the "evoking freedom" technique on an unusual and disturbing request. *Psychological Reports, 116*(3), 936–940. https://doi.org/10.2466/21.pr0.116k31w1

Glaser, R., Dickel, N., Liersch, B., Rees, J., Süssenbach, P., & Bohner, G. (2015). Lateral attitude change. *Personality and Social Psychology Review*, *19*(3), 257–276. https://doi.org/10.1177/1088868314546489

Glasman, L. R., & Albarracin, D. (2006). Forming attitudes that predict future behavior: A meta-analysis of the attitude-behavior relation. *Psychological Bulletin*, *132*(5), 778–822. https://doi.org/10.1037/0033-2909.132.5.778

Glynn, C. J., Hayes, A. F., & Shanahan, J. (1997). Perceived support for one's opinions and willingness to speak out: A meta-analysis of survey studies on the "spiral of silence." *Public Opinion Quarterly*, *61*, 452–463. https://doi.org/10.1086/297808

Gold, G. J., & Raven, B. H. (1992). Interpersonal influence strategies in the Churchill-Roosevelt bases-for-destroyers exchange. *Journal of Social Behavior and Personality*, *7*(2), 245–272.

Gouldner, A. W. (1960). The norm of reciprocity: A preliminary statement. *American Sociological Review*, *25*(2), 161–178. https://doi.org/10.2307/2092623

Green, M. C., & Brock, T. C. (2000). The role of transportation in the persuasiveness of public narratives. *Journal of Personality and Social Psychology*, *79*(5), 701–721. https://doi.org/10.1037//0022-3514.79.5.701

Greenwald, A. G. (1968). Cognitive learning, cognitive response to persuasion, and attitude change. In A. G. Greenwald, T. C. Brock, & T. M. Ostrum (Eds.), *Psychological foundations of attitudes* (pp. 147–170). Academic Press.

Griffin, R. J., Dunwoody, S., & Neuwirth, K. (1999). Proposed model of the relationship of risk information seeking and processing to the development of preventative behaviors. *Environmental Research*, *80*(2), S230–S245. https://doi.org/10.1006/enrs.1998.3940

Griffin, R. J., Dunwoody, S., & Yang, Z. J. (2013). Linking risk messages to information seeking and processing. *Annals of the International Communication Association*, *36*, 323–362. https://doi.org/10.1080/23808985.2013.11679138

Guéguen, N., Marchand, M., Pascual, A., & Lourel, M. (2008). Foot-in-the-door technique using a courtship request: A field experiment. *Psychological Reports, 103*(2), 529–534. https://doi.org/10.2466/pr0.103.2.529-534

Haddock, G., Maio, G. R., Arnold, K., & Huskinson, T. (2008). Should persuasion be affective or cognitive? The moderating effects of need for affect and need for cognition. *Personality and Social Psychology Bulletin, 34*(6), 769–778.

Hafer, C. L., Reynolds, K. L., & Obertynski, M. A. (1996). Message comprehensibility and persuasion: Effects of complex language in counterattitudinal appeals to laypeople. *Social Cognition, 14*(4), 317–337. https://doi.org/10.1521/soco.1996.14.4.317

Hamilton, M. A., & Hunter, J. E. (1998). A framework for understanding: Meta-analysis of the persuasion literature. In R. W. Preiss & M. Allen (Eds.), *Persuasion: Advances through meta-analysis* (pp. 1–28). Hampton Press.

Hample, D. (1977). Testing a model of value argument and evidence. *Communication Monographs, 44*(2), 106–120. https://doi.org/10.1080/03637757709390121

Hample, D. (1978). Predicting immediate belief change and adherence to argument claims. *Communication Monographs, 45*(3), 219–228. https://doi.org/10.1080/03637757809375967

Hample, D. (1979). Predicting belief and belief change using a cognitive theory of argument and evidence. *Communication Monographs, 46*(2), 142–146. https://doi.org/10.1080/03637757909376000

Hample, D. (1981). The cognitive context of argument. *Western Journal of Speech Communication, 45*(2), 148–158. https://doi.org/10.1080/10570318109374037

Hample, D. (1982). Modeling argument. In J. R. Cox & C. A. Willard (Eds.), *Advances in argumentation theory and research* (pp. 259–284). Southern Illinois University Press.

Harkins, S. G., & Petty, R. E. (1981). Effects of source magnification of cognitive effort on attitudes: An information-processing view. *Journal of Personality and Social Psychology, 40*, 401–413. https://doi.org/10.1037/0022-3514.40.3.401

Hart, P. S., & Nisbet, E. (2011). Boomerang effects in science communication: How motivated reasoning and identity cues amplify opinion polarization about climate mitigation policies. *Communication Research, 39*(6), 701–723. https://doi.org/10.1177/0093650211416646

Harvey, J., & Hays, D. G. (1972). Effect of dogmatism and authority of the source of communication upon persuasion. *Psychological Reports, 30*(1), 119–122. https://doi.org/10.1177/0146167208314871

Haslett, D. M. (1976). Distracting Stimuli: Do they elicit or inhibit counterargumentaion and attitude shift? *European Journal of Social Psychology, 6*(1), 81–94. https://doi.org/10.1002/ejsp.2420060107

Hastie, R., & Park, B. (1986). The relationship between memory and judgment depends on whether the judgment task is memory-based or on-line. *Psychological Review, 93*(3), 258–268. https://doi.org/10.1037//0033-295X.93.3.258

Haugtvedt, C. P, & Petty, R. E. (1992). Personality and persuasion: Need for cognition moderates the persistence and resistance of attitude changes. *Journal of Personality and Social Psychology, 63*(2), 308–319. https://doi.org/10.1037//0022-3514.63.2.308

Haugtvedt, C. P., Schumann, D. W., Schneier, W. L., & Warren, W. L. (1994). Advertising repetition and variation strategies: Implications for understanding attitude strength. *Journal of Consumer Research, 21*(1), 176–189. https://doi.org/10.1086/209391

Heath, C., & Heath, D. (2007). *Made to stick: Why some ideas survive and others die.* Random House Publishing Group.

Herek, G. (1987). Can functions be measured? A new perspective on the functional approach to attitudes. *Social Psychology Quarterly, 50*(4), 285–303. https://doi.org/10.2307/2786814

Herek, G. M. (1986). The instrumentality of attitudes: Toward a neofunctional theory. *Journal of Social Issues, 42*(2), 99–114. https://doi.org/10.1111/j.1540-4560.1986.tb00227x

Higgins, E. T. (1987). Self-discrepancy: A theory relating self and affect. *Psychological Review*, *94*(3), 319–340. https://doi.org/10.1037//0033-295x.94.3.319

Hill, S. J., Lo, J., Vavreck, L., & Zaller, J. (2013). How quickly we forget: The duration of persuasion effects from mass communication. *Political Communication*, *30*(4), 521–547. https://doi.org/10.1080/10584 609.2013.828143

Hirsh, J. B., Kang, S. K., & Bodenhausen, G. V. (2012). Personalized persuasion: Tailoring persuasive appeals to recipients' personality traits. *Psychological Science*, *23*(6), 578–581. https://doi. org/10.1177/0956797611436349

Hocking, J. E., Margreiter, D. G., & Hylton, C. (1977). Intra-audience effects: A field test. *Human Communication Research*, *3*, 243–249. https://doi.org/10.1111/j.1468-2958.1977.tb00522.x

Hoffer, E. (1967). *The temper of our times*. Harper & Row.

Hornikx, J., & O'Keefe, D. J. (2009). Adapting consumer advertising appeals to cultural values: A meta-analytic review of effects on persuasiveness and ad liking. *Communication Yearbook*, *33*, 39-71. https:// doi.org/10.1080/23808985.2009.11679084

Hovland, C. I., Harvey, O. J., & Sherif, M. (1957). Assimilation and contrast effects in reactions to communication and attitude change. *Journal of Abnormal and Social Psychology*, *55*(2), 244–252. https:// doi.org/10.1037/h0048480

Hovland, C. I., Janis, I. L., & Kelley, H. H. (1953). *Communication and persuasion: Psychological studies of opinion change*. Yale University Press

Hovland, C. I., Lumsdaine, A. A., & Sheffield, E. D. (1949). *Experiments on mass communication*. Princeton University Press.

Hovland, C. I., & Sherif, M. (1952). Judgmental phenomena and scales of attitude measurement: Item displacement in Thurstone Scale. *Journal of Abnormal and Social Psychology*, *47*(4), 822–832. https:// doi.org/10.1037/hoo53753

Huang, Y., & Shen, F. (2016). Effects of cultural tailoring on persuasion in cancer communication: A meta-analysis. *Journal of Communication*, *66*, 694-715, https://doi.org/10.1111/jcomm.12243

Hunter, J. E., Danes, J. E., & Cohen, S. H. (1984). *Mathematical models of attitude change: Change in single attitudes and cognitive structure*. Academic Press. https://doi.org/10.1016.c2013-0-10881-1

Hunter, J. E., Levine, R. L., & Sayers, S. E. (1976). Attitude change in hierarchical belief systems and its relationship to persuasibility, dogmatism, and rigidity. *Human Communication Research*, *3*(1), 3–28. https://doi.org/10.1111/j.1468-2958.1976.tb00501.x

Hustinx, L., van Enschot, R., & Hoeken, H. (2007). Argument quality in the elaboration likelihood model: An empirical study of strong and weak arguments in a persuasive message. In F. H. van Eemeren, J. A. Blair, C. A. Willard, & B. Garssen (Eds.), *Proceedings of the Sixth Conference of the International Society for the Study of Argumentation* (pp. 651–657). Sic Sat.

Infante, D. A., & Rancer, A. S. (1982). A conceptualization and measure of argumentativeness. *Journal of Personality Assessment*, *46*, 72–80. https://doi.org/10.1207/s15327752jpa4601_13

Innes, J. M. (1978). Selective exposure as a function of dogmatism and incentive. *Journal of Social Psychology*, *106*(2), 261–265. https://doi.org/10.1080/00224545.1978.9924177

Ivanov, B., Rains, S. A., Geegan, S. A., Vos, S. C., Haarstad, N. D., & Parker, K. A. (2017). Beyond simple inoculation: Examining the persuasive value of inoculation for audiences with initially neutral or opposing attitudes. *Western Journal of Communication*, *81*(1), 105–126. https://doi.org/10.1080/ 10570314.2016.1224917

Jacks, J. Z., & Cameron, K. A. (2003). Strategies for resisting persuasion. *Basic and Applied Social Psychology*, *25*(2), 145–161. https://doi.org/s15324834basp2502_5

Jacoby, J. (1975). Perspectives on a consumer information processing research paradigm. *Communication Research*, *2*(3), 203–215. https://doi.org/10.1177/009365027500200302

Janes, L. M., & Olson, J.M. (2000). Jeer pressure: The behavioral effects of observing ridicule of others. *Personality and Social Psychology Bulletin*, *26*(4), 474–485. https://doi.org/10.1177/0146167200266006

Janis, I. L., Lumsdaine, A. A., & Gladstone, A. I. (1951). Effects of preparatory communications on reactions to a subsequent news event. *Public Opinion Quarterly*, *15*(3), 487–518. https://doi.org/10.1086/266331

Johnson, B. T., & Eagly, A. H. (1989). Effects of involvement on persuasion: A meta-analysis. *Psychological Bulletin*, *106*(2), 290–314. https://doi.org/10.1037/0033-2909.107.3.375

Johnson, H. H., & Watkins, T. A. (1971). The effects of message repetitions on immediate and delayed attitude change. *Psychonomic Science*, *22*(2), 101–103. https://doi.org/10.3758/bf03332515

Jones, S. E., & Dieker, R. J. (1968). Effects of choice, justification, and dogmatism on audience responses to a belief-discrepant speech. *Central States Speech Journal*, *19*(4), 263–272. https://doi.org/10.1080/10510976809362939

Katz, D. (1960). The functional approach to the study of attitudes. *Public Opinion Quarterly*, *24*(2), 163–204. https://doi.org/101086/266945

Katz, E., & Fialkoff, Y. (2017). Six concepts in search of retirement. *Annals of the International Communication Association*, *41*, 86–91. https://doi.org/10.1080/23808985.2017.1291280

Katz, E., & Lazarsfeld, P. F. (1955). *Personal influence: The part played by people in the flow of mass communications*. Free Press.

Keller, E., & Berry, J. (2003). *The influentials*. Free Press.

Kelly, J. A., St. Lawrence, J. S., Diaz, Y. E., Stevenson, L. Y., Hauth, A. C., Brasfield, T. L., Kalichman, S. C., Smith, J. E., & Andrew, M. E. (1991). HIV risk behavior reduction following intervention with key opinion leaders of population: An experimental analysis. *American Journal of Public Health*, *81*, 168–171. https://doi.org/10.2105/AJPH.81.2.168

Kelly, J. A., St. Lawrence, J. S., Stevenson, L. Y., Hauth, A. C., Kalichman, S. C., Diaz, Y. E., Brasfield, T. L., Koob, J. S., & Morgan, M. G. (1992). Community AIDS/HIV risk reduction: The effects of endorsements by popular people in three cities. *American Journal of Public Health*, *82*, 1483–1489. https://doi.org/10.2105/AJPH.82.11.1483

Kiesler, C. A. (1971). *The psychology of commitment: Experiments linking behavior to belief.* Academic Press.

Kiesler, C. A., Collins, B. E., & Miller, N. (1969). *Attitude change*. Wiley. https://doi.org/10.1037/h0042717

Kiesler, C. A., & Sakumura, J. (1966). A test of a model for commitment. *Journal of Personality and Social Psychology*, *3*(3), 349–353. https://doi.org/10.1037/h0022943

Kim, D., & Benbasat, I. (2006). The effects of trust-assuring arguments on consumer trust in internet stores: Application of Toulmin's model of argumentation. *Information Systems Research*, *17*(3), 286–300. https://doi.org/10.1287/isre.1060.0093

Kim, M. S., & Hunter, J. E. (1993a). Attitude-behavior relations: A meta-analysis of attitudinal relevance and topic. *Journal of Communication*, *43*(1), 101–142. https://doi.org/10.1111/j.1460-2466.1993.tb01251.x

Kim, M. S., & Hunter, J. E. (1993b). Relationships among attitudes, behavioral intentions, and behavior. *Communication Research*, *20*(3), 331–364. https://doi.org/10.1111/j.1460-2466.1993.tb01251.x

Kim, S., Levine, T. R., & Allen, M. (2017). The intertwined model of reactance for resistance and persuasive boomerang. *Communication Research*, *44*(2), 931–951. https://doi.org/10.1177/0093650214548575

Kleck, R. E., & Wheaton, J. (1967). Dogmatism and responses to opinion-consistent and opinion-inconsistent information. *Journal of Personality and Social Psychology*, 5(2), 249–252. https://doi.org/10.1037/h0024197

Klofstad, C. A. (2007). Talk leads to recruitment: How discussions about politics and current events increase civic participation. *Political Research Quarterly*, 60(2), 180–191. https://doi.org/10.1177/1065912907301708

Kraus, S. J. (1995). Attitudes and the prediction of behavior: A meta-analysis of the empirical literature. *Personality and Social Psychology Bulletin*, 21(1), 58–75. https://doi.org/10.1177/0146167295211007

Krcmar, M., & Green, K. (2000). Connections between violent television exposure and adolescent risk taking. *Media Psychology*, 2(3), 195–217. https://doi.org/10.1207/s1532785xmep0203_1

Krosnick, J. A, & Alwin, D. F. (1989). Aging and susceptibility to attitude change. *Journal of Personality and Social Psychology*, 57(3), 416–425. https://doi.org/10.1037//0022-3514.57.3.416

Krosnick, J. A., Boninger, D. S., Chuang, Y. C., Berent, M. K., & Carnot, C. G. (1993). Attitude strength: One construct or many related constructs? *Journal of Personality and Social Psychology*, 65(6), 1132–1151. https://doi.org/10.1037//0022-3514.65.6.1132

Kruglanski, A. W., & Thompson, E. P. (1999). Persuasion by a single route: A view from the unimodel. *Psychological Inquiry*, 10(2), 83–109. https://doi.org/10.1207/s15327965pl100201

Ksiazkiewicz, A., Klemmensen, R., Dawes, C. T., Christensen, K., McGue, M., Krueger, R. F., & Nørgaard, A. S. (2020). Sources of stability in social and economic ideological orientations: Cohort, context, and construct effects. *International Journal of Public Opinion Research*. https://doi.org/10.1093/ijpor/edz047

Kuhn, D. (1991). *The skills of argument*. Cambridge University Press.

Kumkale, G. T., & Albarracín, D. (2004). The sleeper effect in persuasion: A meta-analytic review. *Psychological Bulletin*, 130(1), 143–172. https://doi.org/10.1037/0033-2909.130.1.143

Kunda, Z. (1999). *Social cognition: Making sense of people*. MIT Press

Lam, S. K., Ahearne, M., Hu, Y., & Schillewaert, N. (2010). Resistance to brand switching when a radically new brand is introduced: A social identity theory perspective. *Journal of Marketing*, 74(6), 128–146. https://doi.org/10.1509/jmkg.74.6.128

LaPiere, R. T. (1934). Attitudes vs. actions. *Social Forces*, 13(2), 230–237. https://doi.org/10.2307/2570339

Latané, B. (1981). The psychology of social impact. *American Psychologist*, 36, 343–356. https://doi.org/10.1037/0003-066X.36.4.343

Lazarsfeld, P. F., Berelson, B., & Gaudet, H. (1944). *The people's choice. How the voter makes up his mind in a presidential campaign*. Duell, Sloan & Pearce.

Levav, J., & Fitzsimons, G. J. (2006). When questions change behavior: The role of ease of representation. *Psychological Science*, 17(3), 207–213. https://doi.org/10.1111/j.1467-9280.2006.01687.x

Levitan, L. C., & Visser, P. S. (2009). Social network composition and attitude strength: Exploring the dynamics within newly formed social networks. *Journal of Experimental Social Psychology*, 45(5), 1057–1067. https://doi.org/10.1016/j.jesp.2009.06.001

Lewan, P. C., & Stotland, E. (1961). The effects of prior information on susceptibility to an emotional appeal. *Journal of Abnormal and Social Psychology*, 62(2), 450–453. https://doi.org/10.1037/h0040869

Lewin, K. (1947). Group decision and social change. In T. Newcomb & E. L. Hartley (Eds.), *Readings in social psychology* (pp. 330–344). Holt.

Lewis, M. A., & Rook, K. S. (1999). Social control in personal relationships: Impact on health behaviors and psychological distress. *Health Psychology*, 18(1), 63–71. https://doi.org/10.1037//0278-6133.18.1.63

Li, F., & Du, T. C. (2011). Who is talking? An ontology-based opinion leader identification framework for word-of-mouth marketing in online social blogs. *Decision Support Systems, 51*, 190–197. https://doi.org/10.1016/j.dss.2010.12.007

Liska, A. E. (1974). Emergent issues in the attitude-behavior consistency controversy. *American Sociological Review, 39*(2), 261–272. https://doi.org/10.2307/1388599

Longshore, D., Ghosh-Dastidar, B., & Ellickson, P. L. (2006). National youth anti-drug media campaign and school-based drug prevention: Evidence for a synergistic effect in ALERT plus. *Addictive Behaviors, 31*(3), 496–508. https://doi.org/10.1016/j.addbeh.2005.05.032

Lowery, S. A., & DeFleur, M. L. (1995). *Milestones in mass communication research.* Longman. https://doi.org/10.1080/08821127.1988.10731159

Lowrey, T. M. (1998). The effects of syntactic complexity on advertising persuasiveness. *Journal of Consumer Psychology, 7*(2), 187–206. https://doi.org/10.1207/s15327663jcp0702_04

Lumsdaine, A. A., & Janis, I. L. (1953). Resistance to "counterpropaganda" produced by one-sided and two-sided "propaganda" presentations. *Public Opinion Quarterly, 17*(3), 311–318. https://doi.org/10.1086/266464

Mackie, D. M., & Asuncion, A. G. (1990). On-line and memory-based modification of attitudes: Determinants of message recall-attitude change correspondence. *Journal of Personality and Social Psychology, 59*(1), 5–16. https://doi.org/10.1037//0022-3514.59.1.5

Marwell, G., Aiken, M. T., & Demerath, N. J. (1987). The persistence of political attitudes among 1960s civil rights activists. *Public Opinion Quarterly, 51*(3), 359–375. https://doi.org/10.1086/269041

Matz, S. C., Kosinski, M. Nave, G., & Stillwell, D. J. (2017). Psychological targeting as an effective approach to digital mass persuasion. *PNAS, 114*(48), 12714–12719. https://doi.org/10.1073/pnas.1710966114

McCrae, R. R., & Costa, P. T. (1987). Validation of the five-factor model of personality across instruments and observers. *Journal of Personality and Social Psychology, 52*(1), 81–90. https://doi.org/10.1037/0022-3514.52.1.81.PMID3820081

McCroskey, J. C. (1969). A summary of experimental research on the effects of evidence in persuasive communication. *Quarterly Journal of Speech, 55*(2), 169–176. https://doi.org/10.1080/00335636909382942

McCroskey, J. C., & Tevin, J. J. (1999). Goodwill: A reexamination of the construct and its measurement. *Communication Monographs, 66*(1), 90–103. https://doi.org/10.1080/03637759909376464

McGuire, W. J. (1960). Cognitive consistency and attitude change. *Journal of Abnormal and Social Psychology, 60*(3), 345–353. https://doi.org/10.1037/h0048563

McGuire, W. J. (1964). Inducing resistance to persuasion: Some contemporary approaches. *Advances in Experimental Social Psychology, 1*, 191–229. https://doi.org/10.1016/S0065-2601(08)60052-0

McGuire, W. J. (1968). Personality and susceptibility to social influence. In E. Borgatta & W. Lambert (Eds.), *Handbook of personality theory and research* (pp. 1130–1187). Rand McNally.

McGuire, W. J. (1985). Attitudes and attitude change. In G. Lindzey & E. Aronson (Eds.), *The handbook of social psychology* (Vol. 2, 3rd ed., pp. 233–346). Random House.

Meppelink, C. S., Smit, E. G., Fransen, M. L., & Diviani, N. (2019). "I was right about vaccination": Confirmation bias and health literacy in online health information seeking. *Journal of Health Communication, 24*(2), 129–140. https://doi.org/10.1080/10810730.2019.1583701

Mercier, H., & Sperber, D. (2011). Why do humans reason? Arguments for an argumentative theory. *Brain and Behavioral Sciences, 34*(2), 57–111. https://doi.org/10.1017/s0140525x10000968

Milgram, S. (1974). *Obedience to authority.* Harper & Row.

Milgram, S., & Sabini, J. (1983). On maintaining social norms: A field experiment in the subway. In H. H. Blumberg, A. P. Hare, V. Kent, & M. Davies (Eds.), *Small groups and social interaction* (Vol. 1, pp. 185–193). Wiley.

Miller, D. T. (1999). The norm of self-interest. *American Psychologist, 54*(12), 1053–1060. https://doi.org/10.1037//0003-066x.54.12.1053

Miller, G. R., & Steinberg, M. (1975). *Between people: A new analysis of interpersonal communication.* Science Research Associates.

Miller, N. (1965). Involvement and dogmatism as inhibitors of attitude change. *Journal of Experimental Social Psychology, 1*(2), 121–135. https://doi.org/10.1016/0022-1031(65)90040-5

Misyak, J., Noguchi, T., & Chater, N. (2016). Instantaneous conventions: The emergence of flexible communicative symbols. *Psychological Science, 27*(12), 1550–1561. https://doi.org/10.1177/0956797616661199

Mongeau, P. A., & Stiff, J. B. (1993). Specifying the causal relationships in the elaboration likelihood model. *Communication Theory, 3*(1), 65–72. https://doi.org/10.1111/j.1468-2885.1993.tb00057.x

Moore, C., & Kaag, J. (2020). The uncertainty principle. *American Scholar. Spring,* 32–43. https://theamericanscholar.org/the-uncertainty-principle

Moscovici, S., & Zavalloni, M. (1969). The group as a polarizer of attitudes. *Journal of Personality and Social Psychology, 12,* 125–135. https://doi.org/10.1037/h0027568

Munch, J. M., Boller, G. W., & Swasy, J. L. (1993). The effects of argument structure and affective tagging on product attitude formation. *Journal of Consumer Research, 20*(2), 294–302. https://doi.org/10.1086/209350

Munroe, R. (2008, February 20). Duty calls. *xkcd.* https://xkcd.com/386/

Neuwirth, K., Dunwoody, S., & Griffin, R. J. (2000). Protection motivation and risk communication. *Risk Analysis, 20*(5), 721–734. https://doi.org/10.1111/0272-4332.205065

Newcomb, T. M. (1961). *The acquaintance process.* Holt, Rinehart & Winston

Newcomb, T. M., Koenig, K. E., Flacks, R., & Warwick, D. P. (1967). *Persistence and change: Bennington College after 25 years.* Wiley.

Noar, S. M. (2006). A 10-year retrospective of research in health mass media campaigns: Where do we go from here? *Journal of Health Communication, 11,* 21–42. https://doi.org/10.1080/10810730500461059

Noelle-Neumann, E. (1974). The spiral of silence: A theory of public opinion. *Journal of Communication, 24,* 43–51. https://doi.org/10.1111/j.1460-2466.1974.tb00367.x

O'Keefe, D. J. (1993). The persuasive effects of message sidedness variations: A cautionary note concerning Allen's (1991) meta-analysis. *Western Journal of Communication, 57*(1), 87–97. https://doi.org/10.1080/10570319309374432

O'Keefe, D. J. (1997). Standpoint explicitness and persuasive effect: A meta-analytic review of the effects of varying conclusion articulation in persuasive messages. *Argumentation and Advocacy, 34*(1), 1–12. https://doi.org/10.1080/00028533.1997.11978023

O'Keefe, D. J. (1998). Justification explicitness and persuasive effect: A meta-analytic review of the effects of varying support articulation in persuasive messages. *Argumentation and Advocacy, 35*(2), 61–75. https://doi.org/10.1080/00028533.1998.11951621

O'Keefe, D. J., & Hale, S. L. (2001). An odds-ratio-based meta-analysis of research on the door-in-the-face influence strategy. *Communication Reports, 14*(1), 31–38. https://doi.org/10.1080/08934210109367734

Olson, J. M., Vernon, P. A., Harris, J. A., & Jang, K. L. (2001). The heritability of attitudes: A study of twins. *Journal of Personality and Social Psychology, 80*(6), 845–860. https://doi.org/10.1037/0022-3514.80.6.845

Ostrom, T. M., Brock, T. C. (1969). Cognitive bonding to central values and resistance to a communication advocating change in policy orientation. *Journal of Experimental Research in Personality, 4*(1), 42–50.

Palmer, D. L., & Kalin, R. (1985). Dogmatic responses to belief dissimilarity in the "bogus stranger" paradigm. *Journal of Personality and Social Psychology, 48*(1), 171–179. https://doi.org/10.1037/0022-3514.48.1.171

Park, H. S., Levine, T. R., Westerman, C. Y. K., Orfgen, T., & Foregger, S. (2007). The effect of argument quality and involvement type on attitude formation and attitude change: A test of dual-process and social judgment predictions. *Human Communication Research, 33*(1), 81–102. https://doi.org/10.1111/j.1468-2958.2007.00290.x

Parker, K. A., Ivanov, B., & Compton, J. (2012). Inoculation's efficacy with young adults' risky behaviors: Can inoculation confer cross-protection over related but untreated issues? *Health Communication, 27*(3), 223–233. https://doi.org/10.1080/10410236.2011.575541

Petty, R. E., & Cacioppo, J. T. (1979). Effects of forewarning of persuasive intent and involvement on cognitive responses and persuasion. *Personality and Social Psychology Bulletin, 5*(2), 173–176. https://doi.org/10.1177/014616727900500209

Petty, R. E., & Cacioppo, J. T. (1980). Issue involvement as a moderator of the effects on attitude of advertising content and context. *Advances in Consumer Research, 8,* 20–24.

Petty, R. E. & Cacioppo, J. T. (1981). *Attitudes and persuasion; Classic and contemporary approaches.* Taylor & Francis.

Petty, R. E. & Cacioppo, J. T. (1986). *Communication and persuasion: Central and peripheral routes to attitude change.* Springer-Verlag.

Petty, R. E., Cacioppo, J. T., & Goldman, R. (1981). Personal involvement as a determinant of argument-based persuasion. *Journal of Personality and Social Psychology, 41*(5), 847–855. https://doi.org/10.1037/0022-3514.41.5.847

Petty, R. E., Cacioppo, J. T., Kasmer, J. A., Haugtvedt, C.P. (1987). A reply to Stiff and Boster. *Communication Monographs, 54*(3), 257–263. https://doi.org/10.1080/03637758709390231

Petty, R. E., Cacioppo, J. T., & Schumann, D. (1983). Central and peripheral routes to advertising effectiveness: The moderating role of involvement. *Journal of Consumer Research, 10*(2), 135–146. https://doi.org/10.1086/208954

Petty, R. E., Kasmer, J. A., Haugtvedt, C. P., & Cacioppo, J. T. (1987). Source and message factors in persuasion: A reply to Stiff's critique of the elaboration likelihood model. *Communication Monographs, 54*(3), 233–249. https://doi.org/10.1080/03637758709390229

Petty, R. E., Wegener, D. T., Fabrigar, L. R., Priester, J. R., & Cacioppo, J. T. (1993). Conceptual and methodological issues in the elaboration likelihood model of persuasion: A reply to the Michigan state critics. *Communication Theory, 3*(4), 336–362. https://doi.org/10.1111/j.1468-2885.1993.tb00078.x

Pierro, A., Mannetti, L., Kruglanski, A. W., & Sleeth-Keppler, D. (2004). Relevance override: On the reduced impact of "cues" under high-motivation conditions of persuasion studies. *Journal of Personality and Social Psychology, 86*(2), 251–264. https://doi.org/10.1037/0022-3514.86.2.251

Poole, G. J., Wood, W., & Leck, K. (1998). The self-esteem motive in social influence: Agreement with valued majorities and disagreement with derogated minorities. *Journal of Personality and Social Psychology, 75*(4), 967–975. https://doi.org/10.1037/0022-3514.75.4.967

Price, E., Ottati, V., Wilson, C., & Kim, S. (2015). Open-minded cognition. *Personality and Social Psychology Bulletin, 41*(11), 1488–1504. https://doi.org/10.1177/0146167215600528

Priester, J. R., & Petty, R. E. (1995). Source attributions and persuasion: Perceived honesty as a determinant of message scrutiny. *Personality and Social Psychology Bulletin, 21*(6), 637–645. https://doi.org/10.1177/0146167295216010

Quick, B. L., & Stephenson, M. T. (2008). Examining the role of trait reactance and sensation seeking on perceived threat, state reactance, and reactance restoration. *Human Communication Research, 34*(3), 448–476. https://doi.org/10.1111/j.1468-2958.2008.00328.x

Radke, M., & Caso, E. K. (1948). Lecture and discussion-decision as methods of influencing food habits. *Journal of the American Dietetic Association, 24*, 23–31.

Regan, D. T., & Cheng, J. B. (1973). Distraction and attitude change: A resolution. *Journal of Experimental Social Psychology, 9*(2), 138–147. https://doi.org/10.1016/0022-1031(73)90005-x

Reimer, T., Mata, R., Katsikoloulos, K., & Opwis, K. (2005). On the interplay between heuristic and systematic processes in persuasion. In B. G. Bara, L. Barsalou, & M. Bucciarelli (Eds.), *Proceedings of the twenty-seventh annual conference of the cognitive science society* (pp. 1833–1838). Erlbaum.

Reimer, T., Mata, R., & Stoecklin, M. (2004). The use of heuristics in persuasion: Deriving cues on source expertise from argument quality. *Current Research in Social Psychology, 10*(6), 69–83.

Reinard, J. C. (1984). The role of Toulmin's categories of message development in persuasive communication: Two experimental studies on attitude change. *Journal of the American Forensic Association, 20*(4), 206–223. https://doi.org/10.1080/00028533.1984.11951266

Reinard, J. C. (1988). The empirical study of the persuasive effects of evidence: The status after fifty years of research. *Human Communication Research, 15*(1), 3–59. https://doi.org/10.1111/j.1468-2958.1988.tb00170.x

Rhodes, N., & Wood, W. (1992). Self-esteem and intelligence affect influenceability: The mediating role of message reception. *Psychological Bulletin, 111*(1), 156–171. https://doi.org/10.1037/0033-2909.111.1.156

Rice, R. E., & Atkin, C. K. (2013). *Public communication campaigns.* SAGE Publications. https://doi.org/10.4135/9781544308449

Robinson, R. J., & Keltner, D. (1996). Much ado about nothing: Revisionists and traditionalists choose an introductory English syllabus. *Psychological Science, 7*, 18–24. https://doi.org/10.1111/j.1467-9280.1996.tb00661.x

Rogers, E. M. (2003). *Diffusion of innovations.* Free Press.

Rokeach, M. (1960). *The open and closed mind.* Basic Books.

Rokeach, M. (1973). *The nature of human values.* Free Press.

Roozenbeek, J., & Linden, S.V.D. (2019). The fake news game: Actively inoculating against the risk of misinformation. *Journal of Risk Research, 22*(5), 570–580. https://doi.org/10.1080/13669877.2018.1443491

Rosen, E. (2000). *The anatomy of buzz: How to create word-of-mouth marketing.* Random House.

Rosenberg, M. (1965). *Society and the adolescent self-image.* Princeton University Press.

Rosenberg, M. (1979). *Conceiving the self.* Basic Books.

Roskos-Ewoldsen, D. R. (1997). Attitude accessibility and persuasion: Review and transactive model. *Communication Yearbook, 20*, 185–225. https://doi.org/10.1080/23808985.1997.11678942

Ryan, B., Gross, N. C. (1943). The diffusion of hybrid seed corn in two Iowa communities. *Rural Sociology, 8*, 15–24.

Ryan, T. J., & Brader, T. (2017). Gaffe appeal a field experiment on partisan selective exposure to election messages. *Political Science Research and Methods, 5*(4), 667–687. https://doi.org/10.1017/psrm.2015.62

Sanaktekin, O. H., & Sunar, D. (2008). Persuasion and personal versus relational bases of self-esteem: Does the message need to be one-or two-sided. *Social Behavior and Personality, 36*(10), 1315–1332. https://doi.org/10.2224/sbp.2008.36.10.1315

Schachter, S. (1951). Deviation, rejection and communication. *Journal of Abnormal and Social Psychology, 46*(2), 190–207. https://doi.org/10.1037/h0062326

Schmälzle, R., Häcker, F. E. K., Honey, C. J., & Hasson, U. (2015). Engaged listeners: Shared neural processing of powerful political speeches. *Social Cognitive and Affective Neuroscience, 10*(8), 1137–1143. https://doi.org/10.1093/scan/nsu168

Schofield, J. W., & Pavelchak, M. A. (1989). Fallout from *The Day After*: The impact of a TV film on attitudes related to nuclear war. *Journal of Applied Social Psychology, 19*(5), 433–448. https://doi.org/10.1111/j.1559-1816.1989.tb00066.x

Schultz, P. W., Nolan, J. M., Cialdini, R. B., Goldstein, N. J., & Griskevicius, V. (2007). The constructive, destructive, and reconstructive power of social norms. *Psychological Science, 18*(5), 429–434. https://doi.org/10.1111/j.1467-9280.2007.01917.x

Sears, D. O. (1986). College sophomores in the laboratory: Influences of a narrow data base on social psychology's view of human nature. *Journal of Personality and Social Psychology, 51*(3), 515–530. https://doi.org/10.1037//0022-3514.51.3.515

Shearman, S. M., & Levine, T. R. (2006). Dogmatism updated: A scale revision and validation. *Communication Quarterly, 54*(3), 275–291. https://doi.org/10.1080/01463370600877950

Sherif, C. W., Sherif, M., & Nebergall, R. E. (1965). *Attitude and attitude change: The social judgment-involvement approach*. W. B. Saunders Company.

Sherif, M., & Hovland, C. I. (1953). Judgmental phenomena and scales of attitude measurement: Placement of items with individual choice of number of categories. *Journal of Abnormal and Social Psychology, 48*(1), 135–141. https://doi.org/10.1037/h0048480

Singhal, A., & Rogers, E. M. (1999). *Entertainment-education: A communication strategy for social change*. Lawrence Erlbaum Associates. https://doi.org/10.4324/9781410607119

Sloman, S., & Fernbach, P. (2017). *The knowledge illusion: Why we never think alone*. Riverhead Books.

Smith, M. B., Bruner, J. S., & White, R. W. (1956). *Opinions and personality*. John Wiley

Snyder, L. B., & Hamilton, M. A. (2002). Meta-analysis of U.S. campaign effects on behavior: Emphasize enforcement, exposure, and new information, and beware the secular trend. In R. Hornik (Ed.), *Public health communication: Evidence for behavior change* (pp. 357–383). Lawrence Erlbaum.

Snyder, M., & DeBono, K. G. (1985). Appeals to image and claims about quality: Understanding the psychology of advertising. *Journal of Personality and Social Psychology, 49*(3), 586–597. https://doi.org/10.1037//0022-3514.49.3.586

So, J., Kim, S., & Cohen, H. (2017). Message fatigue: Conceptual definition, operationalization, and correlates. *Communication Monographs, 84*(1), 5–29. https://doi.org/10.1080/03637751.2016.1250429

Stiff, J. B. (1986). Cognitive processing of persuasive message cues: A meta-analytic review of the effects of supporting information on attitudes. *Communication Monographs, 53*(1), 75–89. https://doi.org/10.1080/03637758609376128

Stiff, J. B., & Boster, F. J. (1987). Cognitive processing: Additional thoughts and a reply to Petty, Kasmer, Haugtvedt, and Cacioppo. *Communication Monographs, 54*(3), 250–256. https://doi.org/10.1080/03637758709390230

Tannenbaum, P. H. (1967). The congruity principle revisited: Studies in the reduction, induction, and generalization of persuasion. *Advances in Experimental Social Psychology*, *3*, 271–320. https://doi.org/10.1016/s0065-2601(08)60346-9

Taylor, M. C. (1983). The black-and-white model of attitude stability: A latent class examination of opinion and nonopinion in the American public. *American Journal of Sociology*, *89*(2), 373–401. https://doi.org/10.1086/227870

Tesser, A. (1993). The importance of heritability in psychological research: The case of attitudes. *Psychological Review*, *100*(1), 129–142. https://doi.org/10.1037/0033-295x.100.1.129

Thagard, P., & Verbeurgt, K. (1998). Coherence as constraint satisfaction. *Cognitive Science*, *22*(1), 1–24. https://doi.org/10.1207/s15516709cog2201_1

Toulmin, S. E. (1958). *The uses of argument*. Cambridge University Press.

Turner, M. M., Rimal, R. N., Morrison, D., & Kim, H. (2006). The role of anxiety in seeking and retaining risk information: Testing the risk perception attitude framework in two studies. *Human Communication Research*, *32*(2), 130–156. https://doi.org/10.1111/j.1468-2958.2006.00006.x

Twain, M. (1884). *The adventures of Huckleberry Finn*. Grosset & Dunlap.

Updegraff, J. A., Sherman, D. K., Luyster, F. S., & Mann, T. L. (2007). The effects of message quality and congruency on perceptions of tailored health communications. *Journal of Experimental Social Psychology*, *43*(2), 249–257. https://doi.org/10.1016/j.jesp.2006.01.007.

Valentino, N. A., Hutchings, V. L., & Williams, D. (2004). The impact of political advertising on knowledge, internet information seeking, and candidate preference. *Journal of Communication*, *54*(2), 337–354. https://doi.org/10.1111/j.1460-2466.2004.tb02632.x

van Dijk, R., Hustinx, L., & Hoeken, H. (2003). A normative and empirical approach to Petty and Cacioppo's "strong" and "weak" arguments. In F. H. van Eemeren, J. A. Blair, C. A. Willard, & A. F. Snoeck Henkemans (Eds.), *Proceedings of the fifth conference of the International Society for the Study of Argumentation* (pp. 265–270). Sic Sat.

van Eemeren, F. H., Garssen, B., & Meuffels, B. (2009). *Fallacies and judgments of reasonableness: Empirical research concerning the pragma-dialectical discussion rules*. Springer.

Verhaeghen, P., & Salthouse, T. A. (1997). Meta-analysis of age-cognition relations in adulthood: Estimates of linear and nonlinear age effects and structural models. *Psychological Bulletin*, *122*(3), 231–249. https://doi.org/10.1037//0033-2909.122.3.231

Verplanck, W. S. (1955). The control of the content of conversation: Reinforcement of statements of opinion. *Journal of Abnormal and Social Psychology*, *51*(3), 668–676. https://doi.org/10.1037/h0046514

Vidmar, N., & Rokeach, M. (1974). Archie Bunker's bigotry: A study in selective perception and exposure. *Journal of Communication*, *24*(1), 36–47. https://doi.org/10.1111/j.1460-2466.1974.tb00353.x

Visser, P. S., & Krosnick, J. A. (1998). Development of attitude strength over the life cycle: Surge and decline. *Journal of Personality and Social Psychology*, *75*(6), 1389–1410. https://doi.org/10.1037//0022-3514.75.6.1389

Vohs, J. L., & Garret, R. (1968). Resistance to persuasion: An integrative framework. *Public Opinion Quarterly*, *32*(3), 445–452. https://doi.org/10.1086/267629

Wang, T. H., & Katzev, R. D. (1990). Group commitment and resource conservation: Two field experiments on promoting recycling. *Journal of Applied Social Psychology*, *20*(4), 265–275. https://doi.org/10.1111/j.1559-1816.1990.tb00411.x

Wansink, B. (2002). Changing eating habits on the home front: Lost lessons from World War II research. *Journal of Public Policy and Marketing*, *21*, 90–99. https://doi.org/10.1509/jppm.21.1.90.17614

Watts, W. A., & McGuire, W. J. (1964). Persistence of induced opinion change and retention of the inducing message contents. *Journal of Abnormal and Social Psychology, 68*(3), 233–241. https://doi.org/10.1037/h0041081

Watzlawick, P., Weakland, J., & Fisch, R. (1974). *Change: Principles of problem formation and problem resolution.* W. W. Norton & Company.

Wesselmann, E. D., Williams, K. D., Pryor, J. B., Eichler, F. A., Gill, D. M., & Hogue, J. D. (2014). Revisiting Schachter's research on rejection, deviance, and communication (1951). *Social Psychology, 45*(3), 164–169. https://doi.org/10.1027/1864-9335/a000180

Weston, A. (2000). *A rulebook for arguments.* Hackett.

Wicker, A. W. (1969). Attitudes versus actions: The relationship of verbal and overt behavioral responses to attitude objects. *Journal of Social Issues, 25*(4), 41–78. https://doi.org/10.1111/j.1540-4560.1969.tb00619.x

Williams, K. D. (2001). *Ostracism: The power of silence.* Guilford Press.

Williams, K. D., Cheung, K. T., & Choi, W. (2000). Cyberostracism: Effects of being ignored over the internet. *Journal of Personality and Social Psychology, 79*(5), 748–762. https://doi.org/10.1037/0022-3514.79.5.748

Wills, G. (1992). *Lincoln at Gettysburg: The words that remade America.* Simon & Schuster.

Wilson, S. R., Aleman, C. G., & Leatham, G. B. (1998). Identity implications of influence goals: A revised analysis of face-threatening acts and application to seeking compliance with same-sex friends. *Human Communication Research, 25*(1), 64–96. https://doi.org/10.1111/j.1468-2958.1998.tb00437.x

Witte, K. (1992). Putting the fear back into fear appeals: The extended parallel process model. *Communication Monographs, 59*(4), 329–349. https://doi.org/10.1080/03637759209376276

Wood, W. (1982). Retrieval of attitude-relevant information from memory: Effects on susceptibility to persuasion and on intrinsic motivation. *Journal of Personality and Social Psychology, 42*(5), 798–810. https://doi.org/10.1037//0022-3514.42.5.798

Wood, W., Lundgren, S., Ouellette, J.A., Busceme, S., & Blackstone, T. (1994). Minority influence: A meta-analytic review of social influence processes. *Psychological Bulletin, 115*, 323–345. https://doi.org/10.1037//0033-2909.115.3.323

Wood, W., & Quinn, J. M. (2003). Forewarned and forearmed? Two meta-analytic syntheses of forewarnings of influence appeals. *Psychological Bulletin, 129*(1), 119–138. https://doi.org/10.1037/0033-2909.129.1.119

Wyer, R. S., & Goldberg, L. (1970). A probabilistic analysis of the relationships among beliefs and attitudes. *Psychological Review, 77*(2), 100–120. https://doi.org/10.1037/h0028769

Yang, Z. J., Aloe, A. M., & Feeley, T. H. (2014). Risk information seeking and processing model: A meta-analysis. *Journal of Communication, 64*(1), 20–41. https://doi.org/10.1111/jcom.12071

Yoon, C., Laurent, G., Fung, H. H., Gonzalez, R., Gutchess, H. H., Hedden, T., Lambert-Pandraud, R., Mather, M., Park, D. C., Peters, E., & Skurnik, I. (2005). Cognition, persuasion and decision making in older consumers. *Marketing Letters, 16*(3–4), 429–441. https://doi.org/10.1007/s11002-005-5903-3

Youyou, W., Kosinski, M., & Stillwell, D. (2015). Computer based personality judgments are more accurate than those made by humans. *PNAS, 112*(4), 1036–1040. https://doi.org/10.1073/pnas.1418680112

Zuckerman, M. (2007). *Sensation seeking and risky behavior.* American Psychological Association. https://doi.org/10.1037/11555-000

Index

CPSIA information can be obtained
at www.ICGtesting.com
Printed in the USA
BVHW022243190523
664487BV00004B/402